Endorsements

This is a must-read for anyone who desires principle-centred leadership. It draws examples and rich principles from the lives of great men and women of God who affected their generation and have left an enviable legacy for us to emulate.

May this book go far to bless many people as we serve our generation.

–Rev Dr Spencer Duncan
President/Founder
International Leadership Development Institute, Singapore.

I have great appreciation for Rev Dr Chandrakumar for his great leadership and scholarship manifested in his ministry in India and abroad. His book on 'Leadership Insights from Bible Heroes' reflects his clear understanding and commitment to the history of the Old Testament and particularly to the great characters described in this exposition. I recommend it gladly to all Bible College students.

–Dr John Thannickal
Principal, New Life College, India.
Executive Member—Pentecostal World Conference.

Leadership Insights from Heroes of the Bible is a book with a purpose and vision. Its intention is to enliven the Christian individuals and communities in the light of a fresh look and appraisal of important characters depicted in the Bible. In his attempt the author has done a good job of selecting and depicting in detail the life and work of many a leader, prophet and visionary who secured for themselves the will of God to lead, to prophecy, to correct and mould not only individuals but also communities in the light of God's plan and will. The inclusion of many a woman in this list ensures the vision of the author in imparting dignity to women. One hopes that the book is well received and used for the enlightenment of all, more so in ensuring the integrity and witness of many a believer.

The author is a prolific writer, speaker, teacher and minister, popular around the world. His ministry extends worldwide to the lay and clergy alike. His books and publications have a ready market among the people. He writes in an easy understandable language and style. One looks forward to more of the kind of ministers in God's vineyard as Dr Chandrakumar.

–Rev Arun Kumar Wesley
Editorial Consultant, CISRS, India.

'If only you could see how much we have appreciated and have benefited with the teachings you have given us . . . .'

–Rev Daniel
Bethany AOG Church, Fiji Islands.

'Your messages and books are very inspiring, practical and helpful.'

–Samson
Kuwait.

Right now I am on a mission trip in Morocco. I am very much inspired with your book, *Leadership Insights from Heroes of the Bible* and it has helped me during my stressful mission to keep my faith firm.

–Christine
France.

Thank you for the book *Leadership Insights from Heroes of the Bible.* I could see a lot of prayer behind this book. You made me to chew, swallow and digest. Tears clouded my eyes with every line of this book and I am a new creation now.

–Pratap
India.

'What a joy it is to see young people committing their lives unto the Lord . . . . I was very much taken up by seeing the ambidextrous approach of your preaching and the conspicuous simplicity of your life.'

–Inbaraj Johnson
Ambassadors for Christ, India.

'Your books are very useful. We would like to buy some books for our young people in our country.'

–Barry and John
New Zealand.

I was at Lorna & John Christian bookstore, and I came across a few of your books, which I find to be very interesting and enlightening.

–Bryant White
Canada.

The blessing has all been ours. We had such a God-given time with you and in those few days you have invested by the grace of God an immense amount of spiritual deposit in our lives and in our ministry for the Lord.

–Chris Seema Sajnendra
Australia.

Dr Chandrakumar Manickam is a global leader who writes with unique biblically based insights that inspire you to fulfil your destiny. Written in his practical and easy-to-read style, this book is a wonderful resource for any Christian desiring to learn the kingdom principles that are revealed through the lives and testing of the leaders of the Bible. Dr Chandrakumar is a man of integrity who exemplifies these time-tested values from God's Word. Read and discover a treasury of wisdom that will bring encouragement and direction for the days ahead.

–Mrs Bev Klopp
President
Gateway Ministries International, USA.

LEADERSHIP INSIGHTS
INSIGHTS
FROM HEROES
OF THE BIBLE

CHANDRAKUMAR MANICKAM

Authentic™

HYDERABAD

Leadership Insights from Heroes of the Bible
by M. Chandrakumar

Copyright © 2007 M. Chandrakumar

First edition 2008
Two Reprint 2008-2009
Revised edition 2010
Reprint 2011
Reprint 2011
Reprint 2012
ISBN: 978-81-7362-828-3

Scripture used in this work, unless indicated otherwise is taken from the *New International Version* of the Bible. Copyright © 1973, 1978, 1984 by the International Bible Society.

Scripture quotations marked *KJV* are from *King James Version*, *NASB* are from *New American Standard Bible*.

Published by
Authentic Books
Logos Bhavan, Jeedimetla Village, Secunderabad 500 067, Andhra Pradesh.
www.authenticindia.in

Authentic Books is an imprint of Authentic Media, the publishing division of OM Books Foundation.

Printed and bound in India by
Authentic Media, Secunderabad 500 067

Contents

Preface to the Second Revised Edition

Leadership Insights from Heroes of the Bible was first published in 2002 under the title *Deep Insights* with 14 chapters by Salt and Sunshine International. The first revised edition with 21 chapters was published in the year 2008 by Authentic India. Since then there has been a tremendous demand for this book internationally and within 12 months Authentic has reprinted 3 times. This book in your hand is the second revised edition with the addition of two more chapters.

The book as its title indicates is about the legendary leaders in the Bible, and attempts to provide the reader with knowledge of characteristics that were par excellence. It is hoped the readers will realize and come to terms with the reality of life, its pitfalls, and merits and how to overcome many of them by gaining awareness for life from the life-sketches of great people.

The effective portraits influence the readers to come back to God and by this to derive strength from Him to lead a good life. It is assumed that the lives of the people given in the book led a victorious life because their goals were set, and they had a definite purpose in life.

It is estimated that nearly 9,000 copies of *Leadership Insights from Heroes of the Bible* (different editions combined)have been sold. It has challenged and equipped several pastors and leaders around the world. We have received feedback from them that this book has brought light into their lives and given them a new hope to carry on even with difficult situations they face in their   ministry. In some places they are using this book as weekly Bible study material, and also many Bible colleges are using this as a textbook for their leadership development courses.

Prof. Dr. Chandrakumar Manickam
International Vice President
International Graduation School of Ministry, U.S.A.

Preface

Leadership Insights from Heroes of the Bible was first published in 2002 under the title 'Deep Insights' with 14 chapters by Salt and Sunshine International. This is the first revised edition with 21 chapters and is published by Authentic India. This book is written on the legendary leaders in the Bible. The book as its title indicates attempts to provide the reader with knowledge of characteristics that were beyond par excellence. The pupose of the book is to give the reader a chance to come to terms with the reality of life, its pitfalls, and merits and how to overcome many of them with gaining awareness for life from the life-sketches of great people.

This book influences the reader to come back to God and by this to derive strength from Him to lead a good life. It is assumed that the lives of the people given in the book led a victorious life because their goals were set, and they had a definite purpose in life.

By the grace of God, we have already sold 5,000 copies of this book. It has challenged and equipped several pastors and leaders around the world in their life in ministry. We have received feedback from them that this book has brought light into their lives and given them a new hope to carry on even with difficult situations they face in their ministry. In some places they are using this book as weekly Bible study material as well as many Bible colleges are using this as a syllabus for their leadership development course.

Prof Dr Chandrakumar Manickam
International Vice President
International Graduation School of Ministry, USA.

Introduction

The book as its title indicates attempts to provide the reader with insights that were beyond the reach of the common person. It attempts to enlarge the horizons of understanding of the reader with facts and interpretations as never before. The insights provided therein assume that they are relevant to us and have a bearing on our lives today. The purpose of the book is to give the reader a chance to come to terms with the reality of life, its pitfalls, and merits and how to overcome many of them through gaining deep insights for life from the life-sketches of great people.

The book establishes the fact that God is the foundation of our lives to lead an honest, faithful and fruitful life. It is assumed that the lives of the people given in the book lead a victorious life because their goals were set, and they had a definite purpose in life. It is assumed that the Bible provides the necessary blueprint for a person to chart his or her course of action and reflection on the reality of life.

The book as well draws the readers' attention to appropriate these insights into their lives as individuals and as members of the church and society as well. To this end the purpose of the book is well served as it narrates the life-stories of these saints and sinners of old in an easy and direct way so as to catch the attention of the reader.

Chapter 1

NOAH
A Leader Who Found Favour with God

The Bible doesn't give us details about the early years of Noah. Bible biography is greatly condensed, but it can give a realistic picture of a person in a sentence, and an ocean of meaning in a few drops of speech. It includes the scars and wrinkles of saints and depicts them as men of passions similar to us.

Noah's Historical Reality

As to the historical reality of Noah himself, his name appears with other historical characters in the genealogy of Genesis 5:28–32. He thus has the same claim to a place in history as Adam or Enoch. He was the son of Lamech, who came of the line of Seth. The record treats him as a historical personage, as does the prophet Ezekiel (Ezek 14:14). The Lord Himself adds His testimony:

> "The coming of the Son of Man will be just like the days of Noah. For as in those days before the flood they were eating and drinking, marrying and giving in marriage, until the day that Noah entered the ark" (Matt 24:37–38).

Apparently, Noah was a farmer and was raising up three sons. There is more to the story of Noah than the ark and the flood. Noah's name means 'rest', but it speaks more of the life he dreamed of than the life he lived.

The word 'rest' is synonymous with the well-known term, 'shalom', peace. Noah was literally responsible for the survival of every land-based living creature, including mankind. Just as Noah's work was not complete until the rains began to fall, our task remains until the clouds part to make way for Jesus' return.

Noah Walked with God

Noah had fellowship with God. He walked with God in the midst of evil. He actually 'walked with God' (Gen 6:9). It means that he had a daily step-by-step fellowship with God. He had God as his companion as he walked through life. Noah's godliness was the godliness of a man who was involved in ordinary life.

God promises those of us who walk with Him by faith that we too will someday enter into His rest. On that day we will enjoy the fulfilment of all the promises He made to us in Christ Jesus. When we walk by faith, we don't find many places to drop our guard and rest.

Once the animals were off the boat, Noah must have thought that at long last he could rest. Now the birds and the goats and the rabbits and the lizards could take care of themselves. Noah thought his work was over and that he could finally rest, but he was wrong. He had new challenges to face.

Noah Obeyed God

He was obedient in spite of the hard task given to him. God saw Noah, the only righteous man on the planet, and saved him and used him to single handedly carry out His purpose and to make a vital difference in the world.

Life was difficult for Noah and his family leading up to that day. By refusing to live like the rest of the world, he put himself at odds with everyone. Building the ark was a huge task, but it must have been a relief of sorts. He thought he might have a chance to rest while he was on board. Noah had to work hard every day. He didn't fit in with the rest of the world and going against the tide can be very taxing. Every day he cried out to God for directives.

Noah Responded through Faith

Noah was a righteous man, by means of his faith. God told Noah about the coming judgement and how Noah himself should make a way of rescue for all who would have faith. He was 'blameless in his generation' (Gen 6:9). He lived in terrible days. The world around him was degraded and depraved, but he was blameless, clean and upright in the midst of it all.

By faith Noah, being warned of God of things not seen as yet, moved with fear, prepared an ark for to save his house; by which he condemned the world, and became heir of the righteousness which is by faith (Heb 11:7).

Seven Salient Features of Noah's Faith

1. The foundation of Noah's faith

God had spoken to Noah and told him the flood was coming, even though there was no indication of it and it seemed utterly impossible. Saving faith simply believes God's Word, without any evidence or proof. It is believing the unreasonable, illogical, unexplainable and supernatural revelation of God just because God says it. True faith asks for no additional evidence. True saving faith is accepting the Word of God just because God says it. Noah was warned of God concerning a most unbelievable flood, and he believed it.

2. The nature of Noah's faith

There is no indication of rain having fallen until the days of Noah. This is very evidently the meaning of the phrase that Noah was warned 'of things not seen as yet'. Rain had never been seen before, but Noah believed the Word of God. This is the nature of faith—believing what we cannot explain, but believing it because God says it.

> The Lord God had not caused it to rain upon the earth, and there was not a man to till the ground. But there went up a mist from the earth, and watered the whole face of the ground (Gen 2:5–6).

It had never rained upon earth until that time; no rain had ever fallen from the sky. But God said it would. The people must have laughed and scoffed at Noah when he told them water would fall from the sky. It did seem unreasonable and unbelievable.

3. The motive of Noah's faith

When God told Noah about the wrath of God and that He was going to destroy thousands of sinners for their rejection of the Word of God, it scared Noah. He was moved with fear. The life of the average man is motivated by fear of existence: We work to obtain money to feed, house and clothe ourselves, because we fear the spectre of hunger, cold and discomfort. Many nations spend billions for defence because they fear invasion. *Any man in his right mind must know some fear of the future and the wrath of God*—Mr De Hann.

Noah was moved with fear before the wrath of God, and it drove him to seek salvation.

4. Exercise of Noah's faith

Noah did something about his faith. It was a working faith. He prepared an ark. Noah's faith was an active faith. It was faith which saved him, and it was his work which proved his faith. Noah did not say, 'Yes, I believe a flood is coming, and my only hope is to find refuge in the ark', and then do nothing about it. Faith without work is pointless.

When the Philippian jailer said to Paul, 'What must I do to be saved?' Paul did not say 'Do nothing', but he said: *Believe on the Lord Jesus Christ, and thou shall be saved, and thy house* (Act 16:31). Have you ever taken the action of inviting Jesus into your heart as your Saviour and Lord? Jesus is knocking at the door of your heart and unless you open your heart, He will not enter into your life (Rev 3:16.).

5. The expectation of Noah's faith

Noah was not wanting to be saved alone, and was deeply concerned about his family. He expected his family to follow him, for he made provision for them in the ark. This is one of the surest evidences of the genuineness of faith. When a person is truly saved, he becomes concerned about others, beginning at home. A parent who is saved, but does not show any concern over the salvation of his children, will find it hard to convince anyone else.

6. The testimony of Noah's faith

By his faith Noah conquered the world and became heir of the righteousness that comes by faith (Heb 11:7). Day after day he laboured on the ark; day after day he preached the coming judgement of the great flood; day after day he must have pleaded with the people to repent and believe. There was no excuse for their perishing in the flood, for they had had ample warning.

There stood the ark nearing completion, as a daily reminder of the impending catastrophe. The building of the ark was a testimony of the faith of Noah. Noah and his family believed the Word of God; all the others rejected it and perished in the flood. Noah, 'by his faith he overcame the world and became heir of the righteousness that comes by faith'.

7. The reward of Noah's faith

Noah was not a sinless man. He was a lost sinner like all others, but he was declared righteous in the sight of God because he had faith in God's Word concerning the ark. I would like to make it clear to you that the ark was Christ. Noah believed God's Word concerning this Christ. Today, the only way of salvation is believing that the Lord Jesus Christ is your Saviour. John says, 'He that believes in the Son of God has the witness in himself; the one who does not believe God has made Him a liar, because he has not believed in the witness that God has borne concerning His Son' (1 John 5:10).

Chapter 2

ABRAHAM
A Leader with Unconditional Obedience

After the flood, the population grew and nations were formed. God wanted a people all His own to be a model of His mercy and a channel of His grace. Searching the world, He found just the man to father such a nation—Abraham, the one through whom, *". . . all the families of the earth will be blessed"* (Gen 12:3).

Abram's father, Terah, lived in a place called Ur of the Chaldees. Ur was a town in Southern Mesopotamia on what was probably then the coast of the Persian Gulf, at the mouth of the Euphrates River, some twelve miles from the traditional site of the Garden of Eden. But preceding the time of Abram, it was the most magnificent city in the entire world; a centre of manufacturing, farming, and shipping, in a land of fabulous fertility and wealth.

For some reason Terah moved his large family, including his son Abram and Abram's wife Sarai, from Ur to Haran, nearly 600 miles to the north. Haran was a bustling trade centre, like Ur. Terah claimed the moon god for his deity. Terah died in Haran and eventually God chose Abram to accomplish the blessing of the earth.

Abraham's Obedience to the Call of God

The Lord told Abram to leave his country, relatives and his father's house and go to the land, which he would show him (Gen 12:1). The call of Abram contained in it not only a command but also a promise from God. The command was to get out—and the promise was that God would show him the Promised Land. The Lord made seven great promises in reference to his covenant. The Lord told Abram,

> "And I will make you a great nation. And I will bless you, And make your name great; And so you shall be a blessing; And I will bless those who bless you, And the one who curses you I will curse. And in you all the families of the earth will be blessed" (Gen 12:2–3).

The Book of Hebrews says, *By faith Abraham, when he was called, obeyed by going out to a place which he was to receive for an inheritance; and he went out, not knowing where he was going . . .* (11:8–10). Abram responded to the command and to the promise by faith. Had Abram remained in Haran, not heeding and obeying the word of the Lord, and not acting upon His promise, he would not have come into the place of blessing that God had appointed for him. God's plan, called for Abram to move toward the blessings; his receiving them depended upon his obedient response.

God deals the same way with us. He has a plan for our lives. He says, *'For I know the plans I have for you,' declares the LORD, 'plans for welfare and not for calamity to give you a future and a hope'* (Jer 29:11).

Paul said, *"For we are His workmanship created in Christ Jesus for good works, which God prepared beforehand that we should walk in them"* (Eph 2:10).

God's plan for our life includes good work that He has prepared ahead of time for us to do. To fulfil His plan we need to obey the Lord and believe in His promises.

If we do not obey God, we will not leave our present circumstances and move towards fulfilling God's plan. There's a sense in which all of us are called to leave something in order to enter into the promise of God. The things that hold us down and keep us back from fulfilling the purpose of God, are oftentimes things to which we have a firm emotional attachment. It might be a particular habit or lifestyle, moving from one career to another.

Whatever it is, unless we are prepared to move from those things in obedience to God's command, we will never enter into the place of His blessing. Unless we are prepared to move out, we will never move in; unless we are prepared to let go, we will never take hold of new things. Such is God's working in our lives.

We must be there where God wants us to be. I would like to draw your attention, to the most important word 'there', which we find in several incidents in the Bible. God told Elijah, that if he wanted the water and food he must go *there*—into the place of God's choice. Are you 'there', in the place of God's will for you? For 'there' is the place of God's provision. When Moses asked God to show His glory, God told him, *"Behold there is a place by Me, and you shall stand there on the rock"* (Exod 33:21).

The call of Abram as recorded in Genesis 12 begins a new chapter in the Old Testament revelation of God's purpose to redeem and save humanity. God intended to have a man who would know and serve Him with devoted faith. From this man would come a family who would know, teach and keep the ways of the Lord. From this family would come a chosen nation of people who would be separated from the ungodly ways of other nations to do God's will. From this nation would come Jesus Christ, the Saviour of the world, the promised offspring of the woman.

Because Abram possessed a faith in God that expressed itself in obedience, he is declared a foremost example of true saving faith. Biblically, any profession of faith in Jesus Christ as Saviour that does not involve obedience to Him as Lord is not true saving faith.

Faith and Obedience

Faith and obedience brought Abram to the Promised Land. While in the Promised Land God promised Abram, that, that land would be given to him and his descendants. His descendants would be as the dust of the earth; yet year after year passed, and Abram had no children, his wife Sarai was getting older. They both were well beyond normal childbearing days. Although God had made the promise and Abram had responded to it, he could not see how it would be worked out.

Abram's father, Terah had bestowed on him the title 'exalted father' by naming him Abram. Four thousand years ago children were viewed as a sign of God's blessing, so an exalted father was a man doubly blessed. The Psalmist says in Psalm 127:3–5, *Behold children are a gift of the LORD, The fruit of the womb is a reward. Like arrows in the hand of a warrior, So are the children of one's youth.*

But Abram's quiver was empty. His wife remained barren as the years ticked by. The childbearing years came and went; the blessing Abram's father bestowed on him had not come to pass.

Abram told the Lord, *"O Lord GOD, what will You give me, since I am childless, and the heir of my house is Eliezer of Damascus?"* (Gen 15:2). According to the code of Hammurabi, (the then prevailing Babylonian law of inheritance) if Abram had remained childless, all that he had, could have passed by his will and decree to a servant whom he had appointed heir.

In their time and culture, no children meant, no future. Further, Abram and Sarai had little understanding of life after death. Rather, they believed that people lived on through their offspring. Families were erased by the absence of a male heir as per the then prevailing circumstance.

Barrenness of Sarai permeated every aspect of her family life. For Sarai and Abram, hopelessness lay beneath the surface of their comfortable life, which they had built together. Underneath it all was a sense of loss and meaninglessness, that all would end with them. However, this was not to be so. The Word of the Lord came to Abram, saying,

> "This man will not be your heir; but one who will come forth from your own body, he will be your heir." And He took him outside and said, "Now look toward the heavens, and count the stars, if you are able to count them." And he said to him, "So shall your descendants be." Then he believed in the LORD; and He reckoned it to him as righteousness (Gen 15:4–6).

Abram believed God, even though there was no external evidence to support God's promise. Abram was 75 years when God made that promise to him. When Abram was 99 years old the Lord established a covenant with him and told him that he would no longer be called Abram, but Abraham—

> "For I have made you the father of a multitude of nations . . . for Sarai your wife, you shall not call her name Sarai, but Sarah shall be her name. I will bless her, and indeed I will give you a son by her. Then I will bless her, and she shall be a mother of nations; kings of peoples will come from her" (Gen 17:1–5; 15–16).

God promised to give Abraham more than he deserved or dared to dream. That's also the Lord's legacy of love for you and me and for all of the faithful. Through the eyes of faith, Abraham believed. He did not go by what his senses told him but as the promise of God—

> In hope against hope, he believed, so that he might become a father of many nations according to that which had been spoken, "SO SHALL YOUR DESCENDANTS BE." Without becoming weak in faith he contemplated his own body, now as good as dead since he was about a hundred years old, and the deadness of Sarah's womb; yet, with respect to the promise of God, he did not waver in unbelief, but grew strong in faith, giving glory to God, and being fully assured that what God had promised, He was able also to perform (Rom 4:18–21).

For us the message is clear, no Word of God is devoid of power.

Jeremiah 1:12 says, 'I am watching over My word to perform it.' Again, in Ezekiel 12:25 we read,

> "For I the LORD will speak, and whatever word I speak will be performed. It will no longer be delayed . . ."

Jesus said,

> "It is the Spirit who gives life . . . the words that I have spoken to you are spirit and are life" (John 6:63).

Therefore, the basis of all faith is the reality of God's Word. The reality is not what we feel, see, or hear but it is God's Word alone. The facts are the promises of God, not what our senses say. Faith is always the determining factor in receiving the promise. The unchanging order is faith not sight.

Sarah conceived and bore a son to Abraham in his old age, at the appointed time of which God had spoken to him. They named him Isaac just as the Lord had said (Gen 17:19). When Isaac was born, Sarah said in grateful praise,

> "God has made laughter for me; everyone who hears will laugh with me . . . Who would have said to Abraham that Sarah would nurse children? Yet I have borne him a son in his old age" (Gen 21:6–7).

'Isaac', means 'laughter'. His birth brought laughter of happiness to Abraham and Sarah. This laughter was different from the earlier unbelieving responses to the miraculous possibility of having a son, which we see in Genesis 18:12. Through this experience, Abraham and Sarah learnt to believe the Word of God; in the midst of difficult situations. We should also understand and believe that His Word will always prevail over the seeming impossibility of natural circumstances.

God alone was sufficient to bring about this change. God was not dependent on any potential in Abram and Sarai. Their possibility for getting a child was long gone. Here is another important concept we learn: God's realm and promise do not depend on our potential, but rest on His power and His faithfulness to us.

Implicit, Unconditional Obedience

God tested Abraham and said to him, *"Take now your son, your only son, whom you love, Isaac, and go to the land of Moriah; and offer him there as a burnt offering on one of the mountains of which I will tell you"* (Gen 22:2).

God leads us to maturity through the valley of testing. In God's school of experience, first we go through the test and then we learn the lesson.

When God told Abraham to take his son and go to Moriah to sacrifice him, Abraham rose early in the morning and saddled his donkey, and took two of his young men with him, and Isaac his son; and he split the wood for the burnt offering, and arose and went to the place which God had told him (Gen 22:3). Hence Abraham was *there* where God wanted him to be. He neither doubted nor argued with God. He didn't wait! He prepared for the trip early in the morning. And he took some wood with him along with Isaac.

Sometimes in life we feel as though God is sending us contradictory messages. We don't understand the direction He is taking us, or the cost that obedience exacts from us. *Destiny is not a matter of chance but a matter of choice. It is not a thing to be waited for it is a thing to be achieved* —W J Bryan. As he set about for the journey, he went with faith.

> On the third day Abraham raised his eyes and saw the place from a distance. Abraham said to his young men, "Stay here with the donkey and I and the lad will go over there; and we will worship and return to you" (Gen 22:4–5).

Abraham took the wood, knife and the fire and walked on together. As they walked on, Isaac told his father that the fire and the wood were there but there is no lamb for the burnt offering. Abraham said,

"God will provide for Himself the lamb for the burnt offering, my son" (Gen 22:8).

Abraham silently, almost compulsively, built the altar, arranged the wood, and he bound his son, laid him on the altar on top of the wood. We do not see Isaac objecting or rebelling against this act. He seemed to have full trust in his father that he will not do anything contrary to the will of God. That is the testimony of a good God-fearing father, and so too of Isaac, an obedient son who trusted his father, Abraham.

Biblical scholars say that Isaac was at least fifteen years old then. So, he would have been a strong young man and would have been able to break away or could have resisted when his father tied his arms together. And I'm sure he could have removed himself from the altar without much difficulty. Abraham and Isaac were alone on the mountain; they had left the servants down at the foot. Think of the faith of the son, so committed to doing his father's will that in the moment of crisis, he asked not a question, moved not a muscle, entertained not a thought in opposition. Isaac was prepared to do whatever his father said.

Abraham took out his knife to slay him, then the angel of the Lord called out to him from heaven, and said,

> "Abraham, Abraham! . . . Do not stretch out your hand against the lad, and do nothing to him; for now I know that you fear God, since you have not withheld your son, your only son, from Me" (Gen 22:12).

After the moment of radical intervention by the angel of the Lord, Abraham looked up and saw behind him in the thicket a ram caught by its horns. God did provide! Here was the substitutionary sacrifice. He offered the ram in place of his son, and so Abraham called the place, YHWH–JIREH, which means, the Lord will provide (Gen 22:13-14). The words became a metaphor for the intervening majesty of God. They have been repeated by succeeding generations during difficulties and have been put on the placards carried before armies and processions.

This incident speaks to our deepest need to trust God for the gift of faith in times of crises, and touches our longing to be reassured of the timely interventions of God.

This story takes us back to another mount a short distance from Mount Moriah—Mount Calvary. There, God did what was truly impossible. He gave His own Son as a sacrifice for the sins of all people, in all ages. What God did not require of Abraham with Isaac, He required of Himself with Jesus Christ, and sacrificed His only begotten Son that we might know that we are ultimately loved and forgiven.

Jesus did not protest but was ready to die on the other hill. Jesus certainly could have escaped the cross. In the garden of Gethsemane, when Peter in a moment of enthusiasm chopped off the ear of Malchus, the servant of the High Priest, Jesus said, *"Put your sword back into its place . . . Or do you think that I cannot appeal to My father, and He will at once put at my disposal more than twelve legions of angels?"* (Matt 26:52–53). But Jesus never did it. If He had done it, then it would have been a spectacular sight; but it would not have been in keeping with the Father's will. Jesus said, *"I do not seek My own will, but the will of Him who sent Me"* (John 5:30). Though He was a son, yet He learnt obedience by the things, which He suffered (Heb 5:8). When the test came, He was able to stand; and so was Isaac.

God asked Abraham to release his first son, Ishmael, to an area outside of his fatherly provision. He obeyed and released him. God then asked of him to sacrifice his dearly beloved son, Isaac, the one promised as his heritage. Abraham was prepared to slay him. No wonder we say that our ancient ancestor, Abraham, is the father of the faithful.

Whenever we are faced with a situation to sacrifice something for God, we may think we are losing the most precious thing in our lives.

But God is no one's debtor. He who gives much will receive much. Jesus said, 'He who loses his life for my sake will find it' (Matt 10:39).

Abraham gave God his Isaac, his future, and his destiny as the father of the multitudes. Abraham refused to doubt God, even when it seemed that God was about to act in a way, which was against God's own nature-requiring human sacrifice.

From the above we learn that, a true servant of God does not live to himself, for himself or by himself.

Faith and Faithfulness of Abraham

Abraham is often referred to as 'The father of faith'. He is also the father of the faithful. Abraham's life was a testimony of faith. In James 2:23, Abraham is referred to as 'The friend of God'. In studying this man of faith and friend of God, we see that faith is not a perfect characteristic or integrity of a person. Rather, it is simply taking God at His word by obeying Him.

His life demonstrates how we benefit from believing and acting upon what God says, despite evidence to the contrary. To walk in the kind of faith that Abraham had, we must believe God's promises to us, and believe, too, that He knows how and when to bring them to pass. When Abraham tried to bring to pass God's promises by his own effort, there were serious consequences (see Gen 16:21). That is why it is so important to avoid striving to fulfil God's promises in our own strength, like Rebecca did to fulfil God's promise in Jacob's life. Doing so, always backfires and produces undesired results, on us.

Your faith may be challenged by fear of the unknown, as Abraham's must have been. And yet, he obeyed God, as we must, even when God's direction takes a different turn and we do not understand His intentions.

We sometimes face difficult and delicate situations. How do we handle them? Life has no questions that faith cannot answer. But where do we get this faith? Obviously, from the Word of God which is the source of our faith. George Mueller the Father of faith, always prayed with an open Bible.

Faith is confidence in action. It not only passively waits on God, but also actively seeks to know and do His will. Work must accompany faith. The object of faith is God Himself. We have to trust Him where we cannot trace Him.

Faith is the sight of the inward eye. Jesus said, *"Blessed are they who did not see, and yet believed"* (John 20:26–29). Faith sees the invisible, believes the incredible and receives the impossible. Faith is daily walking hand in hand with God. Abraham said to his servant, 'The lad and I . . . we will come back.' How did Abraham know that?

There was no way Abraham could have understood what God was about to do, and yet, he obeyed. He obeyed because he so believed that God would keep His word that, if necessary, He would raise Isaac from the dead to do it. Abraham knew nothing about resurrection, as a concept or as an occurrence. It was yet two thousand years before Jesus was raised from the dead! Abraham believed God could do exactly what He said—even if he didn't understand how or why.

Abraham is, in fact, mentioned seventy-three times in the New Testament, more than any other Old Testament figure. He is one of the central figures of the entire Scripture, related not only to those of the Old Covenant, but to those in the New as well. Abraham towers at the very beginning of the Scripture as a man whom God sought out amidst the whole of the earth. He entered into the covenant with, a covenant that has so firmly bound the Lord God to His people that thereafter He was known as 'The Lord, the God of Abraham'.

Chapter 3

JOSEPH
A Leader with Passion, Power and Purity

Doing what is right is no guarantee that everything will turn out right. In a fallen world, sometimes a holy and honest life puts us in conflict with a corrupt society. We may be persecuted because we do not fit in John 15:18–21, but God rewards those who walk uprightly.

What should we do when blessings do not immediately follow obedience to Christ? How should we respond when prayer seems to go unanswered, when things that are important go wrong?

The Book of James provides some insight:

> Consider it pure joy, my brothers, whenever you face trails of many kinds, because you know that the testing of your faith develops perseverance. Perseverance must finish its work so that you may be mature and complete, not lacking anything (1:2–4).

In these verses it is clear, what God seeks to accomplish in our lives when things don't go the way that we expect. Often it is an issue of perseverance, of growing into maturity, of continuing to walk in obedience even through periods of doubt and confusion and, most importantly, of learning not to misinterpret circumstances.

We can see this process at work, in the life of Joseph in the Old Testament. Abraham's grandson, Jacob, had twelve sons. His father especially favoured Joseph. Joseph set his eleven brothers against him by telling them his dream of they bowing down to him. So when his brothers got a chance, they paid him back, they dumped him in a pit and sold him as a slave to the Ishmaelite merchants, who took him to Egypt. Never expecting to see him again, they made up a story and told their father, that wild animals had devoured Joseph (Gen 37:19).

In Egypt, he was falsely accused and thrown into a dungeon. 'What good could come out of my life?' he must have wondered. Still, he remained faithful to the Lord. God had other plans. In Egypt, He gave Joseph the gift of interpreting several dreams. It was a ticket to prominence. Egyptians of that day were fascinated by dreams: archeologists have uncovered lengthy textbooks on dream interpretation.

God lifted up Joseph from the pit and elevated him from the prison to the palace as the Prime Minister of Egypt—a position he later used to save his family from famine and to keep the dream of God's people alive. Later he said to his forgiven brothers, *"You meant evil against me, but God meant it for good in order to . . . preserve many people alive"* (Gen 50:20). When Joseph was tempted to sin, he made the right choice and refused to yield to the temptation. But he was falsely accused and ended up in prison.

Joseph's story is the last of the brotherly battles of Genesis. Cain and Abel, Isaac and Ishmael, Jacob and Esau all quarrelled. Joseph also had problem with his brothers.

He Was Vulnerable but Victorious

The Ishmaelite merchants sold Joseph to Potiphar (Gen 37:28). Potiphar was an Egyptian and the captain of Pharaoh's guard; he recognized that Joseph was no ordinary man. The Scripture goes so far to say that, Potiphar saw that the Lord was with him and that the Lord gave him success in everything he did. Not only did Joseph prosper in all that he did, but also the Lord blessed the household of the Egyptian, because of Joseph. In fact, the blessing of the Lord was on everything Potiphar had, both in the house and in the field. So it was not surprising that Potiphar promoted Joseph to such a high position (Gen 39:3–5).

Potiphar's wife looked with desire at Joseph and said to him, 'Lie with me'. But Joseph did not yield to her request (Gen 39:7–8).

Joseph was in such a situation where the vulnerability of any young man was very high and would have yielded to temptation due to the following reasons:

a) From his life situation we see that Joseph had very little opportunity for physical, or even social, contact with the opposite sex.

b) The woman was persistent. *"She spoke to Joseph day after day, he did not listen to her to lie beside her, or be with her"*(Gen 39:10).

c) Potiphar's wife could create complex problems for Joseph if he refused her. In fact, pleasing a woman of her position might have helped Joseph to get new promotions in his position in Egypt.

d) Joseph was away from his family and probably felt lonely and home sick at times. An invitation to any kind of companionship must have been attractive.

e) It was unlikely that anyone would have known. The only thing that keeps some people from sin is the fear that others will find out. Joseph had nothing to lose; he was an insignificant slave. This was his one chance for a little diversion or pleasure. In spite of such vulnerability, he maintained his moral purity. 'Purity in your heart produces power in your life.'

Three Reasons for Rejecting the Offer

Joseph simply said no to the offer and gave Potiphar's wife three reasons for his refusal:

i) The first reason was regarding his relationship with man. Joseph saw the seriousness of violating that trust, his master had in him.

ii) The second reason, Joseph would not lie with Potiphar's wife was regarding his respect for marriage relationship. He did not want to separate what God had joined together (Mark 10:9).

iii) The third reason was regarding his relationship with God. Since, Joseph maintained a close relationship with God, he was able to be blameless in his moral relationship with Potiphar and his wife.

Without God in the picture, human relationship can be influenced through emotional attractions.

The Strength of Joseph's Character

To have sinned with Potiphar's wife, would have been to sin against God. Only after King David committed adultery with Bathsheba, he realized that he had sinned against God (Ps 51:4). As for Joseph, beyond the face of the adulterous seductress, he saw another face (of God) full of grace and loveliness, which he dared not hurt or displease. The fact that Joseph could resist the same temptation many times reveals the strength of his character.

For Joseph, to be in the presence of Potiphar's wife was like being in the presence of temptation. That is why Joseph avoided her. It is safe to keep away from sources of temptation. Once when none of Potiphar's servants were inside the house, she caught him by his cloak, but Joseph ran out of the house. Perhaps she was looking for such an opportunity, so that there could be no eyewitnesses.

The most important step Joseph took to resist temptation was to run. Paul says, *"Now flee from youthful lusts . . ."* (2 Tim 2:22). Running from a sinful situation, is not a cowardly act but a courageous and a right thing to do. We learn from this story, that in spite of alluring temptations, sin can be avoided.

Satan enters every Eden. He came to tempt Joseph, not in the form of a serpent, but in the form of a beautiful woman. Temptation is all around us. Our eyes, ears, and emotions are constantly bombarded with immorality. It is not always temptation to sexual sin, some feel strongly tempted toward other sins like covetousness, pride, lying, etc. Our consumer-oriented society encourages greed. On the streets we pass through filthy cinema posters and advertisements. Much of the radio and television programmes glorify rebellion, drug abuse and sexual perversion.

The world says, 'There are no absolutes; right and wrong change with the times; past is past and present is present'. It is true that times have changed, and that we are now living in an experience-oriented society; but we cannot forsake godly principles on which our families need operate. Otherwise soon our rules will be mixed with the rules of the world, and our daughters and sons will not know the difference.

In Romans 1 we read that people decided to exchange the truth of God for a lie, and worshipped and served the creature rather than the Creator (Rom 1:25). But deciding to change the truth didn't change it. Deciding to believe that a loaded gun will not kill us if we put it to our head and pull the trigger will not change the fact that it will!

God has set within each of us, a conscience that bears witness and thoughts that alternately accuse or else defend us. The law of God is written in our hearts and they tell us when we cross over the fence (Rom 2:15). The Bible tells us that, there are times when the right feeling can lead to the wrong actions. *There is a way which seems right to a man, But its end is the way of death* (Prov 14:12).

We must avoid nurturing relationships that influence our emotions toward lustful passions, just as Joseph avoided Potiphar's wife. Rather we must be occupied with what God has placed before us to do.

We must remember also that for Joseph, his experience was both a temptation and a trial. This is difficult to comprehend, for God does not tempt—Satan does (James 1:13). God often allows trials in our lives that we might grow spiritually and to prepare us for greater responsibility in His kingdom (1 Pet 1:6-7). God can actually turn evil (which is caused by Satan) to make it work for good (Rom 8:28).

The greatest temptation we all face when someone mistreats us is to seek revenge. Joseph had to face that temptation too. And in doing so, Joseph was not *overcome by evil*. Rather he overcame *evil with good* (Rom 12:21).

How did Joseph overcome this temptation? What held him back from falling into temptation? It was not because he was afraid of Potiphar, nor was it because this beautiful woman did not attract him. He resisted the temptation because he feared God and would not do anything to displease Him. Joseph won the battle because he learnt to say the hardest, little word, 'No'. David had the same kind of temptation that Joseph had, but in a moment of time he forgot God and yielded to temptation.

The most important motivating source for not yielding to temptation should be our relationship with God. Our primary motivation should be as stated by Paul to Titus: *For the grace of God has appeared, bringing salvation to all men, instructing us to deny ungodliness and worldly desires and to live sensibly, righteously and godly in the present age* (Titus 2:11–12).

The Lord Was with Him

When Joseph ran out of the house, the woman concocted a story designed to slander Joseph. This reminds us that doing what is right is no guarantee that everything will turn out right. In a fallen world, sometimes a holy and an honest life puts us in conflict with the corrupt society. We may be persecuted because we do not fit in; but God rewards those who walk uprightly (John 15:18–21). The statement that the Lord was with him in verse 21, is the reason given for Joseph's success.

The presence of God makes all the difference. When Gideon protested that he was unable to deliver the Israelites from the Midianites, God said, *"I will be with you"* (Judg 6:16). When Jeremiah complained that he was too young to serve as a prophet, God said, *"I am with you"* (Jer 1:8). Jesus also promised that he would always be with us (Matt 28:20).

Probably this incident was allowed by God to test Joseph (Ps 105:17–19). Joseph's uncompromising position of moral purity cost him something. He was sent to prison because he refused to succumb to the seductions of Potiphar's wife, causing her to become angry and lie about him. Joseph's life story demonstrates clearly that at times God allows suffering in the lives of His children to accomplish His own special purposes.

Job is a classic illustration of one who suffered. His situation, though much different from Joseph, also had some similarities. In

Job and Joseph's life, God had a special purpose in allowing them to suffer. With Job, it was an unusual demonstration to Satan and us, that, though we do not understand why we are suffering, we can believe and trust God and remain true to Him no matter what the circumstances are.

For Joseph, it was to prepare him for a great task that had not only earthly, but eternal implications. And in every instance where God allows the righteous to suffer in order to use them in a special way, He will certainly make them stronger and more effective following the trail. This indeed is why God allows suffering in the first place. Yet because Joseph obeyed God, God turned the situation around and prospered Joseph in prison. God used this experience as a gateway to future blessing. Joseph learnt to trust and obey God in life's hard places. He learnt that moral purity, although costly, is the pathway to power and great blessing.

Joseph Never Lost His Vision in the Face of Opposition

The first test in his life was being thrown into the pit (Gen 37:24). There was no way, Joseph could see the throne from the pit. But he never lost his vision. You should never loose your vision in the face of opposition.

The second test was on his ability to resist temptations. Sometimes you may say 'yes' to God but do you say 'no' to the devil? (Gen 39:7–12). Joseph was thrown into the prison because of false accusation. Likewise our vision can be tested by false accusation. When Stephen got accused, his vision did not get dimmer but grew stronger and even brighter that he was able to see the Lord.

Remaining true to God-given vision can keep us from sin, as we see in Joseph's life. Joseph was faithful to the vision God had given him and was therefore faithful and loyal in his relationships, as well

(Gen 37:5–10). Remaining faithful to God's vision assures us of finding favour with God and with others and of achieving success in our endeavours (Gen 39:4, 21). Your patient faith will serve as a witness to those who may have scoffed, as you waited for the vision's fulfilment.

As Joseph discovered, sometimes it takes many years to see the fulfilment of a vision received early in life. Waiting patiently is not always easy, especially in the face of adversity. But staying true to God's vision for your life will keep you faithful to Him in all you do, restraining you from compromise and sin (Gen 39:9).

The story of Joseph teaches us that great wisdom and discernment must be exercised in sharing with others, the vision God has given us.

He Waited for God's Vindication

Probably some of us have faced the same kind of mistreatment as that of Joseph. No matter what the emotional or physical pain, we must not allow ourselves to become bitter towards God, for if we do we will only compound our problems. Not that God will turn against us; He never will. His love is unconditional. But if we are angry towards God, then in that state of mind we may be violating all the necessary steps we must take to draw on Him as our divine source of strength and help.

Joseph patiently waited for God to vindicate him, and to honour both his faith and his positive attitudes. So should we! Waiting eleven long years in prison must have been the most difficult thing Joseph had to do.

While in prison, Joseph interpreted the dreams of the king's chief cupbearer and the chief baker. When Joseph interpreted the cupbearer's dream, reassuring him that he would be reinstated to his former position, he asked this high-ranking official to put in a good word for him to the king. This must have been Joseph's first ray of hope for release since his confinement to prison by Potiphar, several years before.

Every day he must have waited for some word, or some indication that Pharaoh was concerned about his plight. After all, if the cupbearer had told the whole story, Pharaoh would have known that Joseph's God had enabled him to interpret dreams accurately. Surely Pharaoh would be interested in discovering more about Joseph's ability. But no word came, days turned into weeks and weeks into months and months into 'two full years'! Now it was thirteen years that he had been in prison paying the price for endeavouring to live a holy life. But Joseph waited patiently for God to set the record straight.

We must remember that God had not revealed to Joseph what was going to happen. The fact that the Lord gave him the supernatural ability to predict someone else's future did not mean that he could predict his own. Joseph had to continue in prison by faith, continuing to hope that God would make it possible for him to be released.

Joseph knew he was innocent and he also knew that this was the time to express it. And I'm glad he did, for it tells us there's a time to defend oneself against false accusation—even though God is the ultimate vindicator. There's also a time to ask someone to put in a good word for us even though we are trusting God with all our heart to help us and to defend us. But it must be emphasized that timing is very important.

Let's think for a moment about Joseph's family relationship. Probably he wanted to return to his family in Canaan (Gen 40:15). It had been thirteen long years since he had seen his father. Furthermore, since Joseph was a sensitive man, he must have grieved deeply for his father who had believed that Joseph was devoured by a wild animal. Fortunately, Joseph had hope beyond hope. That's what kept him from despair all during this terrible ordeal. His hope was ultimately in God, not in Potiphar, not in the cupbearer, not even in the king of Egypt. When men failed him he knew God was still with him even in the prison.

One of the great virtues God was developing in Joseph's life was patience, which is the essence of learning to wait. We read that the chief cupbearer did not remember Joseph; he forgot him. The historical record continues—'When two full years had passed, Pharaoh had a dream' (Gen 40:23; 41:1).

Eventually, when Pharaoh heard about Joseph he was impressed and sent word for him. Pharaoh said, 'I have heard it said of you, that when you hear a dream you can interpret it.' Joseph took absolutely no credit; he told Pharaoh it was not him who could interpret his dreams, but God will give the answer Pharaoh desires (Gen 41:14–16).

Pharaoh related his two dreams to Joseph, and Joseph was able to give an instant interpretation (Gen 41:17–32). Through this dream God was warning Pharaoh of the coming seven years of famine after the seven years of abundance. Not only did Joseph give an interpretation of the dream, but he also made a very wise proposal.

He suggested to Pharaoh that he look for a discerning and wise man—a man he could put in charge of the land of Egypt. He further suggested a plan for storing up food during the seven years of abundance, which in turn could be used and distributed during the seven years of famine. Pharaoh's response to Joseph's plan was positive. He asked his officials, 'Can we find anyone like this man, in whom is a divine spirit?' (Gen 41:33–36).

Pharaoh knew that Joseph's capabilities were from God. Furthermore, he now saw him against the backdrop of all the other magicians and wise men of Egypt.

Proper reasoning would help us to understand, why God allowed this to happen. Had Joseph come before Pharaoh two years before, chances are that it would have been only because of the king's curiosity. There would have been no personal need or sense of the wise men of Egypt. Consequently, there would have been no opportunity for Pharaoh to compare Joseph's success with their failure. The thoroughness with which Pharaoh tried to determine the meaning of his dreams is seen in his conclusion: *"There is no one so discerning and wise as you"* (Gen 41:39).

Had Joseph attempted to vindicate himself in his own efforts rather than waiting for God's moment in his life, he may never have gotten the unique opportunity that came his way that day. Wrong timing often causes legitimate self-defence to appear defensive.

Joseph became the grand vizier of Egypt. He went from 'Prison' to 'Palace'—not only to live there, but also to have authority over the whole kingdom of Egypt. Thus Pharaoh said, *"You shall be over my house . . . only in the throne I will be greater than you"* (Gen 41:40).

All of Joseph's patient waiting, faithful efforts and his positive attitudes over the past thirteen years did not go waste. Waiting time is not wasting time. A period of waiting often allows time for true character to be developed and revealed.

Joseph would have had some understanding of God's supernatural dealing for a greater purpose, when he went through the difficult and painful experience in all these thirteen years. God's divine pattern for his life must have come into focus rather suddenly when he was promoted so quickly and so dramatically. Seldom does any person released from prison, who is a foreigner, even when innocent, suddenly become a primary ruler of the most significant and affluent kingdom in the world.

The privileges, power, and prestige that went with this promotion accentuate, why this event is so dramatic and incredible and indeed a miracle of God. God was preparing Joseph to endure difficult and demanding circumstances. There's a price to be paid on every leadership position. There will be those who will become jealous. There will be rumours and false accusations. There will be misunderstandings and miscommunications. There will be sleepless nights and never-ending problems.

Samuel Rutherford once stated that we should praise God for the hammer, the file, and the furnace. He went on to explain that the hammer moulds us, the file shapes us and the fire tempers us. All three experiences of course are painful, but we can praise God for them because we know and love God who wields them.

Pharaoh gave Joseph an Egyptian name and married him into a prominent Egyptian family. However, Joseph gave his own sons Hebrew names, a practice that suggests he maintained his own identity.

Joseph's Character of Love and Forgiveness

The famine Joseph predicted came not only to Egypt, but it spread throughout the then known world (Gen 41:57). Consequently, Joseph's homeland, Canaan, was severely affected and so Jacob sent his sons to Egypt to buy food. After twenty years of separation, God used the famine to bring the sons of Jacob face to face with their brother Joseph.

Arriving in Egypt to see if they could buy grain, they were ushered into his presence. Imagine for a moment, what must have gone through Joseph's mind or heart when he looked up and saw ten men bowing low before him. Their garb was readily recognizable. Their tan, weather-beaten faces were those of shepherds and their beards set them off from the clean-shaven Egyptian men. Instantly, Joseph knew who they were—his brothers (Gen 42:2–7).

Though Joseph recognized them, he also sensed they did not know who he was. What were Joseph's thoughts and emotions at that moment? We can only speculate they certainly would have been mixed. On the one hand he probably had an intense desire to reveal his identity. On the other hand that approach would not answer the questions that were flooding his mind. What were their attitudes now? Had they changed? Were their hearts towards God?

Seeing his brothers bowing down before him, faces to the ground, suddenly took him back over twenty years to where his troubles actually began. He remembered his own dreams that had created such intense jealousy and hatred. And now, twenty years later, it was happening! His brothers were bowing down before him. He was in a position of honor over them. In fact, what happened that day became a key in unlocking Joseph's understanding regarding why God allowed him to be sold into Egypt?

Joseph needed more information of how his own brother and father were, before he could let them know who he really was.

One of the greatest struggles in life is to forgive someone who has wronged us, even though that person has not acknowledged the wrong nor sought forgiveness. Jesus of course set the example nobly when He hung on a rugged cross and cried out, regarding those who had so cruelly nailed Him there, *"Father, forgive them, for they know not what they do"* (Luke 23:34).

However, one of the greatest temptations to vindicate ourselves or to retaliate comes, when we meet face to face the one who has offended us. At that moment, whether or not we have truly forgiven is put to the test.

Joseph faced that very problem. His brothers had treated him cruelly. But we've seen Joseph's true character and love for his brothers. He held no grudges, nor did he harbour a desire to get even. And what makes Joseph such an outstanding example is that he had numerous options. He could have imprisoned them, and let them know how it felt to be incarcerated in a strange land with no one to represent your case. He could have sent them back to Canaan without food, leading to a slow but certain death. Or he had the authority to accuse them of spying and could have had them executed.

Joseph felt the strain of forgiveness. He wanted to reconcile with his brothers, whom he loved, but it was not easy. And until they had been pushed to the point of admitting and accepting their guilt, reconciliation could not occur.

Repentance and Reconciliation

Twenty years had not erased the brothers' memory of Joseph. Joseph had his brothers put in prison for three days. At the end of three days, he told them,

> "Do this and live, for I fear God: If you are honest men, let one of your brothers be confined in your prison; but as for the rest of you, go, carry grain for the famine of your households, and bring your youngest brother to me, so your words may be verified, and you will not die" (Gen 42:18–19).

The moment troubles began for Joseph's brothers, their guilt surfaced—*They said to one another, "Truly we are guilty concerning our brother, because we saw the distress of his soul when he pleaded with us, yet we would not listen; therefore this distress has come upon us"* (Gen 42:21). Joseph's strategy worked—God began to awaken their seared consciences through Joseph's words. They began to see a connection between what was happening to them in Egypt now and what they had done to Joseph years before.

For Joseph, this drama brought tremendous emotional strain. Five times Genesis records that he broke into tears, once weeping so loudly that people in the next room heard him. Their sins had planted deep-rooted bitterness, and only an emotionally wrenching struggle could pull it out.

Total repentance and taking responsibility for mistakes always bring results, no matter what the mistakes. Judah illustrates this point dramatically. He was the main leader in convincing his brothers to sell Joseph as a slave. And now he takes the primary leadership in voicing out the wrong he had done. He did not blame their father, though he was also the cause to the bitterness he harboured against Joseph. Neither did he blame Joseph, though he certainly could have pointed to his young brother's pride. And most important he didn't blame God. He made no excuses!

God honours a straightforward confession without self-justification and personal rationalizations. We will always be able to find points with which we can defend ourselves. However, if we have done something wrong we should be willing to accept and admit our faults. God always honours that approach.

Reuben, the oldest, became even more specific— 'Did I not tell you not to sin against the boy; and you would not listen? Now comes the reckoning for his blood' (Gen 42:22).

Though they did not realize it, Joseph understood every word they were saying, for he had an interpreter. For the first time in his encounter with his brothers he began to get answers to the most important questions he was concerned about. Were his brothers aware of their sin? More specifically, were they sorry for what they had done?

He retained Simeon and sent the other nine back to Canaan with their bags filled with grain. Unknown to them he had given instructions to put each man's silver back in his sack. That night when they stopped to rest, one of them discovered the money. The results were dramatic, and traumatic for Joseph's brothers. *Their hearts sank, and they turned trembling to one another, saying, "What is this that God has done to us?"* (Gen 42:28).

They were now sure and admitted that God was involved in this whole episode. They were sincerely frightened. How could they explain all of this to their father? Were they being forced to reveal all they had done to their brother Joseph? Would their father even allow them to take Benjamin to Egypt, especially if he suspected what they had really done to Joseph? Furthermore, what would happen if they did return to Egypt? How could they explain the returned money to the Egyptian ruler? (Gen 42:35). Joseph's brothers found themselves in a serious dilemma, as most people eventually do, when they sin and try to cover it up.

It is clear in this story that Joseph was not attempting to vindicate himself or retaliate for what his brothers had done to him. Rather, he was deeply concerned about his brothers' spiritual welfare and wanted to see his brother Benjamin.

The famine was severe in the land, Joseph's brothers ran out of grain they had brought from Egypt. To prevent them from starving to death they had to go to Egypt to get more grain. This means, they would have to take Benjamin along with them, to prove to Joseph that they were not spies. After much persuasion, their father finally gave them the permission to take Benjamin along with them. When Joseph saw Benjamin he went to his chamber and wept. After he controlled himself he came out and dined with his brothers. Finally Joseph made himself known to his brothers, and he wept so loud that the Egyptians and the household of Pharaoh heard it.

Joseph made a statement that must have overwhelmed his brothers even more—

> "Now do not be grieved or angry with yourselves, because you sold me here; for God sent me before you to preserve life . . . God sent me before you to preserve for you a remnant in the earth, and to keep you alive by a great deliverance." (Gen. 45:5, 7).

He categorically said, *"It was not you who sent me here, but God"* (Gen 45:8).

Joseph had not only risen above his circumstances with God's power, but he had also gained strength to forgive his brothers for what they had done to him. In addition, Joseph understood that God had taken their evil intention and had used it as part of His plan to send Joseph to Egypt, where he earned a position of rulership that later allowed him to save Israel.

The story of Joseph is a beautiful picture of God's love for humanity through Christ. It is hard to imagine how Joseph could so completely forgive the sins of his brothers that he would kiss all of them, and weep with joy at being united with them once again. After being thrown into a pit and then sold by them into the hands of slave traders, Joseph holds no hard feelings but has the welfare of his brothers in mind. Calvary is so similar; after being rejected time and time again by rebellious mankind, God still extends His love to us. Then once we have responded in faith to His love, He asks that we do the same to others.

Therefore, pain, tragedy, mistakes, and evil things that were done to us or that have happened to us can be used by God to make something beautiful through our lives. Only God has the power to take pain and change it into gain. The world never seems to recover from pain; often seeming doomed as they rehearse it over and over again in their minds. God's people have been given the spiritual power to forgive by the One who has forgiven them.

Joseph's Family and the Birth of a Nation

Pharaoh changed Joseph's name, and then he gave him a wife. His new name was Zaphenath Paneah (Gen 41:45). Inherent in this name—the title word nath—is the idea that 'God speaks and lives'. This indicates that Pharaoh believed and wanted others to believe that Joseph was a man of God. Joseph's wife was Asenath daughter of Potiphar, priest of On. This man's full identity and position in Egypt is unknown.

However, it is clear he was involved in the religious system, and that his daughter's name included the same idea as Joseph's new name.

After Joseph's promotion and before the years of famine came, we're told his wife Asenath gave birth to two sons (Gen 41:50). The names Joseph gave these two boys, along with his personal explanation as to why he named them Manasseh and Ephraim, are significant clues to understand how God brought healing to Joseph's inner being.

Joseph named his first son Manasseh, literally meaning 'One who causes to forget'. There is a very definite cause–effect relationship between Manasseh's birth and Joseph's ability to forget his painful past. He said, *"God has made me forget all my trouble and all my father's household"* (Gen 41:51). The emotional sting was gone. He was not in bondage to past experiences. There was no lingering bitterness; no emotional sensitivity, Joseph had no regrets. God had healed his memories. Asenath bore Joseph a second son. There are two possible interpretations regarding Joseph's intentions in naming his second son Ephraim—He said, *"God has made me fruitful in the land of my affliction"* (Gen 41:52). By 'fruitful' did he mean that God had given him a wife and two sons? Or was he referring to his position and accomplishments in Egypt? Joseph was in the midst of the seven years of abundance, when his sons were born. The land produced plentiful.

First, God gave Joseph a wife to help him out of his loneliness. We know little of Asenath, but we can conclude that she was a very special lady because her friendship and love brought healing to Joseph's emotional life. And the sons she bore, filled the vacuum in his life and enabled him to forget the deep loneliness he felt all those years when he was so cruelly separated from those he loved. It's also clear that Joseph did not allow himself to be influenced by Asenath's pagan background. For one thing, she was the only woman in his life. She was all that Joseph needed, emotionally and physically.

In a pagan society and government where men in high positions often demonstrated their power and prestige by the number of women in their harem, this is indeed significant. Joseph did not even follow in the footsteps of his father, Jacob. He maintained a monogamist relationship all his life, knowing this was God's ideal plan for marriage.

Joseph closes one chapter in the story of Israel. The children of Abraham were transformed from a chain of individuals to a nation. God did not choose Joseph over his brothers, as he did Abraham over Lot; Isaac over Ishmael; and Jacob over Esau. The brothers' reconciliation opened the way for them to become one family of twelve tribes—a single nation.

God had a plan for Joseph early on in his life. Although Joseph experienced, major ups and downs, God used those negative experiences to shape and mould Joseph. Not only did God use those experiences to bring him to the place of rulership, those negative experiences were used by God to refine and prepare him to be an effective leader. In Joseph we recognize the elements of a noble character—piety, pure and high morality, simplicity, gentleness, fidelity, patience, perseverance, an iron will, and an indomitable energy.

Joseph stands out in the Old Testament as a classic example of one who was repeatedly mistreated. Though difficult to understand, he did not allow bitterness or self-pity to wither his soul. Joseph is a marvellous example of Christlike behaviour in the Old Testament.

At times we too find ourselves trapped in painful circumstances that we don't want. Sometimes the pain comes from physical enemies; other times it comes from spiritual enemies. Sometimes it is the result of making poor choices; other times it is just part of the flow of life in a fallen world. Believers are not exempted from pain. Jesus

Himself confirmed that "*. . . in this world [we] will have trouble*" (John 16:33).

How was Joseph able to handle this incredible and persistent mistreatment so well? He did not turn against God; rather he turned to God even more. And so should we! Many people who are mistreated harbour bitterness toward those who caused it and also direct it towards God. They blame God for allowing it to happen.

No matter what the emotional or physical pain, we must not allow ourselves to become bitter towards God; for if we do, we will only be multiplying our problems. In that state of mind we will loose out on all the necessary steps we must take, to draw on Him as our divine source of strength and help. Not that God will turn against us; He never will. His love is unconditional.

Have you allowed bitterness to capture your soul because someone has related to you unjustly? God says:

> "Get rid of all bitterness, rage and anger, brawling and slander, along with every form of malice. Be kind and compassionate to one another, forgiving each other, just as in Christ God forgave you" (Eph 4:31–32).

Have you allowed any bitterness towards others to become bitterness towards God? God says:

> And we know that God causes all things to work together for good to those who love God, to those who are called according to His purpose . . . Who will separate us from the love of Christ? Will tribulation or distress, or persecution or famine or nakedness or peril or sword? . . . But, in all these things we overwhelmingly conquer through Him who loved us (Rom 8:28, 35, 37).

Have you become vindictive towards those who have mistreated you, seeking to get even? God says:

> Never pay back evil for evil to anyone . . . . Never take your own revenge beloved, but leave room for the wrath of God, for it is written, "vengeance is mine, I will repay," says the Lord

. . . . Do not be overcome by evil, but overcome evil with good
(Rom 12:17, 19, 21).

Joseph handled a 'full cup' very well in spite of his youthfulness. He
not only survived this test of prosperity, but also used it for the honour
and glory of God. He was prepared to handle the prestige and power
that God designed for him. All along the way Joseph passed each test
satisfactorily. He continued to act responsibly and walk in integrity.
Even in the midst of his own suffering, he noticed the pain of others
and offered to help them. He maintained a close relationship with
God that enabled him to forgive those who had hurt him.

He did not become bitter. He had a forgiving spirit. He
maintained a servant's heart. His self-confidence became properly
balanced with his confidence in God. And most of all, he never forgot
the grace of God in sustaining him in his most trying years! Joseph
trusted in the unbreakable Word of God, rested in the unshakable
power of God and enjoyed the undeniable peace of God.

Chapter 4

MOSES
A Leader Who Practised
the Presence of God

Abraham's grandson, Jacob, had twelve sons. God lifted up one of Jacob's sons Joseph from the pit and elevated him from the prison to the palace as the Prime Minister of Egypt—a position he later used to save his family from famine and to keep the dream of God's people alive. Thus Jacob relocated his family to Egypt, and Israel (Jacob) grew from a family to a nation.

The subsequent Pharaohs forgot Joseph and his favourable stance toward the Hebrews. The new Pharaohs embarked on ambitious building programmes, and they conscripted the minority Hebrews (Israelites) as labourers. The Hebrews had thus become slaves of the Egyptian taskmasters, and they cried out to God for deliverance (Exod 1:8–14; 2:23).

In spite of the whips of oppression and hatred, God's plan did not end there, in the mud pits of Goshen. God had chosen a baby named Moses, whom Pharaoh's daughter drew out of the Nile and gave him to his own mother to be brought up for the palace. This is a very interesting analogy. The Bible says that children are a gift from God (Ps 127:3).

God has given children to us not to fashion them or bring them up according to our own whims and fancies, but to prepare them for the kingdom of God. Moses' mother was given the responsibility to bring Moses up for Pharaoh's kingdom. Little did the princess realize that God had already intended Moses for His kingdom.

For forty years, Moses was a prince. Though he was in the royal state he never forgot his mother's teachings on the living God, and so he could not digest the fact that his people were being oppressed by the Egyptians. So, while trying to help his brethren from the hands of the cruel Egyptians, he got into trouble and then, he was forced out of Egypt for another forty years, where he became a humble shepherd. But at the age of eighty, God drew him out once again to become the deliverer of the Hebrews.

Moses was a born deliverer. Even before he met God, he wanted to set people free. One day he saw an Egyptian beating a Hebrew. When no one was looking, he killed the Egyptian and hid him in the sand. The next day he saw two Hebrews fighting. When he asked one of them, 'Why are you striking your fellow companion?' the man replied, 'Who made you a prince or a judge over us? Are you intending to kill me, as you killed the Egyptian?' (Exod 2:13–14). Moses was afraid because he realized that everyone had come to know about what he had done. When Pharaoh came to know about it, he tried to kill Moses, but Moses fled from his presence and settled in the land of Midian.

The Call for Deliverance

While Moses was tending the flock of his father-in-law Jethro; an angel of God came to him in a 'flame of fire', inside a burning bush. It was there God's call came to Moses to deliver His people (Exod 3:3). God told him, *"I have surely seen the affliction of My people who are in Egypt, and have given heed to their cry because of their taskmasters, for I am aware of their sufferings"* (Exod 3:7).

It means that God could actually feel His people's pain; that He experienced oneness with them in their suffering. Sometimes we make the mistake of thinking that God is distant from us. God's whole message in Christ is that He became a man to understand and know the difficulties we face as human beings (compare Heb 2:14–18; 4:14–16).

God heard the cry of His people and intervened to fulfil His covenant or agreement with Abraham and to deliver His people from the cruel taskmasters (Exod 3:7–8).

The message here is that God does not want His people to work as slaves to the world's system and to be in bondage to sin. God chose Moses to act as a deliverer on His behalf to set His people free. Moses foreshadowed Christ, who was the ultimate deliverer and who set God's people free from the bondage of slavery from the world system, of which Satan is the present ruler.

Years later, God reclaimed for His own purposes the deliverance and leadership skills that He had given to Moses. He sent Moses to the Pharaoh of Egypt to free the Israelites from slavery (Exod 3:10). God didn't throw away the skills and the talents that had been with Moses from birth. He simply renewed them and redirected them to their intended use. In essence, Moses was equipped to fulfil God's purpose, in his life and so are you.

God looks for availability and not ability

When God told Moses to go and deliver His people, the Hebrews, from bondage, Moses made a lot of excuses. In the Book of Exodus 4:10–16, we read that Moses felt insecure because of an apparent lack of eloquence (verse 10). Yet God told him that He would give him the words to speak (verse 12). Moses was still terrified of being a spokesperson for God, and so God agreed to let Moses speak through Aaron.

The point is that we do not have to be gifted in speaking. God doesn't use only evangelists, preachers, and eloquent speakers but He also uses ordinary people, who may have limited abilities. Jesus said, 'Do not become anxious about how or what you will speak; for it shall be given to you in that hour what you are to speak' (Matt 10:19). If we are available and open to Him, the Holy Spirit of God will put His thoughts in our thoughts and His words in our words.

Moses took the rod of God in his hand and set out to Egypt. Moses and Aaron went into the presence of Pharaoh and told him, *"Thus says the LORD the God of Israel, 'Let My people go that they may celebrate a feast to Me in the wilderness'"* (Exod 5:1). Pharaoh did not allow the Israelites to go but he commanded the taskmasters not to give the slaves straw to make the bricks, but the quantity of bricks they made each day should be the same.

The Israelites, especially their supervisors reacted to Pharaoh's new production policy by verbally attacking their own leader, Moses, (verses 15–21). Moses went into the presence of the Lord and said, 'O Lord, why hast thou brought harm to this people? Why did Thou ever send me?' The Lord said to Moses, 'Now you shall see what I will do to Pharaoh for under compulsion he shall drive them out of his land' (5:22–6:1).

The word that the Lord had spoken was fulfilled after He sent ten plagues on the Egyptians to break Pharaoh's stubborn will and demonstrate His power over the gods of the Egyptians. The plagues occurred during a nine-month period. After the plague of the first-born, Pharaoh let the Israelites go. God led them out of Egypt by the wilderness of the Red Sea.

While they were in the desert God placed over them a pillar of cloud to guide them on their way and by night a pillar of fire to give them light, so that they could travel by day or night. God placed the pillar of cloud and fire as proof of His presence, love and care for Israel. The cloud and the fire were present with them until they reached the Promised Land, forty years later (Exod 13:21).

Moses faced the test of the impossible when Israel reached the Red Sea. On one side, lay the impossible waste rage of Baal Zephon, on the other side an impossible waste of sand. Before them lay the impossible Red Sea, and behind them the invincible army of Pharaoh. Moses found himself shut up with a dismayed and complaining horde of people. In this unexpected and shattering experience, the morale of the Israelites dropped very low. When the Israelites saw this, they cried out to the Lord and complained to Moses saying, *"Is it because there was no grave in Egypt, that you have taken us away to die in the wilderness?"* (Exod 14:11).

Moses said to the people,

> "Do not fear! Stand by and see the salvation of the LORD, which He will accomplish for you today; for the Egyptians whom you have seen today, you will never see them again forever. The LORD will fight for you while you keep silent" (Exod 14:13–14).

For Moses, the man of faith, relied totally on God. His order of the day sounded like sheer fantasy to the demoralized Israelites, but in fact it was a demonstration of superb leadership.

'Fear not', he cried when there was every reason to fear.

'Stand still' when Pharaoh was rapidly overtaking them, and to stand still meant death.

'See the salvation of the Lord', which seemed a very long distance away.

Moses passed the test of the impossible situation, and God gloriously vindicated him. His positive prediction came true: 'The Egyptians whom ye have seen today ye shall see no more forever.' They saw the salvation of God and the total destruction of their enemies. The bracing lesson is that God delights to shut people up to Himself and then, in response to their trust, display His power and grace in doing the impossible.

In the evangelization of inland China, Hudson Taylor often found himself face to face with such situations. As a result of his experience, he used to say that there were three phases in most great tasks undertaken for God—impossible, difficult and done.

Moses told them to surrender their unbelief and totally believe that God would perform a miracle for them and He did. God delivered Israel through the Red Sea, they crossed over to the other side but the armies of the Egyptians were drowned in the sea. The children of Israel had a real problem with unbelief just like people do today. They constantly doubted whether or not God would perform the miracles.

The Presence of God at Mount Sinai

In the third month, after the sons of Israel had gone out of the land of Egypt, that very day the Israelites came into the wilderness of Sinai and they camped there before the mountain (Exod 19:1). God told him to tell the people to consecrate themselves for two days and on the third day, He would come down upon Mount Sinai in the sight of all the people (verse 9), in order that the people may hear when He speaks with him, that they may also believe in Him forever.

God's presence and power are so awesome that people cannot contain them unless they are holy. We install circuit breakers in electrical systems to protect wiring from overheating and damaging electrical appliances and causing house fires. This can happen if excessive current flows through the wires. In a similar way, when God sends His presence among His people, they must be spiritually prepared to handle it. If they have sins in their lives, they will not be able to handle God moving through them powerfully. Therefore, God told Moses to sanctify the people and gave them instructions so that when God came down upon Mount Sinai, they would not be destroyed.

When God came down on Mount Sinai, it was more amazing than any contemporary science fiction movie. There was smoke, fire, lightening, thundering, a thick cloud and the mighty presence of God. God's purpose was clear: God was coming to make Israel a holy nation and to give His people instruction. We can expect God to do something to effect the same changes in us.

If ever there was an occasion on which God revealed Himself to human beings, it was at Mount Sinai. When the Lord descended upon Mount Sinai, the whole mountain shook. In fact, the sight was so overwhelming that the people trembled with fear (Exod 19:16; 20:18). The Lord called Moses to the top of the mountain and Moses went up.

Clearly, they were convinced that they were standing before God Himself. Yet though the Lord's presence was still hovering over the mountain, the Israelites fashioned a golden calf and began worshipping it (Exod 32:1–6). This incident of the golden calf brought the Israelites very close to being instantly consumed by the Lord's wrath. Only the earnest intervention of Moses averted immediate judgement (Exod 32:31–35).

Moses went down the mountain with the two tablets of the Testimony in his hands. As soon as he came near the camp, he saw the calf and the dancing. So, Moses' anger became hot, and he cast the tablets out of his hands and broke them at the foot of the mountain. Then he took the calf that they had made, burned it in the fire, and ground it to powder, and he scattered it on the water and made the children of Israel drink it (Exod 32:15–20). He again goes into the presence of the Lord to make atonement for the sins of the people. Though Moses pleaded on their behalf, the Lord could not forgive the people for their sin. So, the Lord plagued the people because of what they did with the calf, which Aaron made.

Moses Intercedes for God's Presence

The Lord told Moses to move from Mount Horeb and go to the land flowing with milk and honey. So, the whole company of Israelites along with Moses moved on. Wherever they camped Moses used to pitch a tent a good distance from the camp. He called it the Tent of Meeting. Whenever Moses entered the tent, the pillar of cloud would descend and stand at the entrance of the tent; and the Lord would enter the tent. 'Thus the Lord used to speak to Moses face to face, just as a man speaks to his friend' (Exod 33:1–11).

When Adam and Eve sinned, God dismissed them from His presence, He drove man out of the garden. But God did not give up on man, nor did He cast doom on him as He did on the angels. The story continues as we see God's persistence in revealing His glory to man. The burning bush was an illustration of God's glory, but in Exodus 33 we have a clearer depiction. In verse 12, Moses speaks with God and is a bit upset with God for giving him such a divine responsibility with so little help. *"But You Yourself have not let me know whom You will send with me"* (Exod 33:12).

Moses told the Lord, 'Now therefore, I pray Thee, if I have found favour in Thy sight, let me know Thy ways, that I may know Thee, so that I may find favour in Thy sight. Consider too, that this nation is Thy people.' And He said, 'My presence shall go with you, and I will give you rest.'

Moses further pleads with God that His presence would go with them. For he tells the Lord,

> "How then can it be known that I have found favor in Your sight,
> I and Your people? Is it not by Your going with us, so that we, I

and Your people, may be distinguished from all the other people
who are upon the face of the earth?" (Exod 33:16).

The Lord told Moses that He would do this also for him since he
has found favour in the sight of the Lord and since He has known
him by name. Moses asked the Lord to show him, His glory. But the
Lord replied, 'You cannot see Me face to face, for no man can see Me
and live'. The Lord told him that there was a place by Him and that
he shall stand there on the rock. While His glory passes by, He will
put Moses in the cleft of the rock and cover him with His back, but
Moses would not be able to see His face (Exod 33:17–23).

God answered his desperate cry. Among the Parthians there
was a custom that no parents were to give their children meat in the
morning before they saw the sweat on their faces. That is God's usual
plan, as well-not to give His children the taste of His delights until
they began to sweat in seeking them. Moses was sweating after God's
glory, passed him. Imagine standing a few yards away from the sun.
That would be a very small example of God's glory in its fullness.
God's back passed by Moses while His face was hidden. Exodus 34
tells us what happened to Moses. His face shown like a light bulb
(Exod 34:29). His face shone so much that Aaron and the others
were afraid to come near him. Moses had to put a veil over his face
while he spoke to the people.

Today, we must do the same thing that Moses did. Those of us
who are leaders must carry God's presence into the lives of people.
Most of us do the opposite. We carry people into the presence of
God. We must come down from His presence to minister with
anointing from above. If people trample on the glory of God, that
should not drive us away from returning to the place of blessing to
receive further from God's glory. We are to be men and women bent
on the glory of God. It should consume us as it did Moses. Our
perseverance in bringing God's glory to the people will ultimately
bring lasting results.

Moses Enjoyed the Presence of God

God told Moses, *"My presence will go with you, and I will give you rest"* (Exod 33:14). Psalm 16:11 states, *In Your presence is fullness of joy.* God promises His presence to the people who will worship, obey and walk with Him. When we live in God's presence through the power of the Holy Spirit, He gives us peace and rest. The presence of God should not be a mysterious and distant thing to people who know God. Every believer in Jesus Christ should seek to live in the presence of God. When we walk with Jesus Christ in intimate fellowship, we can enjoy His presence.

Our God is a living God and when we live our lives in worship of Him, His glory and presence begin to fill our lives. Those of us who have accepted Jesus Christ into our lives now have the glory of God living inside us.

Chapter 5

JOSHUA
Enjoyed Presence and Experienced Power of God

After the death of Moses, the Lord spoke to Joshua the son of Nun:

> "Moses my servant is dead; now therefore arise, cross this Jordan, you and all this people, to the land which I am giving to them, to the sons of Israel. Every place on which the sole of your foot treads, I have given it to you, just as I spoke to Moses . . . No man will be able to stand before you all the days of your life. Just as I have been with Moses, I will be with you; I will not fail you or forsake you . . . Only be strong and very courageous; be careful to do according to all the law which Moses my servant commanded you; do not turn from it to the right or to the left, so that you may have success wherever you go" (Josh 1:1–7).

Joshua was Moses' right-hand during the exodus and desert wanderings. In the law-giving at Sinai he was Moses' companion (Exod 24:13). Joshua was one of the 12 spies sent by Moses to spy the land of Canaan When Moses died, Joshua was the obvious choice to succeed him in leading the nation. The Joshua story is a paradigm of the kingdom struggle which goes on every age and a sign for every generation. From Abraham's descendants through Jacob, God created a nation. Through Moses, God brought that nation out of captivity. And through Joshua, He brought that nation into the Promised Land. God is faithful to the promises he made to Abraham.

Joshua's capability and skill as a spiritual and military leader are evident from the success of the Israelites during his lifetime, and their rapid decline following his death. Indeed, not until Samuel's reign hundreds of years later do the Israelites find a comparable leader.

Joshua demonstrates a duality within his character that was missing from that of Moses. While Moses was primarily a spiritual leader, who acted as an intermediary between God and Israelites, Joshua was a capable military commander as well as a religious leader. All the 24 chapters of the Book of Joshua cover a period of approximately seven years. God had promised the land to the Israelites over 400 years before Joshua. He had chosen one man, Abraham, to found a nation of chosen people. He repeated those promises often (Gen 12:1–3; 15:5–18; 17:2–8; 26:3, 23, 24; 28:13, 14) and finally led the Israelites out of Egypt in order to possess the Promised Land. Almost from the beginning Canaan was a vital part of God's plan.

The Book of Joshua describes the conquest and settlement of the Land of Israel during a very significant period of Jewish history. It gives a fresh breeze of a glorious future. It shows us the spirit of victory and success experienced by God's people at that time. It is very interesting to see that the Book of Joshua occupies a key position in the Bible because of its relation to the Three Promises of God to Abraham:

The first promise was that God would give the land of Canaan to Abraham's descendants (Gen 12:1; 15:7). Abraham and Moses failed to possess it. But this promise was fulfilled in the Joshua story.

The second promise was that God would make of its descendants 'a great nation' (Gen 12:22). Towards end of the Joshua story we observe that a new society was established on the land (Josh 13–22). This was foreshadowing the forthcoming Davidic monarchy (2 Sam 5:3).

The third promise was that in Abraham all the families of the earth shall be blessed (Gen 12:3). We understand this from the canonical settings in the Joshua story. Obviously the blessings are received by Rahab because of her help to the chosen race of God and the Gibeonites as they submitted themselves to the leadership of Israel.

The Book of Joshua continues and concludes the events of the Exodus. In a very interesting way we see the recurrence of the Exodus themes in a spectacular new setting:

1. In Egypt the Israelites were liberated from the power of the Pharaoh. In Canaan the Promised Land was liberated from the tyrannous rule of the Canaanite kings.
2. The people of God came out of the Land of Slavery by crossing the sea. By crossing the river they came into the Land of Promise.
3. The newly formed covenant people at Sinai is similar to the new covenant people at Shechem.
4. The people of God receive guidelines for living both at Mount Sinai and at Mount Ebal.
5. The new allies in the wilderness (Exod 18) are parallel to the new allies in Canaan (Josh 2, 9).

In the light of the above observations we should try to understand the Joshua story as a recurrence of the Exodus pattern of salvation in the Promised Land: liberation, covenant bonding, and training.

Joshua Entered the Plan of God

The first four verses of chapter one describes how Joshua entered into God's plan for his life, which was to succeed Moses as leader of the children of Israel. Joshua listened to the voice of God calling and commissioning him. Joshua was given two main tasks. First, he was to direct a military campaign to take control of the land God had promised. Then, he would parcel out the conquered land among all the tribes. The Lord reassured Joshua that the mantle of Moses has fallen on him and that he has to now carry Moses' torch of divine strength. God tells Joshua, *"No man will be able to stand before you all the days of your life. Just as I have been with Moses, I will be with you; I will not fail you or forsake you"* (Josh 1:5).

When God calls you to perform some tasks for Him, He doesn't leave you alone. He becomes the strength in your arms and the voice on your lips. The peace of God guards you and the God of Peace guides you. Not only He exhorts Joshua to be strong and courageous but makes it clear that by keeping the Word of God in his heart, meditating upon it day and night and by doing what it says, he will become an overcomer.

Just like God had a plan for Joshua in the same way, God has a plan for your life too. You can be a person of excellence, success and prosperity if only you would enter into the plan of God by obeying His voice and doing His will. Man's greatest honour and privilege is to do the will of God. This was what the Lord Jesus taught his disciples. Jesus said, *"He who does the will of My Father who is in heaven will enter"* (Matt 7:21). He also said, *"For whoever does the will of My Father who is in heaven, he is My brother and sister and mother"* (12:50). The entire life and ministry of Jesus was to do the will of His father. His daily food was to fulfil His Father's will (John 4:34).

Why is it important to know God's will and plan for your life?
You are incapable of planning your life
Jeremiah says, *I know, O LORD, that a man's way is not in himself...* (Jer 10:23). Sin has deprived mankind of its steering mechanism. We read in Isaiah 53:6: *All of us like sheep have gone astray, Each of us has turned to his own way.*

Only God knows the way you should go

God knows the way, shows the way and leads the way. Without the Way there is no going; without the Truth there is no knowing; and without the Life there is no living. Man's way leads to a hopeless end but God's way leads to an endless hope. Too often you are looking for a road map to the future rather than a relationship with the Way, Jesus. We read in Isaiah 48:17, *"I am the LORD your God, who teaches you to profit, Who leads you in the way you should go"* and also in Jeremiah 29:11, *" 'For I know the plans that I have for you,' declares the LORD, 'plans for welfare and not for calamity to give you a future and a hope.' "* So, you have to ask God to reveal to you step by step His plan and purpose in your life. *Inside the will of God there is no failure. Outside the will of God there is no success* —Bernard Edinger.

Knowledge of God's will brings new assurance

It would not be easy to find a more blessed promise nor a greater incentive to learn what it means to pray 'according to His will'. We read in 1 John 5:14–15: *"This is the confidence we have before Him, that if we ask anything according to His will, He hears us. And if we know that he hears us in whatever we ask, we know that we have the requests which we have asked from Him."* It would not be easy to find a more blessed promise nor a greater incentive to learn what it means to pray 'according to His will'.

The will of God brings blessings in the life to come

Apostle John taught that, only the one who does the will of God abides forever (1 John 2:17). *The center of God's will is our only safety*—Betsie Ten Boom.

God wants you and commands you to know His will

Paul exhorted the Ephesian Christian not to be foolish, but understand what that will of the Lord was for their lives (Eph 5:17).

Paul prayed for the Colossians that they might be filled with the knowledge of God's will (Col 1:9). We must desire to receive God's will. *Make me know Your ways, O LORD; Teach me Your paths. Lead me in Your truth and teach me, For you are God of my salvation; For You I wait all the day (Ps 25:4–5).*

God promises to guide us

The Lord promises us to be actively involved in guiding and leading His children according to His will. He said, *I will instruct you and teach you in the way which you should go; I will counsel you with My eye upon you* (Ps 32:8). One reason He has given us His Spirit to dwell within us is for the specific purpose of leading us. *For all who are being led by the Spirit of God, these are the sons of God* (Rom 8:14). *For such is God, Our God forever and ever; He will guide us until death* (Ps 48:14). *There are no disappointments to those whose wills are buried in the will of God* —Frederick Faber.

God commands you to obey His will

We must let go of our own reasonings. *Trust in the LORD with all your heart, And do not lean on your own understanding. In all your ways acknowledge Him, And He will make your paths straight* (Prov 3:5–6).

We read in Ephesians 6:5, 6: *Slaves, be obedient . . . not by way of eyeservice, as men-pleasers but as slaves of Christ, doing the will of God from the heart.*

Dr. Billy Graham says,

> To know the will of God is the highest of all wisdom. Living in the center of God's will ... puts the stamp of true sincerity upon our service to God. You can be miserable with much if you are out of his will, but you can have peace in your heart with little if you are in the will of God. You can be happy in the midst of suffering if you are in God's will. You can be calm and at peace in the midst of persecution as long as you are in the will of God.

There is no failure inside the will of God and there is no success outside the will of God. It is always safe to be at the centre of God's will.

God's Justification in Driving Out the Canaanites

Israel's inheritance, however, meant sending out the Canaanites. How could innocent people simply be pushed aside, or killed? In answer to this question, the Bible makes clear that the Canaanites were not 'innocent'. Through their long history of sin, they had forfeited their right to the land.

Four hundred years before Joshua, God had told Abraham that his descendants would not occupy the land until the sin of its inhabitants 'had reached its full measure' (Gen 15:16). Later, just days before the onset of Joshua's campaign, Moses stated:

> "It is not for your righteousness or for the uprightness of your heart that you are going to possess their land, but it is because of the wickedness of these nations that the LORD your God is driving them out before you, in order to confirm the oath which the LORD swore to your fathers, to Abraham, Isaac and Jacob" (Deut 9:5)

Historians have uncovered plenty of evidence of this wickedness. Canaanite temples featured prostitutes, orgies, and human sacrifice. Relics and plaques of exaggerated sex organs hint at the morality that characterized Canaan. Canaanite gods, such as Baal and his wife Anath, delighted in butchery and sadism. Archaeologists have found great numbers of jars containing the tiny bones of children sacrificed to Baal. Families seeking good luck in a new home practised 'foundation sacrifice'. They would kill one of their children and seal the body in the mortar of the wall. In many ways, Canaan had become like Sodom and Gomorrah.

The Bible records that God has patience with decadent societies for a time, but judgement inevitably follows. For Sodom and Gomorrah it took the form of fire and brimstone. For Canaan it came through Joshua's conquering armies. Later, God let his own chosen people be ravaged by invaders, as punishment for their sins. The judgement pronounced on Canaan seems severe, but no more severe than what was later inflicted on Israel itself.

The Possibility of Transfer of Ungodly Spirit

Many people have often questioned why the children of Israel were commanded by God to utterly destroy all the nations occupying the Promised Land. God even told them to destroy the infants and animals and not to take any of their possessions into their households. This is due to the possibility of the dangerous transference of wicked and evil spirits. In His sovereignty, God knew that those ungodly nations would not repent. God also knew the children of Israel would become polluted by their sins and idolatries—He knew evil spirits would transfer to His people.

We read in Deuteronomy 20:16–18,

> "Only in the cities of these peoples that the LORD your God is giving you as an inheritance, you shall not leave alive anything that breathes. But you shall utterly destroy them, the Hittite and the Amorite, the Canaanite and the Perizzite, the Hivite and the Jebusite, as the LORD your God has commanded you, so that they may not teach you to do according to all their detestable things which they have done for their gods, so that you would sin against the LORD your God."

The Israelites could not simply settle down as new neighbours among existing Canaanite cities. From the time when the tribes had made a golden calf while Moses was receiving the Ten Commandments (Exod 32), Israelites had shown a fatal weakness to infection from outside. There was an evident transfer of spirit from the neighbours. They seemed particularly susceptible to sins of sex and idolatry, Canaan's national spirit of weakness.

The later history of Israel justifies why God commanded utter destruction of Canaanites. The alarming phrase in Joshua, 'But they did not drive out the Canaanites . . .' (Josh 16:10), hints at trouble to come, and the very next book, judges, tells of the devastating results. The Israelites slid to one of their lowest levels because they had not fulfilled the original mission of cleansing the land of impure elements.

There are even ruler spirits over cities and countries that affect and characterize the people that live in those cities and countries. For example, there is a gambling and party spirit over the city of Las Vegas. It becomes difficult for any natural person to go there and stay for any length of time without finding himself influenced by that same party spirit. There are spirits of self-promotion, false glamour, and sexual promiscuity over the city of Hollywood. People who go there often become seduced by those same spirits. There are also spirits that characterize the people of certain nations and cities. Germans are reputed to be industrious, clean people, while Italians have a freedom of expression and a zest for relaxed life.

God destroyed the cities of Sodom and Gomorrah because the ruler spirits of homosexuality, perversion, and greed had spread like malignant cancer to all the people of those cities so that not even ten righteous people could be found living there. In intercession, Abraham begged God not to destroy the people of those cities.

In Genesis 18:32, Abraham pleaded with God, 'Oh may the Lord not be angry, and I shall speak only this once; suppose ten are found there?' And He said, 'I will not destroy it on account of the ten.' Sadly though, there were not even ten righteous people living there who had not been corrupted by the spirits ruling over those cities.

We need to clearly understand that it is just as easy to acquire negative characteristics as positive ones. We need to constantly check whether our activities are in accordance with the Word of God. Then you can be safe from ignorantly getting trapped by negative spirits. Paul said, 'Put on the whole armour of God, that you may be able to stand firm against the schemes of the devil. For our struggle is not against flesh and blood, but against the rulers, against the powers, against the world forces of this darkness, against the spiritual forces of wickedness in the heavenly places' (Eph 6:11–12).

Repentance Brings Deliverance

The Bible presents the battles of Joshua as a wider struggle: one between those who followed God and those who opposed Him. Apart from the chosen people, even the heathens had an opportunity of being saved. When God judges groups of people as He judged the world in Noah's day or as He judged Sodom and Gomorrah, those few who remained faithful to Him, found a way of escape.

We see a similar incident happening in the Book of Joshua, the story of Rahab, a non-Jew, a typical Canaanite who worked as a professional prostitute. She hid the two Israelite spies in her house. Rahab's action in harbouring the spies stemmed not from fear, but from belief that Israel's God is the true God. She told the two Israelite spies:

> "For we have heard how the LORD dried up the water of the Red Sea before you when you came out of Egypt, and what you did to the two kings of the Amorites who were beyond the Jordan, to Sihon and Og, whom you utterly destroyed.
> When we heard it, our hearts melted and no courage remained in any man any longer because of you; for the LORD your God, He is God in heaven above and on earth beneath" (Josh 2:10–11).

Though the Canaanites' heard of the God of Israel yet only Rahab took the step of faith by acknowledging the God of Israel. If others in Canaan had repented and turned to God, they might well have escaped punishment, as Rahab did. She and her entire family were the only ones who were allowed to escape when the city of Jericho was taken over by the Israelites. Furthermore, she went on to marry a leading Israelite and became a part of the genealogy of the seed of the woman and one of the ancestors of the Messiah Himself, Jesus.

If others in Canaan had repented and turned to God, they would have also escaped punishment, as Rahab did. Similarly, when the angel of death passed by the houses in Egypt; if the Egyptians had sprinkled the blood on their doors their firstborns would have been saved. The same thing happened when the angel of wrath passed by. If the Egyptians had sprinkled the blood on their doors their firstborns would have been saved.

Likewise the healing, deliverance and salvation given by Jesus is open for all who believe. After 40 years of wilderness experience it was indeed a good news and a welcome change for the Israelites to prepare themselves to go into the Land of Promise. It is very much different from the Book of Numbers in terms of discouraging situations and from Deuteronomy in terms of Fatalism. It does not contain a single word about rebellion against a leader or grumbling against God.

Joshua's Jordan Expedition

Joshua rose up early in the morning after the spies had returned and made their report which shows his readiness and alacrity to proceed in the expedition he was directed and encouraged to. 'He who seeks me early shall find me,' says the Lord (Prov 8:17).

For several months the people of Israel encamped at Shittim. This is historically a prominent place where they heard Moses recite the Law to them (contained in Deuteronomy, which means "second law"). From there they conquered the Ammonite kings Og and Sihon on the east side of the Jordan (where the tribes of Reuben, Gad, and part of Manasseh settled).

Now the Israelites had to set out Shittim and came to Jordan and they lodged there. They would have awondered why they should break camp to move such a short distance of six or seven miles and stay such a short time for three days. But there seems to be a reasonable reason for that move of God in their lives. They had actually settled down in Shittim. They had been there for months, perhaps years, and were too accustomed to sedentary camp life. To take possession of the Promised Land, they need to regain or get back into their pilgrim stance once more. It is easy to steer a moving car than a parked one. When we are too comfortable with things in our lives, or perhaps have accepted the compromises for too long, it is difficult to make the changes necessary to re-align ourselves with God's will.

So finally they had to break camp at Shittim and move to a new encampment right on the banks of the Jordan River. Here they stayed for three days watching the flooded river flowing with great force. Joshua then told the people, *"Consecrate yourselves, for tomorrow the Lord will do wonders among you"* (Josh 3:5)

Consecration

Joshua exhorts the people to consecrate themselves in view of the wonders God would work among them on the next day. By this exhortation, he makes it very clear that we need to consecrate ourselves today if we have to experience God's wonderful deeds tomorrow. Very often we forget about today and always focus on tomorrow. Tomorrow never comes. When the next day comes, it is again today. Hence we need to live one day at a time. Especially when we think of doing God's will in our lives, we immediately tend to think of tomorrow. But unless you do God's will today you cannot do it tomorrow.

Every day early in the morning my wife and I sing the song: "Keep me true Lord Jesus keep me true, there is a race that I must run, there are victories to be won, give me power every hour to be true." Yes if I do not complete the race that God has set before me today, I cannot make it up tomorrow. Today if I am not in the centre of God's will I cannot fulfil God's will and plan for tomorrow.

Joshua tells them to consecrate themselves. What does the word 'consecrate' mean? This is not exactly what we might expect from a military standpoint. During those days, the military leader would have said, 'Sharpen your swords and spears and polish your shields!' But God's ways are not our ways. For God's people, spiritual preparation is a very vital element before making any physical attempt.

'Consecrate' is the Hebrew *qadash* and it may mean, 'be hallowed, set apart, consecrated.' In the Old Testament this word is often used (particularly in Exodus and Leviticus) in connection with the Old Testament sacrifices, priesthood, washings, and with regard to the children of Israel as God's people.

Preparation and Dedication

Any great task requires spiritual as well as material preparation. It is very interesting to note the analogy with the Exodus tradition. The three days allowed for preparation are a reenactment of the three days for purification and consecration at the foot of Mount Sinai (Exod 19:10). During this time of spiritual preparation, all impurities are to be removed (verse 10), because God Himself will walk in the midst of their camp, to save them and give them their enemies before them (Deut 23:14). It is not a time for indulgence in ordinary pleasures (1 Sam 21:4–5), but for inner discipline and dedication to the task ahead.

God's command must become our commission, for since God is infinite and eternal; there is no other source of righteousness, justice, law, or holiness. We should submit to Him and go His way or we will have to forever do without His nature, His grace, or His presence. When there is a lack of consecration through confession for the defilement of sin along with a commitment to God's purpose for our lives in service or ministry, we hinder the power of God. A holy and a consecrated life may not be popular but powerful. Holiness is not only what God gives us, but what we manifest through what God has given us.

Holy Desires, Clean Passions, Pure Thoughts

Paul writes, *I pray God your whole spirit and soul and body be preserved blameless unto the coming of our Lord Jesus Christ* (1 Thess 5:23). Sanctification is a work of God through the Holy Spirit that affects the entire nature of man. The body has its own appetites and cravings, which are capable of being perverted through indulgence. When your spirit is brought into a right relationship with God it becomes the controlling force in your life. As you allow the Spirit of God to work in you, you will find that your desires become holy, your passions clean, your thoughts pure, and that your delight will be in fulfilling the will of the Lord.

Holiness is a mysterious treasure of God. Neither human, nor angelic intellect can comprehend the holiness of God. When we consider holiness of human beings, it refers to blamelessness, virginity, righteousness, and moral perfection in general. It is a state of being marked by wholesomeness and godliness in spirit and body. However, holiness, being inclusive of all virtues, also has an essence merely to 'set apart for God'. That is what Joshua meant when he said to the people to consecrate themselves. But there is more included here in this call for consecration. The people of Israel were to expect God to work a miracle. They were to be eagerly looking forward for the wonders to happen.

It was necessary for the people to purify themselves to experience this miracle, because they were about to enter a new path through which their observance of God's Covenant would enable them to transcend natural law. This was one of only three occasions when the Ark was carried not by the Levites but by the Cohanim (priests)—the other two occasions were in the siege of Jericho and when the Ark was returned from the Philistines. When God instituted the Covenant of the Law (the Law of Moses), He set aside one tribe from the twelve to serve Him as attendants. This was the tribe of Levi. Unlike the other 11 tribes, they were given no inheritance in the Promised Land. Instead, their inheritance was the tithes given by the other tribes. The Levites were chosen to be attendants and servants at the Tabernacle and later at the temple.

The family of Aaron, were a member of the tribe of Levi, but God chose their line specifically to serve Him as priests. They were the mediators between God and the Israelites. They were responsible for the sacrifices, as well as other priestly duties such as using the Urim and Thummim (lot-casting objects), and deciding the cleanliness or uncleanliness of disease victims. It was the high priest, and only he, who could go into the 'Holy of Holies' on the day of Atonement, in order to sprinkle the blood of the sacrificial bull on the mercy seat of the Ark of the Covenant. This symbolised the covering of the nation's sins. Nobody but a direct descendant of Aaron's family line could serve as a priest. The Levites were basically temple servants.

Joshua instructed the priests to carry the ark ahead of the people. Because of God's great love for them He would not allow them to go anywhere but where He Himself would go before them and go with them. They have been instructed that the ark should *pass before them into Jordan.* Because of God's great love for them He would not allow them to go anywhere but where He Himself would go before them and go with them.

Carrying the Presence of God

It involves enjoying the presence of God

Now the LORD said to Joshua, *"This day I will begin to exalt you in the sight off all Israel, that they may know that just as I have been with Moses, I will be with you"* (Josh 3:7). God makes a promise that God made to Joshua that he would be with him, just as he had been with Moses. Surely this spells true success and real prosperity—to be conscious all the time of the presence of the Lord, to know that He is with us every moment of everyday and that He will never fail us. The Lord was re-assuring Joshua of both God's *personal presence* and His *powerful provision,* the provision of His vast hosts. The promise of God's personal presence always carries with it the assurance of God's personal care.

Moses prayed to God, *"For how then can it be known that I have found favor in Your sight I and Your people? Is it not by Your going with us so that we, I and Your people may be distinguished from all the other people who are upon the face of the earth?"* (Exod 33:16).

Moses and Joshua very well understood that in the end, the *only* thing that matters, the *only* thing that makes God's people different from all the rest, is the *presence of God* with them. If you are a believer in Christ, God's presence should never be in doubt, because it does not depend on you or the quality of your faith but on your commitment to Jesus Christ. Now He is sitting at the right hand of the Father, and He says to us, 'Surely I am with you always, to the very end of the age.'

'. . . In Your presence is fullness of joy and in Your right hand there are pleasures forever ... I have set the Lord continually before me; because He is at my right hand, I will not be shaken,' said the Psalmist.

It involves experiencing the power of God

In the first chapter of the Book of Joshua, verses 6, 7 and 9 contain God's commands to Joshua to be strong and very courageous. All God's commands are God's enablings. The same gracious and powerful enabling that God promised and made available to Moses and to Joshua, has been made available to us in the person of the Holy Spirit who dwells within us (John 14:16–17).

Exhortation of the Word of God

The Word of God is the authority of prophetic leadership

Joshua said to the sons of Israel, "Come here, and hear the words of the Lord your God" (Josh 3:9). Joshua endeavoured to boost the confidence of the people through trusting the Word of God. He also maintained the fact that the authority of spiritual leaders should be based on Scripture rather than their personality, charisma, or their past experience. *Faith comes from hearing and hearing by the word of Christ* (Rom 10:17).

Joshua said, *"By this you shall know that the living God is among you and that He will assuredly dispossess from before you the Canaanite, the Hittite, the Hivite, the Perizzite, the Girgashite, the Amorite and the Jebusite"* (Josh 3:10). The words, 'by this' in verse 10 refers to the Ark of the Covenant.

The Ark of the Covenant Contained the Presence of God

Joshua told the people, *"Behold, the ark of the covenant of the LORD of all the earth is crossing over ahead of you into the Jordan"* (Josh 3:11). The most important feature of this episode is the Ark of the Covenant. Its prominence is stressed in the number of times it is mentioned in chapters three and four. It is mentioned nine times in chapter 3 and seven times in chapter 4.

What's so important about the Ark? It represented the person and promises of God. It pointed to the fact that as the people of Israel set out to cross the Jordan, invade, and possess the land, they must do so not in their own strength, but in God's for it was God Himself who was going before them as their source of victory. So, carrying the Ark, accounts for carrying the Presence of God.

This statement of Joshua makes it clear that the battle belongs to the Lord and the key is staying focused on His presence and resting in Him. Joshua told the people, *"It shall come about when the soles of the feet of the priests who carry the ark of the LORD, the Lord of all the earth, rest in the waters of the Jordan, the waters of the Jordan will be cut off"* (Josh 3:13).

Since it was the priests who carried the Ark of the Covenant, and since it was the ark that represented God's person and power, they alone were to take the Ark to the edge of the water and stand *still* in the water. What do we gather from this? It reminds us of our part in the plan of God.

We must learn to step out in faith and obedience to the principles and promises of Scripture. It reminds us of the need to rest in God's promises. They were not to run down into the waters. This is just like the words of Moses when they were hemmed in with the Red Sea in front of them and Pharaoh and his chariots behind them. *But Moses said to the people, "Do not fear! Stand by and see the salvation of the* LORD *which He will accomplish for you today; for the Egyptians whom you have seen today, you will never see them again forever. The Lord will fight for you while you keep silent"* (Exod 14:13–14).

Why did God allow this spectacular event to take place? It is in order to teach us a lesson on risk taking faith. Sometimes God does not move until we're on the edge, and by our faith we step into raging waters. The priests, by faith, put their feet into the water. Peter, by faith, got out of the boat and walked toward Jesus. As long as he is sitting in the boat, he will never walk on the water. These were unnatural acts according to nature. But with God, everything is possible.

Rahab believed in God before she ever understood what her belief meant, and she was delivered from Jericho. Perhaps God is encouraging you to trust Him, even on the edge of Jericho, and move ahead without fear.

A prophetic leader should have the same courage as that of the priests who stood in the middle of a dry riverbed with water towering over their heads. Through their faith in action, the priests were a great inspiration to the people of Israel as they walked across the riverbed When they saw the water looming overhead they would have thought, 'What if the water comes down?' But because the priests were examples of faith and strength and they were faithfully and painstakingly holding the Ark of the Covenant, the people walked across the Jordan without fear.

From Oppressed Seven to New Society of Twelve

Joshua told the people *"Now then, take for yourselves twelve men from the tribes of Israel, one man for each tribe"* (Josh 3:12). It is very interesting to note that the narrative places the instruction of Joshua to 'take *twelve* men' (verse 12) immediately after the statement that God Himself will take the power away from (not drive out) the *seven* nations (3:10). In this way the seven and the twelve are placed in relationship to each other. The twelve symbolize the new covenant people or society of freedom and justice that was God's intention for the land. The seven symbolize the entire number of oppressive and corrupt authorities presently ruling the land.

When the 'Lord of all the earth' had taken power away from the seven and given to the twelve, the people who had been under oppressive rule of the seven would be free to join the new society of the twelve. In fact, this is what happened in the course of the struggle for the land.

This powerful demonstration of Yahweh's power and authority over the waters of Jordan is presented as a sign that Yahweh would take control of the land from the seven nations mentioned in Joshua 3:10: *"By this* (by the subduing of waters) *you shall know that the living God is among you."* The Lord of all the earth (3:11) has power over waters of the river (the exorbitant powers of the nature) as well as over the nations.

Crossing over to the Other Side

Joshua told the people when the soles of the feet of the priests who carry the ark of the Lord, rests on the water of the Jordan the waters of the Jordan will be cut off. Then they all will cross over to the other side. Even with God's specific guidance, and with specific guidance from His word, this is still and impressive step of faith for Joshua.

So the people set out from their tents to cross the Jordan with the priests carrying the Ark of the Covenant before the people, and when the feet of the priests carrying the ark touched the water's edge, the water which was flowing down from above stood and rose up in one heap, a great distance away at a town called Adam. The water which was flowing down toward the Sea of the Arabah, the Salt Sea, was completely cut off. So the people crossed over opposite Jericho. Joshua told the people '. . . for you have not passed this way before . . .' (Josh 3:4)

Indeed this was a path indeed not travelled by any; neither them nor any other ever went into Canaan the way they were now going, through the River Jordan as on dry land. Likewise, the way to heaven through Christ is only revealed in the Gospel, and only travelled by believers in Him. It is an amazing fact to note that no one ever went through that path in this manner before and never again after the chosen race of God had once passed through it.

Likewise all the believers in Christ will pass through the clouds into the heavenly abode only once at the time of rapture and no one has ever gone through that way before except probably Enoch and Elijah. Job said, *"He knows the way that I take"* (Job 23:10)

Our Shepherd knows the windings along which He skillfully, gently, and safely leads His flock. He has travelled that way Himself, and has left the traces of His presence on the Milky Way. Jesus became the firstfruit of all resurrection (1 Cor 15:20). All the believers in Christ will resurrect with a new body at the time when Jesus would come on the clouds and they would travel the same way that Jesus Himself mounted up to heaven (1 Thess 4:13–18). *"I will lead the blind by a way they do not know, in paths they do not know I will guide them, I will make darkness into light before them and rugged places into plains. These are the things I will do, and I will not leave them undone"* (Isa 42:14–16).

Though the place named 'Adam' is found only here it is usually identified with Telled–Damiyeh, about 16 miles north of the ford opposite Jericho. A wide stretch of riverbed therefore was dried up, allowing the people with their animals and baggage to hurry across (compare Josh 4:10).

As we consider all that happened it really seems to be a special act of God brought about in a very unusual way ever known to man:

1) It came to pass as prophesied by Joshua (Josh 3:13, 15).
2) It happened at the exact time (Josh 3:15).
3) This tremendous episode took place when the river was at heavily flooded (Josh 3:15)
4) The great wall of water was held in place for several hours, probably for the whole day (Josh 3:16)
5) The river bed which was slushy and wet became dry at once (Josh 3:17)
6) The water returned immediately as soon as the people had crossed over and the priests came up out of the river (Josh 4:18).

Thus God was magnified, Joshua was exalted (Josh 3:5), the people were encouraged and motivated, and the people of the land, the Canaanites, were terrorized (Josh 5:1). God was giving them the land. Indeed, crossing the Jordan, then, meant two things for Israel. First, they must be totally committed to going against armies, chariots, and fortified cities and secondly committed to a focused walk of faith in *Yahweh,* the only true and living God.

For believers in Christ today, crossing the Jordan represents passing from one level of their faith life to another. It is a picture of entering into spiritual warfare to claim what God has promised. This should mean the end of a life lived by human effort and the beginning of a life of faith and obedience.

Faith Is conviction of Unseen Realities

This was a crucial test of Joshua's prophetic leadership. He told the people: *"As soon as the priests who carry the ark of the LORD—the Lord of all the earth—set foot in the Jordan, its waters flowing downstream will be cut off and stand up in a heap"* (Josh 3:13). It was a faith statement for Joshua, and I have been greatly impressed by the fact that the water didn't stop until the priests' feet touched it. Sometimes, God's miracles take place ahead of us which make things easier for us. The

Red Sea was parted and then the people of Israel went through. But sometimes, God waits for us to take steps of faith before the miracle begins. Unless you take that step of faith you will not even see a clue of how it is going to happen.

In order to possess the land given by God, the greatest hindrance or problem for them was the waters of Jordan. They neither prayed against the water nor commanded it to be removed, but simply carried the presence of God and walked into the water. When you carry the presence of God, your problem will automatically be removed.

We observe that in the ministry of Jesus. He met some lepers along the border between Galilee and Samaria. 'Jesus, Master,' they called in a loud voice, 'have pity on us!' Jesus' reply is interesting: 'Go, show yourselves to the priests,' he tells them. 'And as they went,' the Scripture records, 'they were cleansed' (Luke 17:11–14). If they had waited to be cleansed before starting their journey and likewise if the priests had waited for the waters to stop before taking the next step, they would all be waiting still.

But there are times, we have to do all God instructs us to do, and then He does what no one can do but Him. Perhaps you're in that kind of place right now. You feel God is leading you to take a step that will make you look foolish, vulnerable, and you are afraid to take it. Now you know what Joshua felt like. But he did what God told him to do, and announced what God had promised to do, and God came through for him.

Very often we like to see things happen before we believe it. But faith believes before it sees. *We walk by faith, not by sight* (2 Cor 5:7), not because this is our way, but because it is God's way. This is exactly what Joshua did. He delivered the plan of God to the people as he had received it from God. Then he announced the crossing, based on God's Word that he would perform a miracle. And God did, just as he had for Moses at the Red Sea, a generation before.

The Biblical Significance of the Waters of Jordan

The Exodus departure and Jordan arrival are often combined in the Old Testament narratives. The earliest description is found in the 'song of the sea' (Exod 15:1–8). There we read how 'Pharaoh's chariots and his host he cast into the sea' (verse 4), how the people of Canaan 'melted away' (verse 15; compare Josh 5:1), and how God's people 'crossed over' into the land of Canaan (verse 16; compare Josh 3:17; 4:23).

In the Book of Psalms, the two events are combined very briefly: 'He turned the sea into dry land, men passed through the river on foot' (Ps 66:6). The whole of Psalm 114 is devoted to God's victory over the sea and the Jordan. The 'song of the arm of the Lord' (Isa 51:9–11) speaks of the drying up of the sea and making 'a way for the redeemed to pass over' (Compare Josh 4:24) meaning the path through the Jordan waters 'to Zion'.

The Crossing of Jordan by Great Men of God

Because of the limitations of geography, the first crossing could take place only once, while in different times in history Jordan was crossed in different ways by different men of God:

Jacob crossed the Jordan with his families and belongings on his way to meet his brother Esau in the land of Sier, the country of Edom.

Saul, who after the victory at Jabesh Gilead crossed the Jordan to be crowned at Gilgal, as a preparation for liberation of the land from Philistine oppression (1 Sam 11:14–15).

David also crossed the Jordan to the east in his escape from Absalom's forces. (2 Sam 17:22), and then crossed again to the west after the victory had been won. 'So the king came back to the Jordan; and Judah came to Gilgal to meet the king and to bring the king over the Jordan' (2 Sam 19:15).

Elijah crossed the Jordan from Gilead to carry out his ministry, and then crossed to the east to be received up by God.

Elisha crossed to the west again in circumstances recalling the crossing under Joshua, to continue his master's ministry (2 Kings 2:6–14).

Jacob crossed the Jordan with his families and belongings on his way to meet his brother Esau in the land of Sier, the country of Edom.

Much importance has been given to the waters of Jordan in the New Testament. Jesus' ministry begins when He is baptized 'into' the waters of the Jordan, making a decisive 'crossing over' to a new level of ministry. When Jesus 'came up' out of the waters (Mark 1:10; compare Josh 4:19), He heard the voice from heaven ordaining Him to His mission: *Thou art my beloved Son, in whom I am well pleased* (Mark 1:11). This recalls the words of God to Joshua, *"This day I will begin to exalt you in the sight of all Israel"* (Josh 3:7; 4:14).

God Called Joshua to Possess not to Conquer the Land

Joshua was called to help the people come into their inheritance. But it was the responsibility of the people to 'possess' the land, as God's tenants.

The Hebrew verb *yarash* has an original and archaic meaning 'to tread on' grapes, as seen in Micah 6:15, the only available example. There is another parallel and a more commonly used word *darak* which means to tread on grapes (Judg 9:27), or to tread on a land as possessor (Mic 5:5–6).[1] It is this latter word which is used in Deuteronomy 11:24–25 and Joshua 1:3 as symbolic action not of a conqueror, but of a tenant receiving the land from the owner: 'Every place on which the sole of your foot treads (darak) shall be yours.' The Hebrew verb 'yarash' has three meanings when used in relation to land. The first is to receive the land as a gift and to inherit it (Lev 20:24). The second is to occupy and organize the land according to God's teachings.

The Book of Deuteronomy again and again emphasizes that the commandments are to be applied 'in the land to which you are going over, to possess it . . . that it may go well with you . . .' (Deut 6:1–3). Conversely failure to observe the conditions of faithful tenants will mean that the rights of tenancy or 'possession' will be taken away (Deut 4:26; 28:63). The tenants may be 'dispossessed' (Num 14:12).

The third meaning derives from the first two. Obtaining the right of tenancy and living on the land can be effected only if the tenant exercises actual control. For this reason 'yarash' may also mean to take possession by force (Deut 6:18–19) from 'nations greater and mightier' than Israel, who are occupying the land. It is in this sense that the word is sometimes translated 'dispossess', i.e., to take control of the land from the present tenants (Deut 9:1; 19:1–3). This act is justified, only when the old society is wicked and corrupt (Deut 9:5), and when the new society fulfils God's will.

Joshua's Jericho Episode

Jericho was not defeated by earthly weapons and military strategy. Jericho was defeated by the supernatural power of God. The defeat of Jericho demonstrates the power of worship and praise as seen in the leading of the ark, the continual trumpet blowing, and a holy shout. The Jericho Episode portrays the Prophetic Leadership of Joshua.

Supernatural Strategy: Waiting, Walking and No Talking

Joshua received specific instructions from God, about how to possess Jericho. It was a supernatural strategy, which consisted of waiting, walking, and no talking. The children of Israel had marched by faith day after day with no apparent results.

Joshua 6:1–10:

> Now Jericho was tightly shut because of the sons of Israel; no one went out and no one came in.

And the LORD said to Joshua, "See, I have given Jericho into your hand, with its king and the valiant warriors."
"You shall march around the city, all the men of war circling the city once. You shall do so for six days."
"Also seven priests shall carry seven trumpets of rams' horns before the ark; then on the seventh day you shall march around the city seven times, and the priests shall blow the trumpets."
"It shall be that when they make a long blast with the ram's horn, and when you hear the sound of trumpet, all the people shall shout with a great shout; and the wall of the city will fall down flat, and the people will go up every man straight ahead."
So Joshua the son of Nun called the priests and said to them, "Take up the ark of the covenant, and let seven priests carry seven trumpets of rams' horn before the ark of the LORD."
Then he said to the people, "Go forward and march around the city, and let the armed men go on before the ark of the Lord."
"And it was so, that when Joshua had spoken to the people, the seven priests carrying the seven trumpets of rams' horn before the LORD went forward and blew the trumpets; and the ark of the covenant of the LORD followed them."
"The armed men went before the priests who blew the trumpets, and the rear guard came after the ark, while they continued to blow the trumpets."
But Joshua commanded the people, saying, "You shall not shout nor let your voice be heard, nor let a word proceed out of your mouth, until the day I tell you, 'Shout!' Then you shall shout!"

A silent walk

The people had to walk silently. It would have been a difficult task for Joshua to keep such a large number of people in total silence. But Joshua said to them, 'Don't say a word' (Josh 6:10). Some times and in certain situations the most difficult thing in the world is to be totally silent. But, for the people of God the success of their mission involved the control of their tongue.

A faith walk

This faith walk was a test of their obedience and trust (Ps 37:34). They had to exercise implicit, unconditional obedience for seven days. It took amazing self-control and submission to God's will. The people had to walk around the city, not doing a thing to attack it, and maintain absolute silence. Though they were doing nothing, yet followed God's instructions. Then they had to go back to the camp and spend the night there (Josh 6:11). It was a very unusual way of destroying a city!

The second day they got up early in the morning to do the same thing all over again. The people carried on this way for six days.

> So he had the ark of the LORD taken around the city, circling it once; then they came into the camp and spent the night in the camp.
> Now Joshua rose early in the morning, and the priests took up the ark of the LORD.
> The seven priests carrying the seven trumpets of rams' horns before the ark of the LORD went on continually, and blew the trumpets; and the armed men went before them, and the rear guard came after the ark of the LORD, while they continued to blow the trumpets.
> Thus the second day they marched around the city once and returned to the camp; they did so for six days (Josh 6:11–14).

The marching tested the faith of the people: By faith the walls of Jericho fell down, after they had been encircled for seven days (Heb 11:30).

It took faith to continue in obedience without knowing what would happen. It took patience and self-control, and such patience and self-control required faith.

A praise walk

The message to be learnt from the battle of Jericho is that God wants to destroy any fortified cities and strongholds that are erected by the enemy to block the purposes of God. The primary weapons God used here were supernatural weapons of worship and praise. *Thus the second day they marched around the city once and returned to the camp; they did so for six days* (Josh 6:14)

Then on the seventh day that they rose early at the dawning of the day and marched around the city in the same manner seven times; only on that day they marched around the city seven times (Josh 6:15).

The apostle Paul talked about supernatural warfare and the destruction of strongholds. For the people of God, victory does not come through fleshly struggle and worldly weapons. *For though we walk in the flesh, we do not war according to the flesh, for the weapons of our warfare are not of the flesh, but divinely powerful for the destruction of fortresses* (2 Cor 10:3–4).

We are destroying speculations and every lofty thing raised up against the knowledge of God, and we are taking every thought captive to the obedience of Christ (2 Cor 10:5). God has gifted us with spiritual weapons that are far more powerful. The use of spiritual weapon destroys the adversary in the invisible realm, which is where the real battle is waged.

A triumphant walk

The seventh day was the key day. They had already done a lot of silent marching. Nothing had happened. Now Joshua announced that they have to do seven times as much marching. They would have to walk around the town seven times. It was a final test before God would act. After the seven circuits the priests were told to sound the trumpets. At the sound of the trumpet blast Joshua gave the people their instructions. They had to give a great shout. The city was to be destroyed but Rahab and all who lived in her house must be kept safe. Anything that could be easily destroyed should be destroyed. Valuable metals like gold, silver, bronze and iron should be handed over to the treasury of the Lord. The trumpets sounded, the people shouted and Jericho's walls fell.

> Then on the seventh day they rose early at the dawning of the day and marched around the city in the same manner seven times; only on that day they marched around the city seven times.

At the seventh time, when the priests blew the trumpets, Joshua said to the people, "Shout! For the LORD has given you the city.

"The city shall be under the ban, it and all that is in it belongs to the LORD; only Rahab the harlot and all who are with her in the house shall live, because she hid the messengers whom we sent."

"But as for you, only keep yourselves from the things under the ban, so that you do not covet them and take some of the things under the ban, and make the camp of Israel accursed and bring trouble on it."

"But all the silver and gold and articles of bronze and iron are holy to the LORD; they shall go into the treasury of the LORD."

So the people shouted, and priests blew the trumpets; and when the people heard the sound of the trumpet, the people shouted with a great shout and the wall fell down flat, so that the people went up into the city, every man straight ahead, and they took the city.

They utterly destroyed everything in the city, both man and woman, young and old, and ox and sheep and donkey, with the edge of the sword (Josh 6:15–21).

The Peculiar but Precious Ways of God

The Bible is full of peculiar ways of God. We may not understand them but they are very precious in the sight of God. The people marching around Jericho would have been embarrassed, because after that stupendous and spectacular march across the Jordan River, they had to humble themselves to take a simple walk around the town. God gave them victory, but He did it in His time and in His way. Probably He did it in such a peculiar way to help the people to lose some of their pride.

Another example of His peculiar way is baby Moses who was preserved in a tiny boat made of reeds. Moses grew up to become the great liberator of the Jewish people. He is an awesome God.

What about Goliath? He was such a huge giant that tyrannized everybody. No one could even attempt to attack him, but little David could bring him down with a little stone and killed him with Goliath's own sword. That's very creative!

God told Aaron and Moses, that if they wanted water, to hit a rock. God could have just built a stream.

Why would such a great God of the universe send Jesus to be born in a manger? God is not concerned with image but with faith. If you look back, probably some of you may discover that some of your unanswered prayers worked out for the best because they did not happen the way you wanted it.

Joshua's Encounter with Ai

After the great triumph over Jericho, there was a trial over the city of Ai. A major disaster took place and at first it looked as if the conquest of Canaan would be a night mare. Achan took some booty that was to have been destroyed, God was angry and the conquest seemed about to end in failure (Josh 7:1). For a while no one was able to understand what had happened. Some spies went to study Ai, just as they had previously been sent to Jericho. The spies came back speaking confidently. They suggested two or three thousand men would be sufficient to destroy Ai. Everyone was convinced that success was certain and no one—not even Joshua—thought of specially seeking God's counsel. But when the soldiers went they were defeated and the people fell into despair (verses 2–5).

Sin in the Camp
Sin causes failure, blocks progress

God had given specific instructions about the destruction of the treasures that would be available in the battle against Canaan. Joshua had firmly repeated God's instructions (Josh 6:17–19). There was no lack of guidance in this matter. But sin was the problem.

Achan obviously felt that no serious harm would come by taking some of the plunder for himself. No one would know! The conquest of Canaan would continue just as planned, and all would be well for him and for Israel. Oftentimes we who are among the people of God fall into some petty sins and at first do not realize the seriousness of it. Whether it is a small sin or big sin, it is sin. Someone said, 'Christians are not sinless but only sin less'.

Sin causes wider consequences

Like everyone else, you might have gone through various stages of life and have found yourself at some time or another tangled up in one sin or another. At such a time you may feel that it is purely your own personal problem. But this incidence shows us that sin often has wider consequences. Joshua 7:1 does not say 'Achan committed a sin' but it says that the people of Israel committed a sin and that Yahweh's anger burnt against Israel. The sin of one was the sin of the whole people. Everyone was affected by what Achan had done. Everyone lost the next battle. Thirty-six men who had not been personally involved in what Achan had done nevertheless lost their lives (Josh 7:5).

This failure brought great discouragement to Joshua. He was greatly distressed. For a moment he spoke as if God had entirely abandoned Israel, and seemed to be regretting even over crossing the Jordan (verses 6–7). Sometimes we are also tempted to use such foolish words when our plans are badly shattered or when we encounter unexpected problems. Problems are guidelines not stop signs. Welcome problems, they are real stimulators to success. They are intended to make us better not bitter. Every problem is another opportunity. Use your problem creatively. No problem leaves you where it found you. Let your problem lead you to God.

When the clouds of trouble put tears in your eyes, God will put a rainbow in your heart. In the school of experience first we go through the test and then we learn the lesson. Without breaking there is no making. The breaking of the outward man is God's way of blessing the inner man. No matter what storm you face, when you are with God, there's always a rainbow waiting for you.

Sin has to be identified

Joshua's discouragement was only momentary. He says, *"O Lord, what can I say since Israel has turned their back before their enemies?"* (Josh 7:8) and then seems to recover his calmness. He puts the matter before God with more confidence. God told him to stop praying and deal with sin which was the cause of the failure. The Lord said to Joshua,

> "Rise up! Consecrate the people and say, 'Consecrate yourselves for tomorrow, for thus the Lord, the God of Israel, has said, There are things under the ban in your midst, O Israel. You cannot stand before your enemies until you have removed the things under the ban from your midst.
>
> 'In the morning then you shall come near by your tribes. And it shall be that the tribe which the Lord takes by lot shall come near by families, and the family which the Lord takes shall come near by households, and the household which the Lord takes shall come near man by man.
>
> 'It shall be that the one who is taken with the things under the ban shall be burned with fire, he and all that belongs to him, because he has transgressed the covenant of the Lord, and because he has committed a disgraceful thing in Israel' " (Josh 7:13–15).

Israel must purify itself by dealing with the compromise with idolatry. The tribes must be investigated one by one until the cause of failure is found. The person who has caused the problem must be executed. God does not say who the person is. He requires the matter be disclosed indirectly by casting lots. This involves all the people taking note of what is happening. It demands that each part of the nation gives the matter some attention, and it gives Achan time to think of what he has done.

Joshua follows God's instructions. The tribes are investigated; Achan is discovered. Joshua is fatherly and kind but demands to know what has happened. Achan confesses. The booty is found and brought out for everyone to see.

Sin has to be severely dealt with

Achan and his stolen possessions—the silver, the mantle, the bar of gold, his sons, his daughters, his oxen, his donkeys, his sheep, his tent and all that belonged to him were brought to the valley of Achor. All the Israelites stoned them and burnt them with fire. The stolen goods could not be hidden without the help of his family; they had been involved in his sin. They and his stolen possessions are buried and the place is marked by the heap of stones (Josh 7:16–26)

In a young community where idolatry would lead to the extermination of the whole nation, it was necessary that Achan and his family pay a severe price for what he had done. This would serve as a severe warning for anyone who has a temptation to compromise with idolatry, or to steal what was forbidden. The lesson that we can draw from the story is to learn how powerful sin is in blocking the progress of God's kingdom, and how severely it must be cut out of our lives and out of our churches, not by stones and fire but by the rock of God's Word and the fire of the Holy Spirit.

Thus Joshua maintained discipline in the camp by his extended treatment to Achan.

Rahab stands in studied contrast with Achan:

1. Rahab was just a poor Canaanite woman involved in prostitution; Achan was a well-to-do man from the prestigious tribe of Judah (Josh 7:24).
2. Rahab took the spies to the roof and hid them from the king of Jericho (Josh 2:6); Achan *took* the forbidden things and *hid* them from Joshua (Josh 7:21–22).
3. Rahab with her love and kindness served the Israelite spies, protected them and helped them achieve victory (Josh 2:12); Achan bought trouble on Israel by his greed (Josh 7:21, 11, 25).
4. Rahab established a covenant with the Israelites (Josh 2:12–14); Achan broke covenant with God (Josh 7:11).

5. Rahab saved her whole family alive, and they became part of the people of God (Josh 2:13–14; 6:22–23, 25); Achan condemned his family to death and oblivion (Josh 7:25).

Like how we find it in the world today, even in the biblical history we find a remarkable contrast between the unfaithful Israelite and the faithful Gentile or foreigner. King Ahab was a kind of Achan figure. We can find counterparts of Rahab in Ruth the Moabitess (Ruth 2:2), the widow of Zarephath in Sidon (1 Kings 17:9), Naaman the Syrian (2 Kings 5:1), the people of Nineveh (Jonah 3:6–9), King Cyrus (Isa 44:28; 45:1), the centurion of Capernaum (Matt. 8:5, 10), the Canaanite woman of Phoenicia (Matt 15:22–28), the centurion at the cross (Matt 27:54), and Cornelius in Caesarea (Acts 10).

Jesus said, "Many will come from east and west and sit at table with Abraham, Isaac and Jacob in the kingdom of heaven, while the sons of the kingdom will be thrown into the outer darkness" (Matt 8:11–12).

The City of Ai Captured by Clever Strategy

Contrary to their previous judgement, God tells Joshua that the whole nation must be involved in the conquest of Ai and gives them detailed guidance. Two groups of soldiers move into position at night. One group has thirty officers in it. (The common translations say 'thirty thousand' but the Hebrew word for 'thousand' can have other meanings such as 'officer' or 'large company of soldiers'.) Thirty officers move into position to the west of the city; the city gate is apparently on the east side. They will soon have with them five thousand men, but the officers go to look for good hiding places.

A much larger group (with Joshua) approach the city from the east side towards the eastern wall of the town where the city gate is to be found; they will pretend to run away in fear when the defenders of the city come out after Joshua and his men, then the first group will come out from their ambush and will seize the city. The city can then be utterly destroyed.

It all happens as God has planned. At night the thirty commandos hide west of the town, on the far side from the city gate. Joshua stays on the east side among the common people and with another fighting force.

> Now the LORD said to Joshua, "Do not fear or be dismayed. Take all the people of war with you and arise, go up to Ai; see, I have given into your hand the king of Ai, his people, his city and his land. "And you shall do to Ai and its king just as you did to Jericho and its king; you shall take only its spoil and its cattle as plunder for yourselves. Set an ambush for the city behind it." So Joshua rose with all the people of war to go up to Ai; and Joshua chose 30,000 men, valiant warriors, and sent them out at night. And he commanded them, saying, "See, you are going to ambush the city from behind it. Do not go very far from the city, but all of you be ready. Then I and all the people who are with me will approach the city. And it will come about when they come out to meet us as at the first, we will flee before them. They will come out after us until we have drawn them away from the city, for they will say, 'They are fleeing before us as at the first.' So we will flee before them. And you shall rise from your ambush and take possession of the city, for the Lord your God will deliver it into your hand. Then it will be when you have seized the city, that you shall set the city on fire. You shall do it according to the word of the Lord. See, I have commanded you."
> So Joshua sent them away, and they went to the place of ambush and remained between Bethel and Ai, on the west side of Ai; but Joshua spent that night among the people (Josh 8:1–9).

The next day Joshua and the people march towards the city. It is daytime. The citizens of Ai can see what is happening but they know nothing of the Israelites in hiding on the west side of the town. Joshua and his people march around part of the city and camp on the north side. There is a valley to the north of the town, between the people camping in the north and the town itself. Five thousand men (perhaps going along the ravine where they cannot be seen) join the thirty officers in the west and hide there. They spend the night in those positions; Joshua stays in the valley keeping watch on what the men of Ai might be doing.

> Now Joshua rose early in the morning and mustered the people, and he went up with the elders of Israel before the people to Ai. Then all the people of war who were with him went up and drew near and arrived in front of the city, and camped in the north side of Ai. Now there was a valley between him and Ai. And he took about 5,000 men and set them in ambush between Bethel and Ai, on the west side of the city. So they stationed the people, all the army that was on the north side of the city, and its rear guard on the west side of the city, and Joshua spent that night in the midst of the valley (Josh 8:10–13).

This gives the king of Ai time to get his army together. He has seen the army which is now in the valley to the north of the city. The next day he comes out with his army. He hopes to fight the Israelites in the 'Arabah'—a term which normally means the Jordan valley but here it seems to mean the valley to the north of the town. The Israelites pretend to have changed their mind and act as if they are running back eastwards the route called 'the wilderness road', the road that goes down to the Jordan valley. The soldiers of Ai and many of Ai's citizens chase the Israelites who are running eastwards. The city is left unguarded.

> It came about when the king of Ai saw it, that the men of the city hurried and rose up early and went out to meet Israel in battle, he and all his people at the appointed place before the desert plain. But he did not know that there was an ambush against him behind the city. Joshua and all Israel pretended to be beaten before them, and fled by the way of the wilderness. And all the people who were in the city were called together to pursue them, and they pursued Joshua, and were drawn away from the city. So not a man was left in Ai or Bethel who had not gone out after Israel, and they left the city unguarded and pursued Israel. Then the LORD said to Joshua, "Stretch out the javelin that is in your hand toward Ai, for I will give it into your hand." So Joshua stretched out the javelin that was in his hand toward the city. (Josh 8:14–18).

Then the Lord says to Joshua, 'stretch out the Javelin that is in your hand . . .' (verse 18). The five thousand men who were hiding in the west of the town come out of hiding and set fire to the almost empty city. The men of Ai look back and see that their city has been destroyed and they are now without any place of refuge. The Israelites, who were pretending to escape, turn around and start attacking the forces of Ai; and the five thousand also come back out of the town which they have just destroyed. Now the soldiers of Ai are trapped between two Israelite armies and are soon destroyed. The king is captured.

> The men in ambush rose quickly from their place, and when he had stretched out his hand, they ran and entered the city and captured it, and they quickly set the city on fire. When the men of Ai turned back and looked, behold, the smoke of the city ascended to the sky, and they had no place to flee this way or that, for the people who had been fleeing to the wilderness turned against the pursuers. When Joshua and all Israel saw that the men in ambush had captured the city and that the smoke of the city ascended, they turned back and slew the men of Ai. The others came out from the city to encounter them, so that they were trapped in the midst of Israel, some on this side and some on that side; and they slew them until no one was left of those who survived or escaped (Josh 8:19–23).

What is striking about the story is the contrast it forms with the destruction of Jericho. Jericho was destroyed by a sheer miracle; the Israelites did not have to do any fighting for the walls to fall. In the case of the city of Ai, the victory comes by cleverness given by God to Joshua. It was not a miracle; it was God-given strategy.

Joshua's Exploit for the Gibeonites

Gibeon was one of the royal cities of the Hivites (Josh 9:7). It was a greater city than Ai; and its inhabitants were reputed mighty men (Josh 10:2). It fell within the territory allotted to Benjamin and was one of the cities given to the Levites (Josh 18:25; 21:17).

The Deception of the Gibeonites

Terrified by the fall of Jericho and Ai, some of the Gibeonites disguised as ambassadors from a far country, their garments and shoes worn-out, and their provisions mouldy as from the length of their journey, went to Joshua at Gilgal, and persuaded him and the princes of Israel to make a covenant with them.

The Israelites did not ask counsel of the Lord in accepting the Gibeonites to dwell with them. Three days later the deception was discovered and the wrath of the congregation of Israel aroused. In virtue of the covenant their lives were secured; but for their duplicity Joshua cursed them, and condemned them to be woodcutters and water-carriers for the congregation and for the altar of the Lord (Josh 9:23).

Gibeonites were ready to purchase life on any terms. They told Joshua: *"Now behold, we are in your hands; do as it seems good and right in your sight to do to us"* (Josh 9:25). But the Gibeonites would have been better off if they had dealt honestly with Israel. Their deception brought them only disgrace and slavery. It was a great humiliation to those citizens of a royal city. Thus through all their generations, their servile condition would testify that God hates falsehood.

This submission of Gibeon to the Israelites who were considered to be invaders, filled the kings of Canaan with dismay. Five revengeful Canaanite kings allied themselves against Gibeon. The Gibeonites were unprepared for defense and sent a message to Joshua at Gilgal. *"Do not abandon your servants; come up to us quickly and save us and help us, for all the kings of the Amorites that live in the hill country have assembled against us"* (Josh 10:6).

The danger threatened not only the people of Gibeon but also Israel. This city controlled the passes to central and southern Palestine, and Israel must hold it in order to conquer the country. The besieged Gibeonites had feared that Joshua would reject their appeal because of their deception. But since they had submitted to Israel and had accepted to worship the God of Israel, Joshua felt obligated to protect them. And the Lord said to Joshua, 'Do not fear them, for I have given them into your hands; not one of them shall stand before you' (Josh 10:8).

Due to the enablement of his prophetic gift, even before the allied princes could muster their armies around the city, Joshua pounced upon them. The immense host fled from the Israelites up the mountain pass to Beth Horon, and from the top they rushed down the steep descent on the other side. The Lord sent a fierce hailstorm upon them and they died. The number who died from the hailstones was more than those whom the sons of Israel killed with the sword (verse 11).

Joshua's Prophetic Insight

In the midst of a fierce battle, while the Amorites were fleeing in panic, Joshua had a Prophetic Insight as he looked down from the ridge above and saw that the day would be too short to accomplish his work. If on that very day the enemy was not fully defeated, they would renew the struggle. 'Then Joshua spoke to the Lord..., and he said in the sight of Israel: "Sun, stand still over Gibeon; and Moon, in the valley of Aijalon." So the sun stood still in the midst of heaven, and did not hasten to go down for about a whole day.' This confirms the prophetic leadership of Joshua.

God's promise to Joshua had been fulfilled before it was dark. The enemy had been given into his hand. The events of that day would long remain in the memory of Israel. *There was no day like that, before it or after it, when the Lord listened to the voice of a man; for the Lord fought for Israel* (verse 14.)

Sun and moon stood in their places; they went away at the light of your arrows, at the radiance of Your gleaming spear. In indignation You marched through the earth; In anger You trampled the nations. You went forth for the salvation of your people (Hab 3:11–13). Even though Joshua had received the promise that God would overthrow these enemies of Israel, he still put forth an effort as earnest as though success depended on the armies of Israel alone. He did all that human energy could do, although he had already called out in faith for divine aid.

The secret of success is the union of divine power with human effort. It is the same man who commanded the sun and the moon to stand still, prostrated himself flat on the earth for hours in prayer at Gilgal. If you prostrate yourself with fear and trembling before God, you can stand before people with power and authority.

The Strength of Joshua's Character

Joshua was a member of one of the largest tribes in Israel, the tribe of Ephraim, the son of Joseph. His name originally was, 'Hoshea' ('salvation'), but Moses renames him 'Joshua', which means 'Yahweh saves' (Num 13:16).

The most salient fact about Joshua's life and personality is that he was a Prophetic Leader. By studying him we can see how leaders are made and what qualities a leader should have. Joshua was a leader, trained by the master, taught by experience. He learnt that success does not ultimately come from one's own efforts. Success comes from the Lord. It comes through the direct intervention of God Himself. He was filled with the spirit of wisdom (Deut 34:9; Num 27:18) which came from the Lord. He enjoyed the presence of God (Josh 1:5; 6:27). Yet Joshua was obedient to the will of God. He followed God's instructions exactly. It is easy to follow instructions that make sense; it takes total development to follow what seems like craziness.

While Moses was alone before God at Sinai, Joshua kept watch; in the Tent of Meeting. He was probably 17 years old and from that time he learnt to wait on the Lord; and in the years following something of Moses' patience and meekness was doubtless added to his valour (Exod 26:13, 32:17, 33:11; Num 11:28). When he was 40 years old, when the Amalakites attacked the Israelites at Rephidim, before the people could reach Mount Sinai, Moses called on Joshua as the military field commander to organize an army to repel them. From that time he was formally consecrated as Moses' successor to lead the people in coordination with Eleazar the priest (Num 27:18, 34:17).

When representatives of the twelve tribes are chosen to spy out the land, Joshua (leader of the prominent tribe of Ephraim) is chosen along with Caleb. Joshua also learnt from experience. When he was leading the fight against the Amalekites (Exod 17:8–16), Moses stood on a hill in plain view. As long as his hands were up, the Israelite army gained ground; but when they dropped, the army lost. The point was to make it clear to the Israelites that God was doing the fighting, and victory, therefore, belonged to Him alone. When the battle was won, the Lord said to Moses, *"Write this on a scroll as something to be remembered and make sure that Joshua hears it"* (Exod 17:14). Joshua must learn from this experience that victory is the Lord's.

Joshua's leadership potential was being moulded by opening his eyes to what God was doing around him, and he was learning from those experiences. Joshua occupied and consolidated the area of Gilgal, fought successful campaigns against Canaanite confederacies, and directed further operations as long as the united efforts of Israel were required.

Settlement of the land depended on tribal initiative, which Joshua sought to encourage by a formal allocation at Shiloh, where the national sanctuary was established. The time had come for him to dissolve his command and set an example by retiring to his own lands at Timnath Serah in Mt Ephraim. It was perhaps at this time that he called Israel to the national covenant at Shechem (Josh 24:25).

In Joshua's farewell speech, he recounted God's mighty deeds in the past and left them with this challenge: *". . . choose for yourselves today whom you will serve. . ."* (Josh 24:15). Joshua died when he was

110 years old, and was buried near Timnath Serah.

God is looking for someone to stand in the gap.

Walking with God like Enoch

Full of faith like Abraham

Persevering like Jacob

Decisive like Moses

Courageous like Joshua

With a remarkable faith like Rahab

A prophetic judge like Deborah

A prophetic leader like Elijah

Holy and powerful like Joseph

Above reproach like Daniel

Bold and sacrificial like Esther

Self-reliant like Nehemiah

Committed like Peter and John

Long-suffering like Paul

Will you be that someone?

Chapter 6

RAHAB
A Remarkable Woman of Faith

There was a sharp knock on her door. She thought probably another travelling merchant had come seeking her charms. But as she opened the door she knew instinctively the two men standing there were Israelites, sent from the mighty Jehovah, who had dried up the Red Sea.

Rahab was a harlot whose very name means 'insolence and fierceness'. Probably she was a temple prostitute, a practitioner of the vile Canaanite religion, which raised immorality to an act of worship. Certainly the Law of Moses marked her for death, which would come to pass once Israel's army took Jericho. Yet God saved her! How and why He did so is a great lesson in grace that we have to learn.

Joshua sent two men to spy out Jericho because he was going to take it by force (At that time Joshua did not know that God was going to work a miracle, and Jericho would fall). These two men, hiding from the King of Jericho, sought shelter in the house of Rahab the prostitute. Because her's was a public house, it was common for people to be seen coming and going. It seemed the perfect place to stay (Josh 2:1–13).

However, the rumour of Joshua's plan reached the King of Jericho; he sent his soldiers to Rahab's house, to look for the men. Rahab helped the spies to escape because she had heard about the God of Israel and all the miracles He had performed. Although she was a prostitute, Rahab had faith and believed in God. Rahab's name is listed in the 'Hall of Fame of Faith' (Heb 11:31).

Rahab's house of ill repute was next to the fortress wall of Jericho. It was only six miles to the Jordan River, which was at this time on its annual rampage. The valley was flooded, which was a great help because on the other side were encamped millions of people who had suddenly appeared from the wilderness. Rahab would have spent hours watching them. She had heard they were called Israelites.

They terrified the people of Jericho who like their neighbours, lived in a state of tension. Even their temple priests gave them no hope. The people of Jericho understood that the God of Israel was superior to the gods of Jericho. They knew that their situation was hopeless. No matter how strong its walls, the city and all who lived in it lay under a death sentence!

Rahab had already heard the Israelites' miraculous story . . . how the Lord dried up the water of the Red Sea when they came out of Egypt and what they did to the two kings of the Amorites—Sihon and Og who were on the other side of Jordan, whom they utterly destroyed (Josh 2:10).

Rahab Took a Risk of Faith

Rahab opened wide her door and welcomed in the two strangers. They wanted a place to hide since the king's soldiers were behind searching for them. The spies promised her that they would leave as soon as it became dark.

Rahab took them to the flat roof of her house, high up on the fortress wall. Standing there one could look straight down at the great spring, which the prophet Elisha would one day sweeten; to the south, were the brooding waters of the Dead Sea; just behind were the wall of the mountain, where one day the Son of God would have His great battle with the tempter.

Rahab had been drying some flax on the roof. She made the spies get under it and went back down to ward off the soldiers of Jericho.

When the soldiers enquired Rahab about the spies, she answered them,

> "Yes the men came to me, but I did not know where they were from. And it came about when it was time to shut the gate at dark that the men went out; I do not know where the men went. Pursue them quickly, for you will overtake them" (Josh 2:4–5).

Once they had gone, she returned to the roof and said to the men,

> "I know that the LORD has given you the land, and that the terror of you has fallen on us, and that all the inhabitants of the land have melted away before you . . . Now therefore, please swear to me by the LORD, since I have dealt kindly with you that you also will deal kindly with my father's household, and give me a pledge of truth" (Josh 2:9–12).

So the men said to her, "Our life for yours if you do not tell this business of ours; and it shall come about when the LORD gives us the land that we will deal kindly and faithfully with you" (Josh 2:14).

Then she let the men down with a rope since her house was on the city wall, and the spies disappeared into the night. But before they had swung down into the blackness, they had said to her,

> "We shall be free from this oath to you which you have made us swear, unless, when we come into the land, you tie this cord of scarlet thread in the window through which you let us down, and gather to yourself into the house your father and your mother and your brothers and all your father's household" (Josh 2:17–18).

The scarlet cord is symbolic of the redemptive work of Jesus Christ that saves us from destruction. Rahab's faith in God saved her from death, and our faith in Jesus Christ saves us from spiritual death.

To offer hospitality to two total strangers, whose identity she guessed, was a courageous act on Rahab's part. But it was also an act of treason for which she could expect no mercy if discovered. Behind her action there was a strong motivation. From her testimony, it is clear that the inhabitants of Canaan and Jericho were well informed about the victories God had given Israel, and they were afraid; a fear which she herself shared. "She confessed, 'I know that the Lord has given you the land, and that the terror of you has fallen on us . . ." (Josh 2:9–11, 24).

Probably Rahab would have sensed that this was a heaven-sent opportunity to change sides, and so she would have made up her mind to switch her allegiance and identify herself with Israel and their God. That is why she took a risk of her life by offering hospitality, to these men.

The Saving Faith of Rahab

So profound was the impression made on Rahab by the miracle at the Red Sea, and the rout of the mighty Amorite kings Sihon and Og, that while it struck terror into her heart, it also kindled a spark of faith. Faith comes by hearing. She heard, and tremblingly believed. Her faith was born of the supernatural evidence she had seen in the experience of God's people, and so she transferred her allegiance to their God. In her heart she believed God, and by faith God saved her.

The environment in which Rahab lived made it very difficult for a young woman to retain her virtue. This makes her faith and subsequent career more remarkable, for she was the only person in Jericho to respond readily to the call of God. She was a glowing example of the fact that faith can flourish in a most inhospitable environment.

Real faith is not that which a person holds, but that which takes hold of him or her. Real faith is not that which a person assents to, but that which he or she submits to. It is not an object of worship, but an impulse of life. *It is not thy joy in Christ that saves thee; it is not even thy faith in Christ, though that be the instrument; it is Christ's blood and merit.* Spurgeon said,

He saved us, not on the basis of deeds which we have done in righteousness, but according to His mercy, by the washing of regeneration and renewing of the Holy Spirit (Titus 3:5).

One is justified by faith, not by works, or character, or by anything else. The only thing we have to hold out to God is the weak hand of faith. Then He will do the rest.

Even in her house of prostitution, Rahab could still respond to the cries of faith rising from her wanton heart. She would come to this great God, just as she was. The great Apostle Paul who wrote of her much later said: *By faith Rahab the harlot did not perish along with those who were disobedient, after she had welcomed the spies in peace* (Heb 11:31).

The fact that Rahab could place her faith in the Living God, shows that God is willing to accept and forgive anyone who comes to Him in faith. The whole message of the Bible is that we come to God through faith, and the story of Rahab is of a woman whom God accepts on the basis of her faith and not because of her 'good works'. Rahab's faith proved genuine by her willingness to hide the spies at the risk of her own life (Josh 2:18–21).

In his letter James has asserted that Rahab showed her faith by her deeds (James 2:25). Faith provides the motivation for obedience. Before she helped the men escape down the wall, she obtained from them the promise that she and all in her house would be spared.

But the promise was conditional. First, safety would be guaranteed only to those who remained in the house (Josh 2:19). Second, an identifying scarlet cord must be bound in the window (Josh 2:18). Third, the mission of the spies must be kept secret. If the conditions were fulfilled, all in Rahab's house would be spared.

There is an interesting parallel between some features of the Passover and this incident. In the Passover observance, the prohibition was, "*. . . none of you shall go outside the door of his house until morning*" (Exod 12:22). In Rahab's case the condition is, "*Anyone who goes out of the doors of your house into the street, his blood shall be on his own head, and we shall be free*" (Josh 2:19).

Their safety from impending judgement, in both cases depended on their remaining under the shelter of the specially marked house. At the Passover, crimson blood was smeared on the door. In Rahab's case, a scarlet cord was bound in the window. When God saw the blood, He passed over them as He promised. When Joshua saw the scarlet cord, the house and its inmates were divinely protected from destruction as promised. In the two symbols, it is not difficult to see the redemption and salvation from judgement procured by the blood on the cross and how it ought to be personally appropriated.

What significance can be seen in the scarlet cord? It meant (1) That Rahab and her family had now chosen to identify themselves with the God of Israel and His people. (2) That all who sheltered in the house were equally under the protection of God. (3) That each had taken this step of faith individually and voluntarily. (4) That they were immune from divine judgement. Just as the Hebrew families could eat the Passover Feast in perfect safety behind the blood-sprinkled door, so the little company gathered in Rahab's house could wait for deliverance in perfect confidence and without fear, behind the scarlet cord. (5) That Rahab was now included in the covenant of promise, and was thus eligible to become a progenitor of the Jewish Messiah.

The Blessing Rahab Received

When Jericho fell, Rahab was spared because she had sheltered the two spies Joshua had sent. The scarlet emblem meant salvation for Rahab and her family. And she needed saving from her immoral life, from the evil that seemed to continually spawn in her desperate heart. She needed saving from the wrath of God that was about to come upon her in the city of Jericho.

Rahab was rescued not only physically but also spiritually. God used her marvellously in His great plan of redemption. The people of Jericho saw Rahab only as an object, but God knew her great value. She was well worth saving from her evil life; not only for her own sake, but also for the place she had in God's plan.

She later married an Israelite—perhaps one of the spies she had sheltered. Through a sovereign and miraculous act of God, the union produced linkage with the divine lineage that gave us Jesus Christ. For Rahab mothered Boaz, who married Ruth, from whose son Obed, Jesse the father of David came, through whose line Jesus was born.

Rahab was listed in the genealogy of Jesus. Whenever a woman's name is included in a genealogical listing in Jewish history, you can be sure she has made a significant contribution to her generation. To be a part of the genealogical listing of Jesus, the Son of God, was indeed a high honour. Only four women are included in this list, each having played a unique role in preparing the world for God's Son.

Rahab's story is miraculous. And it proves that no matter how far a person has fallen, how deeply he or she has fallen into sin, it's never too late and never too far to come back to God.

Rahab became one of God's heroines. She became a wife and mother. God blessed her and her husband Salmon with many children, among them the illustrious Boaz (Matt 1:5).

Now what about you, my friend? Can you imagine yourself different from what you are today? Can you picture yourself being touched by God Himself and lifted to new dimensions of living? It is not a matter of what you have been that is so important. Not even what you are! The thing that matters is what you can become through Jesus Christ.

That's what the Gospel is all about—*"For God did not send the Son into the world to judge the world, but that the world might be saved through Him"* (John 3:17). If it was not too late for the harlot Rahab, with the avenging Israelites storming the gates of her city, then it's not too late for you. If Rahab had not gone too far to be reached by God's mercy, then you haven't either.

How can anyone today receive hope for a new life from God? Jesus said,

> "Come to Me, all you who are weary and heavy-laden, and I will give you rest. Take My yoke upon you, and learn from Me, for I am gentle and humble in heart; and you will find rest for your souls. For My yoke is easy and My burden is light" (Matt 11:28–30).

But as many as received Him, to them He gave the right to become children of God, even to those who believe in His name (John 1:12).

If you want to receive Jesus right now in your heart, please say the following prayer: Lord Jesus, I realize that I am a sinner and I need you in my life. Please forgive me and cleanse me through your blood and come into my life and accept me as your child. I accept you as my personal Saviour and the Lord of my life. Please protect me from evil and guide me and lead me till the end of my life. In your name I pray, Amen.

Now, having prayed this prayer believe that Jesus has definitely come into your heart and you are His child. Now you are born again or born into the kingdom of God (John 3:3–5). The Bible says, *Therefore if anyone is in Christ he is a new creature; the old things passed away, behold, new things have come* (2 Cor 5:17). Therefore now, you should start living a new life, spending much time in prayer and reading the Bible and obeying the Word of God.

Chapter 7

Deborah
A Prophetic and Prudent Leader

During the time of Joshua and his generation, God helped Israel subdue and conquer her enemies. Israel became so captivated by her enemies—their idolatry and sin; that she imitated them and lived as they lived. She served their gods and thus did evil in the sight of God.

After Joshua's death, Israel was without a king, a strong leader, and spiritual advisors . . . . *everyone did what was right in his own eyes* (Judg 21:25), i.e. the people did not acknowledge God as their King and were disloyal to Him and His rule (Judg 3:7). Thus God led the nations to rob, plunder and prostrate her. Each time Israel cried out for relief, God raised up a leader one they called 'judge'. Thus began a cyclic pattern of apostasy, oppression, crying out for relief, and divine deliverance.

Israel had fifteen such judges; each of these judges was 'raised up' by God to that office. They did not seek the votes of the crowd; but the crowd went out to them, attracted by a magnetism they could not understand. These judges attempted to keep the nation from idolatry;

they were eager to improve the morals of the people, reform the land and break the chains of Israel's oppressors.

The fifth judge was a woman — Deborah in Hebrew meaning 'bee'. Science states that the bee ranks among the highest in intelligence of all in the animal kingdom. So also, Deborah ranks among the wisest of all Old Testament women. She was the wife of 'Lappidoth'. 'Lappidoth' signifies 'lamps', 'lightning flashes' or 'torches'. The Rabbis say that Deborah was employed to make wicks for the lamps in the Tabernacle. There is no account of her children in the Bible, which may mean that she did have children but had no bearing in the story so their names were omitted. Or, that she was actually childless. In Judges 5:7 Deborah refers to herself as 'mother in Israel'. *"Until I, Deborah, arose, Until I arose, a mother in Israel."* Commentators say, that this meant she was a spiritual mother to the nation.

The uniqueness of Deborah was not that she was the only woman judge but she was also a prophetess, an encourager, a ruler, a military leader, a poetess and 'mother of Israel'. She was a combination of authority and responsibility held by only two other Israelites, Moses and Samuel. Deborah was, perhaps, only one of many women who held such high and honourable positions. In the following pages, I would like to take you through the setting, scene and the plot of this historical narrative to show you how well Deborah fulfils each of her roles or gifting.

Deborah As a Prophetic Judge

Deborah held her court under a Palm tree (which is the symbol for fruitfulness) which was called ever after as the Palm of Deborah. She dwelt in this area between two cities Ramah and Bethel in the hill country of Ephraim. Ramah means 'high', and Bethel means 'house of God'. Deborah did not judge as a princess by any civil authority conferred upon her, but as a prophetess, as the mouthpiece of God, redressing grievances and correcting abuses. She did not use her own head knowledge or opinion to judge, but received it directly from God. Such judgements never bring confusion or controversy, but clear revelation and fulfillment. This drew the people to her, she did not need to run and canvas people.

This appears to be the same kind of 'judging' we see Moses doing (Exod 18:13–27), and later his 70 helpers (Num 11:16–30). The judicial system in Israel was established upon the advice of Jethro, Moses' father-in-law, to assist Moses in settling disputes on behalf of God. He advised him:

> ". . . select out of all the people able men who fear God, men of truth, those who hate dishonest gain; and you shall place these over them as leaders of thousands, of hundreds, of fifties and of tens. Let them judge the people at all times; and let it be that every major dispute they will bring to you, but every minor dispute they themselves will judge" (Exod 18:21–22).

'Judges and officers' were appointed for every town to judge difficult cases of the people. A judge with priests as assessors tried more important cases (Deut 17:8–13). A judge had jurisdiction over the entire nation of Israel, some judging from a fixed location and some from a circuit (Judg 4; 1 Sam 7:16–17). Deborah's judging, like that of Moses and his helpers, was enabled by the Holy Spirit. It may be that the gift of prophecy she possessed first became evident in her judging. Who is better to 'judge' a matter than one who can 'see' the situation exactly as it is? She exercised a prophetic gift. Prophesying does not necessarily include the gift of foretelling future events, but it meant essentially that they were a voice of God in revealing His will and purpose for the people.

As the word got out that God's will, could be known through Deborah, many came to her for judgement. It would seem that she was but one of a very few judging prophets, and even more likely that she was the only person gifted and functioning in this way at that particular time. Thus she was the first woman to be honoured in the

Scripture. Although some will not accept women prophetesses or ministers, we find many such women in the Old Testament whom God ordained and used. But this prophetess did not take any authority over man. The Word of God declares she was a prophetess, the wife of Lapidoth, and a judge of Israel.

Deborah As a Strong Deliverer

During Deborah's time Israel faced a crisis. The crisis is given in the opening verses of Judges chapter 4.

> "Then the sons of Israel again did evil in the sight of the LORD, after Ehud died. And the LORD sold them into the hand of Jabin king of Canaan, who reigned in Hazor; and the commander of his army was Sisera, who lived in Harosheth-hagoyim. The sons of Israel cried to the LORD; for he had nine hundred iron chariots, and he oppressed the sons of Israel severely for twenty years" (verses 1–3).

For twenty years, the Canaanites had reigned rough shod over the Israelites. Their superior military might enabled them to make Israel a vassal state. The 900 iron chariots gave the Canaanites military superiority over Israel. Nine hundred iron chariots were too many for a single city to have. It also signifies how advanced Jabin's forces were in terms of military equipment, and how desperate and hopeless the situation was in the eyes of the Israelites.

The highways were virtually deserted, because it was heavily patrolled by the Canaanite chariots. Villages were likewise abandoned because there were no walls to protect the people from being pillaged and robbed by the Canaanites. The Israelites seem to have retreated to the walled cities, and even these did not really protect them. If the Canaanites had their chariots, swords, spears, and shields, it would seem that the Israelites were not allowed to possess any weapon. Israel may have been able to muster 40,000 warriors, but they would have had to fight unarmed. In the light of this we are told that they cried to the Lord for help and the help God gave them was in the person of a woman. Deborah was raised up by God to deliver the nation in a time of crisis. God gave a promise of deliverance to Deborah, *"I will draw out to you Sisera, the commander of Jabin's army, with his chariots and his many troops to the river Kishon, and I will give him into your hand"* (Judg 4:7).

Deborah summoned Barak, whose name means 'thunderbolt'. He was the son of Abinoam, and was from Kedesh in Naphtali. He is included in the 'heroes of faith' (Heb 11:32). Barak was commissioned to fight Sisera, Jabin's army commander and his army. She said to him,

> "Behold the LORD, the God of Israel has commanded, 'Go and march to Mount Tabor, and take with you ten thousand men from the sons of Naphtali and the sons of Zebulun. I will draw out to you Sisera, the commander of Jabin's army, with his chariots and his many troops to the river Kishon, and I will give him into your hand'" (Judg 4:6–7).

He was commanded to muster an army of 10,000 men from Naphtali and Zebulun. He was commanded to meet Sisera's army at Mount Tabor. The tribes of Zebulun and Issachar shared borders at Tabor. Sisera's army, including his chariots and troops would be 'lured' to the Kishon River by the Lord.

The Kishon River is about twenty-five metres in length, originating in the northern hills of Samaria and ending at the Mediterranean Sea, by Mount Carmel. The Kishon River passes through the Valley of Jezreel (Esdraelon Valley). In times of storm the Kishon River floods the Valley of Jezreel making it virtually impassable.

Deborah As a Wise Counsellor

When it comes to the other 'judges', we are told of their military powers, fighting skills, and their bravery. Only of Deborah is it said that she had this input into the daily lives of the people by helping them with their disputes and problems. One thing we can say with certainty therefore is that she could relate to other people; they found her to be a ready listener and a woman to whom they could talk. Other women have reigned besides Deborah—but not by the vote of the people. Jezebel reigned, Athaliah reigned; but their empire was regarded with hatred by the community.

Barak refuses to fight Sisera unless Deborah accompanies him. Barak said to her, *"If you will go with me, then I will go; but if you will not go with me, I will not go"* (Judg 4:8). What caused Barak to respond in this way? Maybe, he lacked confidence and the faith to act without Deborah. But what did Barak fear? What was it he felt Deborah would contribute by coming along? It was surely not her battle skills.

She was not a David, who could handle a Goliath on her own. She was just a wife and a judge. It may be that Barak feared no one would follow him. Canaanites oppressed the Israelites for twenty years and were well armed. Many had been coming to Deborah for judgement. Perhaps they would follow her into battle, even if they would not follow Barak. Or, perhaps it was simply that Barak wanted to have this prophetess with him so that he would have a means of obtaining divine guidance at this critical time. Whatever his fears, she encourages Barak by assuring him of her support and presence by agreeing to go with him, but tells him that he will not get the glory for the victory over the Canaanites that God has promised: *"Very well"*, Deborah said, *"I will surely go with you; nevertheless the honour shall not be yours on the journey you are about to take, for the Lord will sell Sisera into the hands of a woman"* (Judg 4:9). This proves she was not hungry for honour from anybody, but desired to exalt God, giving all glory and honour to him. I pray we have a humble spirit like Deborah.

Deborah As a Brave Military Strategist

What a sight it would have been, if one could have seen these two armies setting out for battle. Barak set out with his men, armed with little or nothing (Judg 5:8), but Sisera had his well-armed soldiers, and 900 iron chariots. Barak set out with 20 years of defeat behind him; Sisera set out with 20 years of military dominance. Sisera must have been accompanied by a number of top military strategists; Barak is accompanied by Deborah, a wife and mother in Israel.

Deborah and Barak went to Kedesh where Barak summoned 10,000 men of Zebulun and Naphtali (Judg 4:10). Deborah and Barak and the army went to Mount Tabor and camped there. Word was brought to Sisera that Israel's army had gone up to Mount Tabor. Sisera, his 900 chariots and his army, assembled in the Valley of Jezreel.

> "Then they told Sisera that Barak the son of Abinoam had gone up to Mount Tabor. Sisera called together all his chariots, nine hundred iron chariots, and all the people who were with him, from Harosheth-hagoyim to the river Kishon" (Judg 4:13).

Militarily speaking the battle plan God had given Barak made little sense. Chariots were very effective on the plains, but they were of little or no value in the mountains. God ordered Barak to muster his troops on Mount Tabor, and then to lead them down from the mountain and onto the plains. This is precisely where the chariots had the advantage and could do the most damage. But in retrospect we can see how wise God's plan was. Because the Israelite army would come on the plain, Sisera felt that his chariots were the perfect weapon. He ordered all of his chariots to engage the Israelites in battle. It looked like a slaughter, which is exactly the way God wanted it to appear.

God created a rainstorm, turning the plains to mud, causing the river Kishon to overflow its banks, sweeping the Canaanites away. God 'went before Israel' (Judg 4:14). The powers of heaven, i.e. rain and floods, fought for Israel in the Valley of Jezreel (Judg 5:20–21). The horses seem to have panicked, and because of that they probably killed their share of Canaanites. No wonder God had instructed Barak to bring his army down from Mount Tabor to the plains, near the river

Kishon. Now the wisdom of His plan is apparent. Deborah makes her contribution to the battle. *She orders Barak, "Arise! For this is the day in which the LORD has given Sisera into your hands; ... " She hid herself saying, "... behold, the Lord has gone out before you"* (Judg 4:14).

Today, many go in the name of the Lord to make a name for them and for self-glory. But Deborah knew surely and sincerely that God had sent them up a certain mountain to do battle for God. Therefore she committed herself and the entire army to God, and God worked on their behalf. That is why the result was victory!

Deborah urged Barak and his army to advance upon the Canaanites whose superior numbers and equipment were nullified by their inability to manoeuvre the chariots in the flooded slushy condition of the valley floor. The Canaanite army panicked, and fled before the Israelites (Judg 4:15). Barak's army pursued, overtook, and slew the remainder of the Canaanite army, even going as far as Harosheth Haggoyim, the camp of the Canaanite army (Judg 4:16). Harosheth Haggoyim was likely on the opposite side of the Jezreel Valley. Mount Tabor sits at the eastern end of the Jezreel Valley, 11 miles (17 km) west of the Sea of Galilee. Its elevation at the summit is 1,843 feet (575 m) high. It is used in Scripture as a symbol of majesty. Jeremiah 46:18 (NASB) *"As I live," declares the King Whose name is the Lord of hosts, "Surely one shall come who looms up like Tabor among the mountains, Or like Carmel by the sea"* (Compare Ps 89:12).

It was not really the Israelites who overcame the Canaanites. The victory was the Lord's. He routed Sisera and all his chariots (Judg 4:15). All that the Israelites did was only a 'mop up' operation. They could go about the bodies of the Canaanites, making sure each soldier was dead, and then plundering their weapons. When Sisera saw that defeat was certain, he too fled, leaving his chariot behind and running with all his strength, hoping to find a place of safety with his own people. He fled to the camp of Heber the Kenite, which was near Kedesh. *Now Sisera fled away on foot to the tent of Jael the wife of Heber the Kenite, for there was peace between Jabin the king of Hazor and the house of Heber the Kenite* (Judg 4:17).

Heber whose name means 'ally' was a Kenite. The 'Kenites' were a loosely knit clan of metalworkers (Kenite means 'metalworkers' or 'blacksmiths') living in Canaan. Kenites were descendants of Hobab, the father-in-law of Moses, so they had close ties with Israel (verse 11). Heber had separated from the rest of the Kenites (verse 11) and allied himself with Jabin king of Hazor (verse 17). He may have done this because he was a metalworker and Jabin had 900 iron chariots and that would have helped his trade. Also may be because Jabin seemed to be the undisputed ruler of the area and Heber wanted to be on a winner's side.

Since, Sisera and Heber shared friendly relations, Sisera expected to receive 'hospitality' from Heber. A Middle Eastern custom promises shelter, food, and protection, even to one's enemies for three days under normal circumstances. He came to the tent of Jael, Heber's wife. Jael whose name means, 'wild or mountain goat' or 'gazelle'. She lived by the great tree in Zaanannim, near Kedesh. We do not know her ancestral background, but compared to her husband, her loyalties were with the Israelites.

The tents of women, in Near Eastern customs, were off-limits to any men other than their husbands. Sisera believed he would be safe there from discovery by the pursuing Israelite army. Heber was not home so Jael went out to meet Sisera and said to him, *"Turn aside, my master, turn aside to me! Do not be afraid . . ."* (verse 18). So he entered her tent, and she covered him with a rug. Sisera asked her for water to drink, instead she gave him milk because he was exhausted (verses 19, 21). This was probably goat's milk. Why did she give him milk instead of water? It would have been as easy for her to give him the water he asked for, than the milk, but only milk would have acted as a natural sedative on an exhausted man. She did not really want to offer 'hospitality' to him, which an offer of water usually guaranteed. To be invited to come into someone's home and to receive water was to be acknowledged as a guest and entitled to the benefits of the custom of 'hospitality'. When he drank the milk, Sisera said to her, *"Stand in the doorway of the tent, and it shall be if anyone comes and inquires of you, and says, 'Is there anyone here?' that you shall say, 'No'"* (verse 20). She assured him of safety, when he fell asleep she gathered her weapons and approached her enemy.

> But Jael, Heber's wife, took a tent peg and seized a hammer in her hand, and went secretly to him and drove the peg into his temple, and it went through into the ground; for he was sound asleep and exhausted. So he died (verse 21)

Putting up tents and taking them down was the woman's work, and so Jael had the tools of her trade close at hand and knew how to use them. While Sisera was deep in sleep, she seized a tent peg and drove it through Sisera's skull and into the ground.

Barak came in pursuit of Sisera, and Jael went out to meet him. *She said "Come, and I will show you the man whom you are seeking"* (verse 22). So he went in with her, and there lay Sisera with the tent peg through his temple—dead. The glory did, indeed, go to a woman, and not to Barak.

We are not told why Jael decided to put Sisera to death. Quite obviously, Jael's loyalties were not the same as those of Heber, her husband. Her loyalty was to Israel, and not to the Canaanites. She refused to be bound by the covenant of peace that her husband had made with the Canaanites. From Sisera's arrival and subsequent actions Jael must have realized that the Israelites were prevailing in the battle with the Canaanites. She must have sensed this was her opportunity to come to Israel's aid by putting Sisera to death. She was acting in accordance with God's will that a woman would kill Sisera (verse 9).

That day God humiliated Jabin, king of Canaan, before the Israelites. Israel's power continued to overwhelm Jabin, king of

Canaan, until they did away with Jabin, king of Canaan. *So God subdued on that day Israel pressed heavier and heavier upon Jabin the king of Canaan, until they had destroyed Jabin the king of Canaan* (verses 23–24).

These verses are important because they tell us that this victory over Sisera and his army is not the end of the story, but rather the first of a series of battles by which the Israelites overcame the Canaanites. This victory not only eliminated some of Jabin's top warriors, but it deprived him of his greatest weapons—his 900 iron-rimmed chariots. The spoils of this victory would also have provided armor and weapons for many Israelite soldiers. This was a great disadvantage for the Canaanites, and levelled the playing field for future battles.

Deborah As a Poetess

Deborah was a poetess as well; she composed the famous historical poem of that period on the morrow of the victory. It is in this poem recorded in Judges, chapter five that we learn what precisely brought about Sisera's defeat compared to the narrative in chapter four. This poem was in all likelihood the expression of her prophetic gift, as it tells forth the acts of God.

The Song of Deborah

> On that day Deborah and Barak son of Abinoam sang this song:
> "When the princes in Israel take the lead,
> when the people willingly offer themselves—
> praise the LORD!
> "Hear this, you kings! Listen, you rulers!
> I will sing to the LORD, I will sing;
> I will make music to the LORD, the God of Israel"
> (Judg 5:1–3)

God has ordained in his Word that men should exercise the prophetic gift, through the preaching ministry, but there are also other ways.

Like Deborah, some have the gift of poetry, and this can be a very powerful instrument the Spirit may use for the presentation of divine truth. For example, Charles Wesley who wrote nearly 9,000 hymns, many of which have been so mightily used of God in acts of worship and in proclaiming the way of salvation.

It is similar in form and substance to the 'song of deliverance' which the Israelites sang after they passed safely through the Red Sea, when the Egyptian army was drowned (Exod 15). As the prophetess Miriam may have had a hand in writing the 'song of the sea'. She ordered the soldiers to sing the triumphant song as they marched through the land that all the people might catch the strains and that generations might proclaim the victory.

The song of Deborah has been preserved from the twelfth century BC with its language practically unmodernised, and is thus one of the most archaic passages in the Old Testament. It is also an important source of information on tribal relations in Israel at the time. It may be divided into eight sections: an exordium of praise (Judg 5:2-3); the invocations of Yahweh (verses 6-8); the mustering of the tribes (verses 9-18); the battle of Kishon (verses 19-23); the death of Sisera (verses 24-27); the description of Sisera's mother awaiting his return (verses 28-30); and the epilogue (verse 31). In verses 2 and 3, Israel praises God because the leaders actually lead, after years of little or no leadership at all. And because the leaders led, the people (at least some of them) followed. Many volunteered to join their Israelite brethren in going to war against the Canaanites.

All these raise a question with which we are only too familiar today in the life of the nation, the church and the family. Why do we see so many men failing to take responsibility in the leadership role, and so many women taking on that role themselves? We gain the impression from Deborah's song that she would have been only too happy if the leaders in Israel had accepted the responsibility. *"That the leaders led in Israel, That the people volunteered"* (Judg 5:2).

The New Testament is clear in its teaching about the headship or leadership of the man in God's scheme of things. *For the husband is the head of the wife, as Christ also is the head of the church* (Eph 5:23). Paul is here talking about Christian's marriage, but the principle of the headship of the man applies in other directions. There are many church fellowships today where women are engaged in leading, guiding, teaching in Sunday school and, in general, giving direction and counsel; not that they particularly aspire to these positions, but because the men are either not available or, if they are, they simply opt out of leadership responsibility. The same is true of missionary work. The number of women taking up the challenge of overseas mission invariably outstrips that of men.

Many pastors will relate the experience of wives complaining to them that their husbands are not giving the lead in the home, and that the responsibilities of disciplining the children and taking family devotions have fallen on them, or else it isn't done. This abdication by men of the leadership role is something, I believe, most believer women are deeply unhappy about, and they would much rather accept in practice the doctrine of the headship of the husband. God will not allow his cause to fail because the modern Baraks will not take it on. He will always raise up a Deborah.

Verses 3–11 link the giving of the Law at Sinai with the deliverance of the Israelites from the Canaanites under Deborah and Barak. At Sinai, God made a covenant with Israel. His presence and power at Sinai were demonstrated as He employed nature to accomplish His purposes. The earth quaked and the heavens brought forth rain, testifying to the presence of God (verses 4 and 5). That was in the past, and it was witnessed by the first generation of Israelites to be delivered from Egyptian bondage. Now, the second generation of Israelites sing a similar song, based upon the deliverance God gave Israel from her Canaanite oppressors. Here, too, Israel's deliverance was due to God's grace and power. The Israelites were ill-equipped and powerless before the Canaanites and their chariots, but God intervened, employing nature to defeat those who oppressed His people.

The tribes who volunteered to go to battle is found in verses 14 and 15. They came from Benjamin, and from the half-tribe of Manasseh well as those from Zebulun. Issachar and Reuben also took part in the battle. In verses 16–18, we see a stark contrast being made between the 'workers' (Zebulun and Naphtali, verse 18) and the 'shirkers' (e.g., Gilead and Dan, verse 17). If there were those like Zebulun and Naphtali, who were first to volunteer, there were also those who shrunk back from their duty. It may well be that they were far away from the conflict that they felt no obligation to involve themselves in this fight. Though they were part of Israel it did not motivate them to come to the aid of their brethren. And for this they are condemned.

Verses 19–23 describe, in poetic language, the battle that was fought between the Canaanites and the Israelites. Verses 24–27 are poetic, but very graphic, description of the slaying of Sisera, at the hand of Jael. Here, she gets the glory that would have been Barak's. She is blessed as a woman among women. Three times in verse 27 it is said that Sisera bowed at the feet of Jael. This refers, I think, to his posture in sleep, but the song sees more to it than that; in so doing, he symbolically submits himself to Jael as the greater one.

Verses 28–30 paint a very dramatic picture. Note that once again this is given 'from a woman's point of view'. If Deborah, a 'mother of Israel', represents the women of Israel, Sisera's mother represents the grieving Canaanite women whose losses have been so great on this day. The songwriter focuses on the mother of Sisera, waiting for her son to return, triumphant in battle, as he has done so many times before over the past 20 years. But time passes, and the sound of hoof beats is not heard. Why the delay? Has something gone wrong? The maidens wisely attempt to assume the best. Surely the victory was so decisive and the spoils so great that more time was required to gather them and to bring them home. That was it; it must be.

Verse 31 concludes the song with blessing and cursing. If Deborah saw the power of God at Sinai repeated in the war with Sisera, she now sees this battle as a prototype of God's future dealings with men. Let all the enemies of God perish, just as the Canaanites have in this battle. And let all those who love God be blessed, rising like the sun in all its glory and power. This is similar to the Abrahamic Covenant in (Gen 12:1–3): *"And I will bless those who bless you, And the one who curses you I will curse, And in you all the families of the earth will be blessed."*

Those fellow-Israelites who came to the aid of their brethren were blessed. Those who refused to help were cursed, not unlike the Canaanites who opposed God's people.

Deborah the Extraordinary Prophetic Leader

Although quite an ordinary woman in one sense, being a wife and mother, Deborah nevertheless was quite extraordinary in the part she played under God's direction in the history of Israel. God uses ordinary people in his service and for the furtherance of the gospel. We can assume that Deborah was an able and gifted woman, and yet we are not told of any particular quality of leadership she may have possessed or of any other position she may have held as the reason why God chose her to be the judge of his people. Indeed, her own words in her song —'until I arose, a mother in Israel'— suggest that she was as surprised as anyone that God should have called her to be Israel's deliverer in the time of crisis. But God often works in that way and it ought to be a great encouragement to those of us who feel we are just 'ordinary' people without any special gift or talent.

This brings to our attention Apostle Paul's words:

> For consider your calling, brethren, that there were not many wise according to the flesh, not many mighty, not many noble;

but God has chosen the foolish things of the world to shame
the wise, and God has chosen the weak things of the world to
shame the things which are strong, and the base things of the
world and the despised God has chosen, the things that are not,
so that He may nullify the things that are, so that no man may
boast before God (1 Cor 1:26–29).

This is often God's way, to choose the ordinary. When Philip excitedly
told Nathaniel that he had met Jesus of Nazareth whom the prophets
had foretold; he replied with deep scepticism: *Nathanael said to him,
"Can any good thing come out of Nazareth?" Philip said to him, "Come
and see"* (John 1:46). He clearly felt that Nazareth was far too ordinary
and insignificant to make it the source of any great blessing, let alone
the home of God's own Son. And we may be equally sceptical about
ourselves when it comes to the question of God using us in His service.
'Who, me? No way I don't believe it, I'm just an ordinary person with
no special gifts.' God does in fact use ordinary people like us.

It is all the more intriguing, therefore, that in the roll-call of the
great Old Testament heroes of the faith, in Hebrews 11 the writer
refers to Barak, who played a subsidiary role under Deborah, but
makes no mention of Deborah herself, who was the woman of God's
choice. The question should arise in our minds, If Barak is listed in
the 'hall of faith', and then why is Deborah not named? I think the
answer is found in verse 34. Barak was one who 'gained strength in
weakness', and 'became mighty in battle'. Barak was weak in his faith,
and he became strong. In our story, Deborah was strong in her faith all
along. Indeed, I believe Deborah was the primary reason why Barak's
faith was strengthened. The absence of Deborah's name here is not
an insult to her; it is a compliment. She invested her faith and time
in developing a great leader. She was a great prophetic leader.

Chapter 8

GIDEON
A Strong and Decisive General

After the death of the fourth judge Barak, Israel returned to idolatry and God delivered them into the hands of the cruel Midianites for seven years.

Israel had known little peace since they stepped into the Promised Land. As nomadic people, they were ill trained for an agrarian life. They tried to learn the methods of being an agricultural people and would have done well if it had not been for a fatal mistake on their part and the persistent invasion of the Midianites and the Amalekites. To be sure of the agricultural success, they adopted a blatant syncretism of religion, worshipping both the Baal god of fertility and Yahweh. They set up Baal shrines in their fields, along with that god's female counterpart, the Asherah, emulating the pagan religion of the land.

The worship of Yahweh was blended with fertility rites and rituals. If their purpose was prosperity, it was short lived. The ravaging forces of Midian and Amalekites would sweep down during the harvest season and carry off the fruit of their hard labour, their cattle, and their possessions. Such raids continued relentlessly. Israel was never out of danger.

Whenever they turned to God for deliverance, He answered the cry of the people by sending them a prophet who here is being left out nameless (Judg 6:7–8), although there is a Jewish legend to the effect that he was Phinehas, the son of Eleazer. The prophet's message was that of needful rebuke, as well as of assurance that the divine deliverance from oppression was at hand.

Gideon was the next judge through whom God delivered the people of Israel from the Midianites. He was hesitant and fearful but God drew out Gideon's hidden potential and patiently brought him to the point of courage and confidence in the living God. The Lord encouraged, directed, and transformed him overnight to become a strong and a decisive general.

The Undeniable Call of God to an Unlikely Person

An angel of the Lord supernaturally appeared to Gideon at Ophrah and commissioned him from threshing wheat to thrash the enemies of Israel (Judg 6:11–14). To thresh wheat openly was to invite the occupying Midianite army to confiscate it. That's the reason Gideon was threshing wheat by hand in the bottom of a grape press to hide it from the Midianites. The Midianites dominated Israel so thoroughly that Israelites could rarely harvest crops; some lived in caves in fear of them.

The angel of the Lord said to him, *"The LORD is with you, O valiant warrior"* (Judg 6:12). Gideon was just an ordinary man, but when he had a supernatural encounter with God he became an extraordinary man. Actually according to the original version it was Yahweh, who is referred to be mighty in valour. The divine visitation was to remind Gideon of the greatness of God.

God looked at Gideon and did not see him as he was, but how he was going to make him to be. Gideon could not see himself as God saw him. He needed to renew his mind. His response to the angel was one of doubts, confusions, and excuses. This led to the obvious question by Gideon:

> "If the LORD is with us, why then has all this happened to us? And where are all His miracles, which our fathers told us about, saying, 'Did not the LORD bring us up from Egypt?' But now the LORD has abandoned us and given us into the hand of Midian" (Judg 6:13).

Gideon complained as though if it was the Lord's fault. There was no confession of apostasy or seeking to know what he and Israel might have done to bring the calamity on themselves. So often, our demands 'if' and 'why', seem to hold the Lord accountable for all that happens to us.

'And the Lord looked at him.' God does not look at the failure but at the faithfulness of man. The Lord told him, *"Go in this your strength and deliver Israel from the hand of Midian. Have I not sent you?"* (Judg 6:14). If the Lord calls, commissions and sends us we don't need any extra strength or ability, but our availability to fulfil his mission. Like some of us, Gideon started giving excuses about his family situation and probably about his inexperience as the youngest in his house. But the Lord did not leave him. He assured him, *"Surely I will be with you, and you shall defeat Midian as one man"* (Judg 6:16).

Gideon's lack of courage asked for a sign, some clear proof that the angelic appearance was no mere vision, but that the message he heard was really from God. Gideon went into his house and prepared a meal for the angel. The angel commanded Gideon to lay the meal of meat and unleavened cakes upon the rock and then pour broth upon it. Obeying the angel's command, Gideon witnessed a miracle, for the angel took a staff, touched the offered meal, and fire came out of the rock and consumed it. Immediately the miracle-worker vanished out of Gideon's sight. He had seen the angel of God face to face but did not die. The belief that death or misfortune would be the result of looking on any divine being was universal among the Jews (Judg 13:22; Gen 16:13; Exod 33:20, etc).

The Lord Is Peace

Gideon, receiving a divine benediction, built an altar at the scene and called it 'The-Lord-Is-Peace' or (Yahweh Shalom). The God who was able to bring water out of a rock can also produce fire—the common sign of His presence and of His acceptance of an offering—out of a rock (2 Sam 22:13).

The fire out of the rock consuming the flesh has a spiritual significance. Fire is a symbol of the Holy Spirit (Acts 2)—the Rock, a type of Christ, smitten of God. Fire came out of the rock, and the mission of the fire is to consume the flesh (Rom 8:1–13).

The word 'Shalom' means 'wholeness', 'security', 'well-being', 'prosperity', 'peace', and 'friendship'. Some people keep God at an arm's length. They know about God, they discover how loving and kind He is, but they do not know Him very personally. But Gideon had discovered a new and deeper personal relationship with God.

Gideon who was called for battle knew the meaning of both 'the peace of God' and 'peace with God'. For Gideon it signified God's favour, affirmation, and blessing.

Gideon Called to Unswerving Obedience

Gideon's first task as the Lord's warrior was to tear down the altar of the heathen god Baal and build an altar to the Lord. He did this in obedience to God's command (Judg 2:2; 6:25).

Gideon's father and the people were involved in worshipping the false god Baal, a wooden image or cult object representing the Canaanite goddess Asherah (Judg 6:25–34). Gideon was going to smash the idols that his father built. Although God had commanded us to honour our father and mother (Exod 20:12), people of God must not partake in the heathen practices of their parents or ancestors. In fact, they must cut down anything that is idolatrous or sinful.

Gideon obeyed God; even though it must have been very difficult for him to destroy the altar his own father had built. He replaced it with an altar to Jehovah (Judg 6:25–27). He knew this act of obedience to the Lord would surely bring threat to his life from his neighbours who were passionately committed to Baal in addition to their allegiance to Yahweh.

He destroyed the altar of Baal at night. In the morning when Joash came to know of the daring action of his son he changed his name from Gideon to Jerubbaal, which meant 'the antagonist of Baal'. Gideon, true to his name, which signifies 'the hewer', was not afraid to stand almost alone among a cringing and apostate people as a true worshipper of Jehovah. After Gideon obeyed God, the Spirit of the Lord came upon him. He then blows a trumpet and sounds a call to arms (Judg 6:34–35).

The Lord could not bless Gideon with victory over the impossible until He knew that he would obey His will without questioning. Gideon had an unconditional, implicit and total obedience. He did exactly what the Lord had told him.

Is there anything in our life that corresponds to the worshipping of an idol. Are there people, position, possession, plan, or purpose that stands in the way of complete obedience? That's the reason why we do not have much spiritual power or vision. The reason, often, is that we have blended our commitment to God with a god of our own. The Israelites feared total dependence on Yahweh and hence they also depended on Baal. How often we believe in God but draw our security from what we are or what we have, or on our accomplishments, our self-image, and because of the approbation of others.

The obedience of Gideon brought the spirit of the Lord upon him and he blew a trumpet. *"The Spirit of the LORD came upon Gideon; and he blew a trumpet . . ."* (Judg 6:34). The more accurate translation of the Hebrew is, 'The Spirit of the Lord clothed Himself with Gideon'. Natural talents were maximized and extraordinary gifts were given. This anointing from the Lord replaced fear with faith, compromise with courage and charisma with character in the life of Gideon. This enabled Gideon to rally his clan, the Abi-ezrites, to the call and challenge of God. But he needed fresh encouragement and confidence for the battle ahead and so asked for a double, divine sign.

Sign of the Fleece

Gideon asked for a sign from the Lord. One evening, he told the Lord that he would put a fleece of wool on the threshing floor. If by morning, dew was only on the fleece, and the ground around it was dry, then he would be sure that God would deliver Israel through him as he had promised. The next morning when he was awake, he found God's answer. He squeezed the fleece, and it was so full of dew that he could fill a bowl full of water. Then just to be doubly sure, Gideon asked the Lord, 'Please let me make a test once more with the fleece, let it now be dry only on the fleece, and let there be dew on all the ground'. God was faithful to the test. In the morning the fleece was completely dry and the ground was covered with dew. Twice, Gideon was reassured concerning his call by God (Judg 6:36–40).

After presenting our needs to the Lord, we need to wait on Him and be assured that He will accomplish what concerns us (Ps 138:8). The Lord promises to be actively involved in guiding and leading His children according to His will. He said, *"I will instruct you and teach you in the way which you should go; I will counsel you with My eye upon you"* (Ps 32:8).

Sometimes the Lord uses events and influences only as a confirmation of what He has been telling us in our prayers and through the Word of God. We can take into account providential circumstances, but should carefully check whether God has arranged certain events to give us positive guidance.

God does not will every circumstance; but he does have a will in every circumstance —J Kenneth Grider. God says in Revelation 3:8, *"I know your deeds, Behold I have put before you an open door which no one can shut".* We should examine ourselves whether we have continued inner peace as we consider the above factors in prayer.

To know the mouth of the harbour, the captain of the ship should keep looking at the three lights in the harbour till they line up behind each other as one. When he sees them so aligned, he knows the exact position of the harbour's mouth. In the same way, there are three lights that help us to know the will of God. According to F B Meyer, they are: 'the inward impulse', 'the Word of God', and 'the trend of circumstances'. God in our heart impels us forward; God in Bible corroborates what He says in our heart, and God in circumstances, indicates His will. Never start until these three lights agree.

We must check whether we experience restlessness, impatience or inner conflict. We read in Isaiah 32:17: *And the work of righteousness will be peace, And the service of righteousness, quietness and confidence forever.* There should be nothing, ordinarily, to disturb our assurance that we are in God's will. We are promised: 'The peace of God which passeth all understanding. . .' (Phil 4:7).

The Psalmist says in Psalm 119:165: *Those who love Your Law have great Peace. Let the peace of Christ rule in your hearts* . . . (Col 3:15).

If this peace is absent, then there is something wrong. Let us return to God's Word and pray and re-examine the circumstances.

God Looks for Quality not Quantity

God is not interested in quantity but quality. He has always been looking for obedient men and women to accomplish His purposes.

Hence He made Gideon's job more formidable by reducing his army from 32,000 to 300 heavenly commandos who were on the cutting edge of obedience to him. With these 300 he would face 135,000 enemy troops. Probably, God specifically wanted a small number of men so that Israel would not think that it was their own strength that won them the victory (Judg 7:2).

Often, God deals with us in the same way He did with Gideon's army. Sometimes He allows us to go through situations where we feel very weak and reduced to absolute powerlessness and then He gives us the victory. His strength is made perfect in weakness (2 Cor 12:9).

Probably He wanted the Israelites to understand that only through humble dependence upon Him that they could possibly win their battle. Humility should be understood in terms of God's principle that, spiritual victory does not depend upon natural strength or ability. We are to rely totally upon God's enablement and strength, refusing to build any monuments to our own success or victories (Judg 8:27). Building our own empires in our ministries can create occasions of stumbling for us and for others.

God instituted a test to check the people of their faithfulness. He asked Gideon to bring the people down to the water. When Gideon brought them to the water, God asked him to separate all those who lap the water with their tongue like a dog; and all those who kneel to drink. The faithful and alert people were three hundred men those who lapped like dogs, without bending or putting their faces in the water. God chose them to fight the battle.

The selection of Gideon reminds us of the fact that throughout the Bible, God used weak and foolish to accomplish great things for His kingdom (1 Cor 1:26–27).

At a time when women were regarded as second-class citizens, (see 9:54; 19:24), God chose Deborah to lead. Jephthah was a social outcast, and the leader of a gang of outlaws, but God chose him as one of the judges. Israel was not chosen either because of its great size or sophistication. Time and again, the Israelites proved themselves faulty. So did their leaders. God did not seek the most capable people, nor the most naturally 'good'.

Paul had a clear understanding of this concept and he wrote about it a thousand years later,

> For consider your calling brethren, that there were not many wise according to the flesh, not many mighty, not many noble; But God has chosen the foolish things of the world to shame the wise, and God has chosen the weak things of the world to shame the things which are strong, and the base things of the world and the despised God has chosen, the things that are not, so that He may nullify the things that are, so that no man may boast before God (1 Cor 1:26–29).

Therefore, as it is written: *"LET HIM WHO BOASTS, BOAST IN THE LORD"* (1 Cor 1:31).

If you want to be used by God for His service, believe that God strengthens those He calls and commissions, trusting in the promise of His abiding presence (Judg 6:14,16). Also be careful to heed God's warning. Do not continue to rely upon your fleshly wisdom and ability, lest He limit you to those resources rather than releasing His wisdom and power through you (Judg 10:13–14).

Even the talents and abilities we have from birth can be corrupted by sin and therefore must be energized by the Holy Spirit to bear fruit for God. Proverbs 3:5, 6 says, *Trust in the LORD with all your heart And do not lean on your own understanding. In all your ways acknowledge Him, and He will make your paths straight.*

We should be careful not to follow any leading that is our own, and also those that are not from God. The devil is very clear in presenting his ideas in a way that makes them seem harmless, and possibly even inspired by God (2 Cor 11:14). But God calls us to test and confirm any sense of divine leading, to refuse to move impulsively, and to be certain of His direction before stepping out in any venture. If we do that, we will move ahead in greater confidence, knowing that we are following God's leading and moving in His strength (Judg 6:36–40).

God Builds Up Our Courage and Confidence

Before the battle with the enemy, God showed Gideon that there was no question about his success. Gideon was told to take his servant, Purah, and sneak secretly into the camp of Midian late at night. They made it past the sentries and crouched beside one of the black tents where they heard two of the Midianites talking inside. One was telling about his frightening dream in which a barley loaf came tumbling into the camp and struck their tent turning it upside down. The soldier interpreted the dream as a special gift to Gideon from the Lord. *"This is nothing less than the sword of Gideon the son of Joash, a man of Israel,"* the interpreter said. *"God has given Midian and all the camp into his hand"* (Judg 7:14).

God was so gracious to inflame courage in Gideon by letting him know that Midian knew of him and feared his growing power in Israel, and that his victory was secure. We are comforted by the persistent efforts of the Lord to build up our confidence as He did to Gideon. The result was that Gideon was able to thank God in advance for the liberation of Israel.

Thanking God in advance for what He has promised provides us with the liberty to imagine what it will be like to receive the promise to unlock the prevailing impossibilities of our life. That requires prayer, attentive listening, and awareness of the messages He sends us through unexpected circumstances and people. Once the image of the victory is firmly set in our minds, the resolution of problems, the reconciliation of broken relationships, or the success in the projects or programmes He assigns us can be accomplished with courage.

God gave Gideon an excellent military strategy. The children of Israel under God's military leadership tricked the enemy. He used light and sound for scare tactics, enabling His little flock to scatter the large enemy.

At midnight Gideon divided his 300 men into three attacking columns, and they were to follow him in the blowing of trumpets and the breaking of pitchers, so that their hidden lamps could shine forth suddenly in the face of the foe. Attacking the Midianites, the 300 had to shout the war cry, *The sword of the Lord, and of Gideon!* (7:18, 20). The 300 had to stand still as if each trumpet holder seemed to have a company behind his back.

The Midianites and the Amalekites were awakened from sleep by the frightening sound of blaring trumpets and battle cries. They staggered out of their tents in confusion. Because they were so confused in the darkness, they began to attack and kill one another. But note the Lord's part: 'The Lord set the sword of one against another even throughout the whole army.' Of the 135,000 men, 120,000 were slain by one another, thinking they were battling Gideon and his men. The other 15,000 fled when they realized what was happening. It was the Lord's victory for Gideon and Israel from start to finish. And all the praise was given to Him. The Lord of the impossible had done it again.

Prayer is the key. When we spread out before the Lord the impossibilities we face, surrendering it to Him completely, we are given a confidence to press on. Our courage grows the more we depend on Him. We do not need to be defensive, self-justifying, or timid.

Gideon Lived in the Glory of His Past Victories
The men of Israel asked Gideon to be king, but Gideon rejected the

invitation to rule because he believed that God Himself should be king of Israel. *"I will not rule over you, nor shall my son rule over you; the Lord shall rule over you"* (Judg 8:22–27). Gideon knew that it was only because of the Lord's power, which ruled his life that he was able to accomplish something worthwhile that made the people adore him.

However, Gideon went on to do a strange thing: he asked the men for the gold earrings that they had captured during war. The weight of these earrings amounted to 1,700 shekels of gold or 73 pounds; and from the earnings, he made an ephod.

This gold ephod may have been a garment patterned after the short outer vest worn by the high priest, but it was not made for that purpose. Rather, it was erected and worshipped as an idol. Gideon was a man divinely appointed to deliver Israel from idolatry and oppression, yet he caused Israel to stumble by making an idol for them to worship.

He placed it in his hometown of Ophrah. Judges 8:27 says, *And all Israel played the harlot with it there, so that it became a snare to Gideon and his household.* What is implied is that the ephod became a shrine of memorial worship of the great things Gideon had done in defeating Midian and Amalekites. It focused their attention not on what God had done in the past rather than what He would do in the future. Gideon lived in the glory of his past heroics. He took the glory for himself, which previously he had been so careful to give to God.

The Baal shrine he had vigilantly removed was back in another form. It can, and does, happen to us. When the pressure that forced us to depend on God is relieved, we forget who got us through the tumult. Endless tales of what we accomplished replaces praise and worship and thanksgiving. The past becomes more exciting than the future, heritage more precious than hope. What the Lord has done in the past should give us the key to unlock the impossibilities of today and all our tomorrows.

Chapter 9

SAMSON
A Leader Who Played with God's Anointing

Anyone can fall if his intention is to act contrary to his basic convictions or moral principles of God, and if his judgement has been clouded by 'desire' or overwhelmed by 'passion'. Man develops character through his concrete decisions. Our decision determines our destiny. Circumstances do not make a man; they set before you a temptation so alluring that by your own strength you'll not be able to overcome it. Our trouble is not that we are tempted, but that we don't turn to God for deliverance and turn to someone else for counselling.

The same is true in Samson's story. The people of Israel were forever sinning and repenting. The anger of the Lord became hot against Israel so much so that He permitted the people to be vexed and oppressed by heathen kings for eighteen years. As the people cried and repented, God became grieved at their misery. Fresh apostasy, however, engulfed Israel, resulting in God delivering them into the hands of the Philistines for forty years. Samson's birth found Philistines power in the ascendancy.

Israel was in a desperate need for a deliverer. God decided to deliver His people from their oppressors. He chose Samson as the one to deliver them out from under the oppression of the Philistines. So the angel of God appeared to the wife of Manoah and said to her,

> "Behold now, you are barren and have borne no children, but you shall conceive and give birth to a son... and no razor shall come upon his head, for the boy shall be a Nazirite to God from the womb; and he shall begin to deliver Israel from the hands of the Philistines" (Judg 13:3–5).

The woman then went and reported to her husband all that the angel had told her. Just as the angel had said, a son was born to Manoah and his wife and they named him Samson. He grew up to live a life of a Nazirite. The Nazirites were not supposed to drink wine or eat anything that came from the vine such as raisins and grapes. The reason was the 'fruit of the vine' indicated of earthly joy, a cheer to the heart. But the Nazirites were not to find joy in anything on this earth. There is joy only in the things of God.

There is no record that Samson found his joy in the things of God ever in his life! He was always finding his pleasure in the things of this world. Second, a Nazirite was not supposed to cut his hair. He never had a haircut until Delilah gave him one. Why was this necessary? Because the Bible tells us, *Does not even nature itself teach you that if a man has long hair, it is a dishonor to him, but if a woman has long hair, it is a glory to her? For her hair is given to her, for a covering* (1 Cor 11:14).

The Scripture makes it very clear that long hair dishonours a man. But the Nazirites were expected to be willing to bear the shame for God. He was to be different. John the Baptist was a Nazirite, which was the reason for the way he looked. A razor had not touched his head or face. Third, a Nazirite was not supposed to come near a dead body. When a loved one died, he was not to go to the funeral or have anything to do with it. In other words, he had to put God first, above his relatives and loved ones.

Samson gave a fresh start to the humiliated and depressed condition of the people of Israel. He was appointed by God to deal with the existing emergency. Self-denial should have reached its highest significance in his life. He should have been a living embodiment of Israel's calling as a consecrated people. Although he judged Israel for twenty years, he did not have a fitting personal character. Samson took advantage of his special endowment, thinking his special gift enabled him to accomplish extraordinary deeds. He yielded to fleshly sins and personal gratification.

Yet in spite of his spiritual and moral decline, God continued to give him the gift of supernatural strength. Considering the life he lived, he was given more space than any other judge, because, amongst all the judges, Samson was the only Nazirite.

The Secret of Samson's Strength

Strength is the first thing that comes to mind, when we think of Samson. He was a physical giant but a moral weakling. His whole life was a scene of follies and sin. He mastered others, but he could not discipline himself. Samson could not be defeated by anyone as long as he had his long hair, and as long as he was under the anointing of God. The Bible says, the spirit of God would move on Samson, and he would rise up and accomplish feats with supernatural power (Judg 13:25). But Samson had a big weakness: He loved the world and what it offered him. He wanted the very thing his vows prohibited.

Samson had seen a beautiful girl in Timnah, one of the daughters of the Philistines. He wanted her as his wife. As a Nazarite, he was not supposed to marry anyone from the pagan culture. Since the woman looked good to him, he insisted that he have her (Judg 14:1–3). Then, Samson went down to Timnah with his father and mother. When they came as far as the vineyards of

Timnah, a young lion came roaring toward them. When the Spirit of the Lord came upon Samson mightily, he tore the lion with his bare hands (verses 14:5–6).

While Samson was in Timnah he proposed a riddle to the thirty companions who were with him. He gave them seven days to answer his riddle. At the end of seven days, through Samson's wife, the men were able to get the answer to the riddle. Then the Spirit of the Lord came upon him and he went down to Ashkelon and killed thirty of them and took their spoil, and gave the changes of clothes to those who had answered the riddle (verses 12–19). The marriage ended in a matter of days and resulted in the death of many people.

On another occasion, when Samson felt that the Philistines had mistreated him, he caught 300 foxes, and took torches, and put one torch between two tails. When he had set fire to the torches, he released the foxes into the standing grain of the Philistines; thus burning up both the stocks and the standing grain, along with the vineyard and grooves (Judg 15:4–5).

He then went and lived in the cleft of the rock of Etam. The Philistines marched against Judah to take revenge on Samson. The men of Judah went down to the cleft of Etam to take Samson and hand him over to the Philistines. This is the time when Samson first began to play with God's anointing. He considered himself invincible, and allowed the Israelites to tie him up and hand him over to the Philistines. They bound him with two new ropes and brought him up from the rock. When the Philistines met them at Lehi, the Spirit of the Lord came upon Samson so mightily, that the ropes that were on his arms were like flax that burned with fire and his bonds dropped from his hands. Samson found a fresh jawbone of a donkey; he took it and killed a thousand Philistine men with it (verses 9–15).

He thought he was mocking his enemies, but actually he was setting himself up for his downfall. Samson had a great anointing, but he came to a place in his life where he thought he could do all that he wanted and get away with it. Today, many men of God are in that same place. They are very much under the mighty anointing and have a wonderful ministry with signs and wonders. Because of the signs, the wonders and the miracles, they begin to think they can do anything they want.

Shortly after the incident in the Philistine camp, Samson again opted to toy with the anointing. Scripture says that he went to Gaza, where he saw a harlot there, and went in to her. When the Gazites knew that Samson was there they surrounded the place and lay in wait for him all night at the gate of the city planning to kill him early in the morning. Samson lay until midnight, then he arose and took hold of the doors of the city gate and the two posts and pulled them up along with the bars, then he put them on his shoulders and carried them up to the top of the mountain, which is opposite to Hebron (Judg 16:1–3).

Where did he get all his strength? His strength was not in his arms, although he killed a thousand Philistines at one time with them. His strength was not in his back, although he carried the gates of Gaza on his back, which was a remarkable undertaking. And note very carefully; Samson's real strength was not even in his hair, although he was weak when it was cut. His strength was from God. In each instance we see that the Spirit of the Lord came upon him. If God would not have intervened each time, he would have been as any other man.

Samson is forever strongly recorded in our memories, as the man who relinquished his anointing for the love of an adulterous woman. Samson, the mighty strong man is not remembered for great victories, but rather for his fall. God called Samson to defeat Israel's enemies, but a woman named Delilah robbed him of his strength. Samson's story warns us that if we play with God's anointing we can even loose it.

The Cause of Samson's Weakness

Samson, the strongest man of his generation, unfortunately was unable to control his lust. First, he fell for the woman at Timnah, second, he went into a harlot at Ghaza and Delilah was the third woman who dallied or played around with him. When thousands of men had failed to overcome Samson, a wheedling woman succeeded. Desire was his only rule.

The Philistines came to Delilah with a proposition, *"Entice him, and see where his great strength lies and how we may overpower him that we may bind him to afflict him. Then we will each give you eleven hundred pieces of silver"* (Judg 16:5). Delilah was not a woman of character and was not faithful to Samson. She said to him, *"Please tell me where your great strength is and how you may be bound to afflict you"* (Judg 16:6).

Samson told her if they bound him with seven fresh cords that have not been dried, then he shall become weak and be like any other man. She bound him with the seven fresh cords that the Philistines had given her and she cried, *"The Philistines are upon you, Samson!"* But he snapped the cords as a fire breaking a slender thread (Judg 16:9).

Delilah tried again:

> "Behold, you have deceived me and told me lies; now please tell me, how you may be bound." He told her, "If they bind me tightly with new ropes which have not been used, then I shall become weak and be like any of other man" (verses 10–11).

Again when she cried out, he rose up and broke the ropes like you would a thin string. Rather than seeing Delilah as a viable threat, Samson took God's anointing for granted. The key to his anointing was still a secret even after Delilah tried to know a couple of times. But Delilah didn't give up. The next time she tried to coax Samson to reveal the key to his anointing, he came closer to telling her the secret. He even mentioned part of the secret: his hair. She said, *"Up to now, you have deceived me and told me lies; tell me, how you may be bound"* (Judg 16:13).

The devil will come to us constantly, trying to find the key to the anointing on our lives—just as Delilah did with Samson. Samson said *"If you weave the seven locks of my hair with the web and fasten it with a pin then I will become weak and be like any other man"* (verse 13). She did this and the same thing happened. He again came out as strong as ever. Samson had played with Delilah on the previous occasions, but now he was starting to touch the very source of God's anointing on his life—*It came about when she pressed him daily with her words and urged him, that his soul was annoyed to death* (verses 15–17). That's what Satan wants to do. He wants to wear us down. He wants to get us to a place where we act upon our hearts and compromise with things of God.

Finally, Samson yielded and told Delilah the secret of his strength. He said,

> "A razor has never come on my head, for I have been a Nazirite to God from my mother's womb. If I am shaved, then my strength will leave me, and I shall become weak and be like any other man" (verse 17).

Samson said that his strength was, in his hair. This shows that he merely depended on his anointing. If he had said that his strength was in his God, he would never have fallen. Our anointing or our spiritual gifts cannot take us to heaven, but only our obedience to the will and the Word of God.

Samson had begun to think that even if they shave his hair, he would be invincible. But he had lost the anointing. There are people in churches today who have lost the anointing and don't know it. Some of them are even deacons, elders and pastors. In the end, Samson was captured by the Philistines and his eyes gouged out and taken to Gaza and bound with bronze chains, and was put in the prison.

The lure of sexual fantasy can begin like the wisp of a wind, but it will eventually tear through your life like a tornado, devastating everything and everyone in sight. Satan attacks the individual Christian, mostly through temptation. He will seek to tempt a believer to become absorbed into the world's system:

* By creating a desire for the material blessings that the world offers.
* By focusing our attention towards the honour and recognition of this world.
* By making comfort and luxury as the basis for security.

There can be a 'Delilah' in the life of every child of God—not necessarily a woman, but a weakness or a craving for the things and the pleasures of this world. The Bible says: *Do not love the world, nor the things in the world. If anyone loves the world, the love of the father is not in him* (1 John 2:15, James 4:1–4, 1 Tim 6:6–11).

It was in the areas of the world and the flesh that Satan won his original victory in the tempting of the first man and woman, and these are still his tactics today. Based on the foundation of the great victory won for us by Christ, you can defeat any attack from Satan. Because of his defeat at the cross, the devil's only strength now is found in a Christian's ignorance (Hos 4:6). But when a Christian knows the complete work of the cross and resurrection in his life, the devil is stripped of any weapon against him.

Keep away from obvious areas of temptation. Do not set any vile thing before your eyes (Ps 101:3, 1 Tim 6:9–11).

The Result of Samson's Failure

Sin blinds people. It blinds them of their duty to God and also blinds us of our duty to our fellowmen. When we sin, we not only loose our power, we also loose our peace. The pitiful thing about Samson was he did not know that his strength was gone. When Delilah had shaven the seven locks of his hair she said, *"The Philistines are upon you, Samson!"* and Samson woke up from his sleep and said, *"I will go out as at the other times and shake myself free."* But he did not know that the Lord had departed from him (Judg 16:20).

Delilah cut off Samson's locks. Along life's pathway many Delilah's shear us of power, peace, prayerfulness and position. Surely we must take heed lest we fall. While in prison, Samson must have thought of the mercies and blessings of the Lord. He must have surely repented of his sin and turned back to God.

One day the Lords of the Philistines came together for a great feast. They came together to celebrate the capture and humiliation of their enemy, Samson. They began to eat and drink and be merry, giving their god Dagon, the glory for their victory. As the feast moved to a climax they said, 'Call for Samson that he may amuse us'. So they called for Samson from the prison and made him stand between two pillars and he had to entertain them. The house was full of men and women and all the Lord of the Philistines were there. And about 3,000 men and women were looking from the roof while Samson was amusing them.

Samson asked a little boy who was holding his hand to help him feel the pillars on which the house rests, so that he could lean against them. Then Samson called out to God and said, *"O Lord GOD please remember me and please strengthen me just this time, O God, that I may at once be avenged of the Philistines for my two eyes"* (Judg 16:28).

At the very least, he began to call upon God again, even if his motive was vengeance. God heard his prayer and supernaturally strengthened him one last time. He took hold of the two main pillars that held up the house and pulled on them with all his might. The house fell killing not only Samson, but also everyone in the house. The number he killed at his death were more than he killed in his lifetime (Judg 16:30).

Who—or what—is your Delilah? Loose relationships? Unforgiveness? Pride? You must locate it and deal with it in your life before it kills you.

Samson was a Nazarite in outward appearance, but it is quite evident from the narrative that he knew little of the inward heart —separation from the Lord. He was not to touch or go near dead things. After he killed a lion, bees began to make honey in the dead body after-a-while. Samson took the honey that was in the carcass of the dead lion and ate it, and gave some to his parents. He became ceremonially and spiritually unclean because he violated God's law not to touch dead things (Judg 14:8-9).

In the lives of believers there are things that God does not want us to touch or involve with. These things can make us spiritually unclean. We should keep up our commitments and vows and not fall into a worldly pattern of life.

Despite all of Samson's weaknesses, God used him. He is mentioned in the Bible 'Hall of Fame' as a hero of faith along with Gideon, Barak, and Jephthah, all from Judges (Heb 11:32). Barely conscious of what it meant to live for God; and given to fits of lust and temper, Samson still had great physical strength, which came supernaturally from God. With it, he pushed back the Philistines— more by accident than by intention and kept Israel intact.

Don't ever let the devil steal the anointing from you like he did from Samson. Do not try to live in yesterday's anointing. Seek for a fresh anointing every day. We must do whatever it takes to keep in close touch with God. David says, . . . *the nearness of God is my good* (Ps 73:28).

Chapter 10

HANNAH
An Honourable Leader's
Graceful Mother

By the time, the Lord fashioned the woman out of Adam's rib, He was into His sixth day of work. A humorous story is told about an angel appearing before the Lord and commenting upon the intricacies of God's creation of the woman.

One of the angels asked the Lord, 'Why are you spending so much time on making the woman?' The Lord replied the angel by saying, 'Have you seen the work sheet on her? She needs to be totally washable, but not plastic, have 100 movable parts, all replaceable, run on a cup of tea and leftovers, have a lap that can hold two children at one time, have a hug and a kiss that can cure anything from a scraped knee to a broken heart, and have six pairs of hands'. The angel was surprised at these requirements and said, 'Six pairs of hands. No way'.

The Lord replied, 'Oh, it's not the just six pairs of hands but the mothers must have three pairs of eyes.' 'What for?' the angel asked. The Lord replied, 'One pair of eyes is to see what her children are doing, another pair at the back of her head to see what her husband needs and the third pair in front of her head to supervise the maid in her work.'

The angel came closer and touched the woman and exclaimed 'But you have made her so soft, Lord.' The Lord replied, 'Yes she is soft, but I have also made her tough with a great power to endure.' The angel then touched the woman's cheek, and said there seems to be a leak in this creation. The Lord objected and said, 'That's just a tear. Which is her way of expressing her joy, her sorrow, her disappointment, her pain, her loneliness, her grief, and her pride.' Now the angel was really impressed and said, 'Lord, You are a genius in creating the amazing woman'.

There is another story told about a family that was travelling to Shiloh. Every year they would travel from their native place to the temple of God to worship and sacrifice. They were the pilgrims from Ramathaim—Zophim from the hill country of Ephraim, to give sacrifice and offerings to the Lord of hosts. The man, Elkanah and his two wives Penninah and Hannah were with him. The children were hopping and running around their parents. A festive gaiety was shone on their faces except on Hannah.

Hannah had no children. She was barren. She felt very sad that she was not doing the duty of a wife. Penninah provoked her bitterly to irritate her, because the Lord had closed her womb (1 Sam 1:6). Now all Hannah wanted was a baby boy.

In Shiloh, in the house of the Lord things were different. Eli, the high priest of the Temple of God had two sons, Hophni and Phinehas, the successors of Eli. They were breaking the laws of the Lord (1 Sam 2:12 –17, 22). It was customary for the priests to have their portion of meat after the sacrifice, but the sons of Eli forced the Israelites to give them their portion first. They also lay with the women who came to the House of the Lord. Now the God of hosts who was fighting for His holy temple was looking for someone to take care of the temple and perhaps Hannah arrived at the temple at the right time.

The birth of a child to a barren woman is not a common occurrence. The birth is first of all an occasion for celebration. The deepest yearning of Hannah had been inexplicably fulfilled. Her dignity, and her rightful place with her husband were restored. Second, birth is an assertion that concerns the entire community of ancient Israel. It is a confirmation that the life and future of Israel (like the womb of Hannah) have been reopened. The birth was not a private wonder, but a gift of the possibility for all of Israel.

The Book of 1 Samuel records the transition in Israel from the period of the Judges to the Kings. This change in national life revolved around three men, Samuel—the last of the great judges, Saul—Israel's first King—and David who underwent adventures before coming into power.

The Gracious Hannah

The name Hannah means 'gracious', 'graciousness' or 'favour'. Hannah was the favourite wife of Elkanah, a Levite of Ramathaim—Zophim, who belonged to one of the most honourable families of that priestly portion of Jacob's family, the Kohathites.

Hannah is not recorded as having any particular outward beauty, but we see in her the beauty of a meek and quiet spirit. She is a beautiful example of how the most unpleasant and unfavourable circumstances can produce a character of blessing to the world.

The story of Hannah presents a sharp contrast with that of Deborah, another significant woman of Ephraim from the period of Judges. In contrast to Deborah's career impact on Israelite society through political clout, judicial leadership, and prophetic activity, Hannah's effect on Israel's society came through the gentle forces of faith and motherhood. Through Hannah, the point is made that women of faith played a legitimate and even formative role in shaping Israel's history.

Hannah's Attitude towards Irritation

When Elkanah went to Shiloh, to worship, he would make a portion of his offering for Peninnah and her children. But to Hannah he gave double. Because of this Peninnah would constantly taunt Hannah. What was the cause of Hannah's irritation? The Bible says,

> Her rival, however, would provoke her bitterly to irritate her, because the LORD had closed her womb. It happened year after year, as often as she went up to the house of the LORD, she would provoke her; so she wept and would not eat (1 Sam 1:6–7).

Hannah never forced herself on anyone. She never expressed herself to anybody. She opened herself, only to the Lord of Hosts who would stand by her in the battlefield, she was facing. Sometimes God allows thorns in our life. When we ask Him to remove it, He says, *"My grace is sufficient for you, for power is perfected in weakness"* (2 Cor 12:9), as He told Paul. The negative attitudes of others helped Hannah to overcome her situation. A blessing in disguise.

Peninnah, on the other hand whose name means 'pearl' or 'coral', does not seem to be as precious as a jewel or pearl, but as hard as one. *"Jealousy is as severe as Sheol; Its flashes are flashes of fire, The very flame of the LORD* (Song 8:6). Peninnah was jealous because Elkanah loved Hannah more, and gave her more portions. Although Peninnah was fruitful in the womb, she couldn't be thankful and graceful. She acted proud and haughty, an adversary and enemy to Hannah and she constantly provoked her. She brought continually before Hannah the fact that she was barren, taunting her, implying that the Lord did not favour Hannah.

It is better to examine yourselves and see if you have any 'Peninnah' attitudes. Penninah was irritated to see her husband love Hannah. She was jealous of Hannah's portion of meat. Are you jealous of your sister or brother in Christ? Are you irritated because of your sister's beauty, wealth, health, her ministry and even her commitment to God? The Creator is willing to accept you as you are. He created you in His own likeness. You are unique in the sight of the Lord.

We all face irritations, and they are waiting out there in the world to grab us. Therefore, how can one cope with the cause and effect of irritation? The secret of overcoming irritation lies in adjusting. I know that it is not easy. Here we have a lesson to learn from the oysters and its pearls.

Pearls are the products of much pain. The shell gets pierced when external substance or a grain of sand gets inside it. On the entry of that foreign irritant all the resources within the tiny, sensitive oyster rush to the spot and begin to release healing fluids that other wise would have remained idle. Gradually, the irritant is covered and the wound is healed by the formation of a pearl. A pearl is the symbol of stress, a healed wound, a precious tiny jewel conceived through irritation, born of adversity, nursed by adjustments.

Had there been no wounding, no irritation, no interception, there would not have been any pearl. 1 Corinthians 2:16 encourages us to live with the mind of Christ. 'For who has known the mind of the Lord, that He should instruct him? But we have the mind of Christ.' He who goes to bed angry has the devil for a bedfellow. Never take your anger or enemies to bed with you. Do you have enemies? Have you forgiven them whole-heartedly? If you don't forgive, it breaks the bridge you have to cross.

A pastor preached in a church about talents. He told the congregation that God made each one of us in a unique way; He has blessed us with at least one talent. None of us is without a talent. After the service, a lady came to him and said, 'Pastor, God has blessed me with a talent of irritating others'. The pastor exclaimed, 'O, that's great! Do you know what the man with only one talent did?' The lady replied, 'Yes of course, he dug a hole and hid his talent.' 'Do the same,' said the pastor.

Life of a Barren Wife

That year, as they went up to worship and sacrifice at Shiloh; as usual Peninnah provoked Hannah bitterly to irritate her. Hannah wept and refused to eat. Elkanah her husband consoled her saying, *"Hannah why do you weep and why do you not eat and why is your heart sad? Am I not better to you than ten sons?"* (1 Sam 1:8).

Elkanah described marriage with a spiritual insight that is out of keeping with cultural norms. He saw the relationship of husband and wife as having value in itself entirely apart from giving birth to children. His words to Hannah reveal that the union of marriage is a true becoming of 'one flesh of a child' belonging to both of them. Elkanah saw something that Hannah, in her anguished failure to live up to her culture's norms for wives, was incapable of seeing. He saw that, while children are an additional blessing in a marriage, marriage has meaning even without children.

The deepest meaning of marriage lies in the freely given love between a husband and wife. Elkanah longed for that kind of love from Hannah. But Hannah also desired the affirmation of the society in which she lived, and so she prayed for a child.

If you are married, I would like to assure you, that God had a special plan when He united both of you. Even if you don't have children, that doesn't mean that your marriage is not complete. You should not allow such thoughts to ruin your marriage. Waiting for something to happen is not a curse. In fact God always uses it to produce a blessing if we remain faithful to Him. Keep your trust in God. That is what Hannah's life reflects.

Elkanah's Love for His Barren Wife

How can a man love his barren wife? First, Elkanah loved his Creator, and then he loved his wife. When the vertical relation between God and you is healthy, naturally your horizontal relationship with your spouse will be perfect too. 1 Samuel 1:21 says, *Then the man Elkanah went up with all his household to offer to the LORD the yearly sacrifice and pay his vow.* He had a vow too. He came every year to fulfil his promised vow.

Elkanah respected Hannah's vow. He was very serious about that. He says in 1 Samuel 1:23, *"Do what seems best to you. Remain until you have weaned him; only may the LORD confirm His word."* Elkanah consulted his wife to plan for the trip that year. He respected her opinion. He consulted her decision-making. This helped Hannah to fulfil her vow and thus this family gave birth to a young prophet.

Hannah's Prayer Life

Hannah went near the doorpost of the temple of the Lord and prayed to the Lord and wept bitterly. She poured out her heart to the Lord. Her prayer life was one of a bitterly wounded heart.

It is often easier for the people of God to pray when they are in deep trouble. The trouble produces a kind of desperation in us, and we spend more time with God and are willing to come to terms with Him. Trouble may lead us to pray with fervency, with energy, with determination, with persistency. Hannah was praying so fervently that Eli thought she was drunk.

It was a prayer from the very depth of her heart. It is the custom of Orientals to pray audibly, but as she stood beside Eli's seat (1 Sam 1:26) she spoke in her heart; her lips moved, but her voice was not heard. This indicates that she had come to know the secret of heart-fellowship with God. Her's were not vain repetitions, but such an interaction of spirit with Spirit, of the human with the Divine, which requires no speech, for speech could not convey those groanings that cannot be uttered in a normal way.

The Bible admonishes us to go to the presence of God to hear rather than to speak. Do not be hasty in word or impulsive in thought to bring up a matter in the presence of God. For God is in heaven and you are on the earth; therefore let your words be few (Eccl 5:1–2).

You should not reason with unprofitable talk or with speeches with which He can do no good (Job 15:3–4). God already knows what is in your heart, but you do not know what He wants to convey to you and hence it will be profitable to you, if you would spend more time to hear and listen to His still and clear voice. He will admonish you and guide your steps and actions.

I would urge you to pour out your heart to the Lord. You may not understand all that you go through, but one thing is sure: Those that put their trust in God are never put to shame. God always hears the prayer that comes from the depth of the heart of a righteous person (James 5:16). Remember that Christ has made us righteous (1 Cor 1:30) and hence we too can come boldly to His presence to receive our requests from Him (Heb 4:14–16).

How many of us have prayed so intensely that our fervour could be mistaken for drunkenness or perhaps a mental or nervous disorder? Many of us are afraid to sweat, and instead of praying fervently, we would rather sit back and watch others pray. At Gethsemane, Jesus prayed so hard that He was sweating blood (Luke 22:44; 18:1–8).

It is such praying that prevails with God. Many of our prayers do not reach anywhere because we do not persist in praying. But prayers such as Hannah prayed storms the fortress of heaven.

Hannah prayed publicly
We seem to feel that public prayer is appropriate only for pastors and other Christian leaders. Hannah had no training in prayer, but she prayed publicly (1 Sam 1:10–11). And even though her voice was

soft and perhaps hoarse with the intensity of emotion, she prayed. God does not regard professionalism in prayer as important. It's the heart that matters and the fact that one prays at all.

Hannah practised the presence of God

Like Hannah, you must pray in such a way that, external realities fade away and you become aware only of the presence of the Lord. She was so much overwhelmed by the presence of God that words came so naturally and she didn't even notice that Eli was watching her. She became oblivious to all external distractions. This requires practising a regular on-going prayer life. How long does it take for you to let go of your burdens, responsibilities and get absorbed into the presence of the Lord?

As soon as you pray, the problem may not be solved or the pain may not subside but you may feel the peace of God. This is the assurance that you get in prayer. Even when there is no visible sign of the answer to your prayer, you will no longer be downcast. You will find strength to go about your daily activities as if you had already got the answer from God. Through this peace of God that passes all understanding you should know that your prayers have been heard. And the time taken for the answer to reach you is no longer a matter of concern.

You need to keep on praying till you reach this moment of transition. It is at this point that the burden is lifted from your hearts and the peace from God fills the vacuum instead. God may use different persons or methods to imprint this assurance in your heart.

Eli's Role As a Priest and Judge

Eli served as both priest and judge in Israel. As a judge, Eli dispensed justice between opposing parties. As a priest he oversaw an entire nation's relationship with God. Once each year, Eli entered the temple's Holy Place and offered a sacrifice for Israel's sins. No king or prophet in Israel's history was ever permitted to do that. People depended on him for their social, political and religious well being.

Thinking that Hannah was drunk, Eli rebuked Hannah for her drunkenness— *"How long will you make yourself drunk? Put away your wine from you"* (1 Sam 1:14). When Eli saw her trembling lips; he perhaps thought she was one of the women who gathered at the doors of the tabernacle of the congregation.

This shocking rebuke would have been a painful experience for her. Childless in the home, provoked on the way, and now rebuked in the house of the Lord. This could have broken her heart.

Eli's attitude of judging others

One of the most common mistakes we make is jumping to conclusions before getting to know all the facts. Eli observed Hannah and immediately concluded that she was muttering out of drunkenness. Since it never occurred to him that there might be another explanation for her behaviour, Eli misjudged Hannah's character and intentions. A good leader does not judge according to appearances, but according to facts. Looking can be deceptive just as hearing can too, but knowing for sure is the truth.

Judgement belongs only to the Lord. Let us not do God's work. Stop judging others by externals. When Samuel went to Bethlehem to anoint David, as the King of Israel, the Lord said, *"Do not look at his appearance . . . for God sees not as man sees, for man looks at the outward appearance, but the LORD looks at the heart"* (1 Sam 16:7). Romans 14:13 says, *Therefore, let us not judge one another any more, but rather determine this—not to put an obstacle or a stumbling block in a brother's way.* Deuteronomy 1:17 says, *"You shall not show partiality in judgment."*

Eli's inability to distinguish appearances from reality

On the one hand, Eli appeared to be doing his job, vigilantly guarding the sanctuary from possible desecration by Hannah; on the other hand he was actually demonstrating his incompetence. Though Eli was a high priest of Shiloh and a man of exceptional spiritual maturity he was unable to distinguish between appearance and reality. He was a man who watched lips instead of perceiving hearts, who misjudged profound spirituality to be indulgence in spirits.

But Eli proved quite capable of fulfilling his priestly role. Learning the true nature of Hannah's actions, he validates her prayer with a wish and a blessing. Eli did more than conduct the formalities of his office: he ministered to his people.

Hannah's gracious response

Hannah did not react but calmly and graciously responded to Eli's misjudgements. Hannah whose name means 'grace' is seen being gracious, and gives margin to aged Eli. She corrects his misjudgement gently. She said,

> "No, my Lord, I am a woman oppressed in spirit; I have drunk neither wine nor strong drink, but I have poured out my soul before the LORD. Do not consider your maidservant as a worthless woman, for I have spoken until now out of my great concern and provocation" (1 Sam 1:15–16).

In Proverbs 15:1, 4 we read that, *A gentle answer turns away wrath, but a harsh word stirs up anger . . . A soothing tongue is a tree of life.* Her gentle answer turned Eli's anger and he blessed her. He said, *"Go in peace; and may the God of Israel grant your petition that you have asked of Him"* (1 Sam 1:17). Her soothing tongue gave life to her dead womb, gave birth to a 'Samuel', and also it revived the dead Israel. Her tongue was a tree of life. The tree of life had lots of branches, to give life to others too. It bore fruit for the Lord. Beloved is your tongue, a tree of life? Does it bring life to others? Or does it stir up anger? Let us examine ourselves.

Hannah's Persistent and Triumphant Faith

Hannah's departure from the sanctuary was an example of faith triumphant. Though she had approached the Lord in the depths of despondency she left the sanctuary elevated and transformed. Hannah's spiritual victory, won through the labour of tearful prayers.

Hannah knew exactly what she desired. She did not have any selfish reasons when she desired a child. Barrenness was viewed as a curse in that day, in fact it was grounds for divorce, and fortunately Elkanah loved his wife. When she prayed to the Lord and asked for a child, she made a vow,

> "O Lord of hosts, if You wilt indeed look on the affliction of Your maidservant and remember me, and not forget Your maidservant, but will give Your maidservant a son, then I will give him to the Lord all the days of his life, and a razor shall never come on his head" (1 Sam 1:11).

God took her prayer seriously. Actually, that was precisely what He wanted. Because the leadership of Israel was so corrupt, He needed someone to reveal Himself to and so start a new leadership in Israel altogether. When our will and God's will come together, things are bound to happen. The Holy Spirit was at work in leading Hannah to make this offer to God.

He gives us the heavenly wisdom to deal with the problems we are undergoing. The Bible says, *If any of you lacks wisdom, let him ask of God, who gives to all generously and without reproach, and it will be given to him* (James 1:5). Spend time to ask for it. Hannah asked for it and got the wisdom to deal with her rival. She spent time in the presence of the Lord, her face was no longer sad.

Moses spent 40 days and 40 nights up in Mount Sinai in the

presence of the Lord. His face was glowing. His face was glowing so much that no one could come near him. Jesus said, 'When you pray, go into your inner room and when you have shut your door, pray to your Father who is in secret and your Father who sees in secret will repay you' (Matt 6:6). When you pray in secret, the Lord will do the miracle that every man can see it as the Lord's doing. When He does so, it will be marvellous in the eyes of men.

Your unshakeable faith in the Word and in the promises of God makes your prayer strong and gives you patience to wait on God. Faith believes that God is a rewarder. No truth is more clearly revealed and none is more encouraging in Scripture than this. Matthew says, *Thy Father which seeth in secret himself shall reward thee openly* (Matt 6:4). Faith gives its hearty consent to this precious truth. God is a rewarder of those who 'diligently seek him' (Heb 11:6). Faith rests its case on diligent seekers after God, and they are richly rewarded.

Chapter 11

DAVID
A Leader Who Inhaled the Flame of Passion

David was a man of God's own heart. God chose him for a definite purpose, to become Israel's greatest king and spiritual leader. Like Moses in the first half, David dominates the latter half of the Old Testament history. His exploits fill the books of First and Second Samuel, and the songs he wrote can be found in the Book of Psalms. All of the kings of Israel and Judah were measured against the standard he set during his forty-year reign.

David was around fifty years old when he became king and he had been Israel's king for about two decades. He was a gifted musician and a valiant warrior. Yet, he had a flaw in his character:

> And David realized that the LORD had established him as king over Israel, and that He had exalted his kingdom for the sake of His people Israel. Meanwhile David took more concubines and wives from Jerusalem, after he came from Hebron; and more sons and daughters were born to David (2 Sam 5:12–13).

Polygamy violated the precepts God gave in Deuteronomy 17:17.

169

How Are the Mighty Fallen?

We see him at one time living so close to God and serving Him in such a wonderful way. Then, we are greatly distressed and embarrassed to read of his great sin. Using his own words we can say, 'How are the mighty fallen?'

During springtime when kings go out to battle, David stayed in Jerusalem and sent Joab and his servants with him and all Israel, and they destroyed the sons of Ammon and besieged Rabbah (2 Sam 11:1). Fighting the battle for Israel was the responsibility given to David by God. But when the battle was raging, David was just relaxing at home not keeping himself busy in the Lord's work. It was at this time that he indulged in the act of adultery. It proves the fact that, 'An idle mind is the devil's workshop'.

Our greatest battles do not come when we are out working hard; they come when we have time on our hands.

> Now when evening came David arose from his bed and walked around on the roof of the king's house, and from the roof he saw a woman bathing; and the woman was very beautiful in appearance (2 Sam 11:2).

One look at this beautiful woman and David's lust was inflamed. When a sinful desire enters the mind, it will grow until the deed is executed, if it is not checked at once. As a rule, the mind eventually acts out what it dwells on. David is an example of this truth. First he saw the beautiful woman bathing, and then he delighted in what he saw. We can call this 'the second look'. Always this *second look* is very dangerous. He allowed his mind to dwell on what he saw and the delight turned into desire which we call lust. This desire brought about a decision to fulfil that lust and thus, he immediately sent messengers and inquired about the woman. One of them said that she was Bathsheba, the daughter of Eliam, the wife of Uriah the Hittite.

David sent his messengers who brought her to him. David lay with her and when she had purified herself she returned to her house. He deliberately committed sin with Bathsheba, resulting in the death of her husband and of her first son, born through David. Because he did not nip temptation in the bud, he went on to put his thoughts into action and fell into sin.

Later one day Bathsheba found out that she was pregnant. Then she sent word to David saying she was pregnant (2 Sam 3:4–5). At that time, instead of facing his sin and confessing it before God and his counsellors, David panicked and chose to develop a cover-up plan trading his integrity for hypocrisy and deceit.

David's plan was to bring Bathsheba's husband Uriah back from battle so that he would lie with his wife and assume that she had conceived his child. Then David sent word to Joab, saying, 'Send me Uriah the Hittite'. So Joab sent Uriah to David. When Uriah came to David he questioned him regarding the welfare of Joab, the people and the state of the war. David's questioning was not one of genuine concern but was mixed with hypocrisy.

David told Uriah *"Go down to your house, and wash your feet"* (2 Sam 11:8). And Uriah went out of the king's presence and a present from the king was sent out after him. Sending a gift to Uriah was another ploy from David's deceitful hands. Nevertheless, David's efforts to get Uriah home to his wife didn't work.

For we read: *But Uriah slept at the door of the king's house with all the servants of his lord, and did not go down to his house.* It was reported to David, saying, *"Uriah did not go down to his house." David said to Uriah, "Have you not come from a journey? Why did you not go down to your house?"* (2 Sam 11:9–10).

Uriah's response to David must have pricked David's conscience with guilt.

> Uriah said to David, "The ark and Israel and Judah are staying
> in temporary shelters, and my lord Joab and the servants of my
> Lord are camping in the open field. Shall I then go to my house
> to eat and to drink and to lie with my wife? By your life and the
> life of your soul, I will not do this thing" (2 Sam 11:11).

Israelite soldiers had no sexual relations while they were preparing for battle (1 Sam 21:5). Uriah refused to sleep with Bathsheba because he preferred duty before pleasure. He was one among the thirty-seven, a group of leading warriors under David (2 Sam 23:39).

David at last tried to get Uriah to go home to his wife. He wined and dined with him until he was drunk. But still, Uriah wouldn't go home, he went and lay on the bed of his Lord's servant. Finally David's cover-up plan turned to cold-blooded murder. Uriah's single-minded devotion to duty spoiled David's plan. And David rewarded Uriah with murder.

The next morning David sent a message with Uriah to Joab saying, *"Place Uriah in the front line of the fiercest battle and withdraw from him, so that he may be struck down and die"* (2 Sam 11:15). David knew he would surely be killed. As a result of David's plan, not only did Uriah die, but a number of other innocent soldiers as well.

When the word of Uriah's death reached David, he sent a message to Joab saying ". . . *do not let this thing displease you, for the sword devours one as well as another; make your battle against the city stronger and overthrow it, and so encourage him"* (2 Sam 11:25).

But the thing that David had done was evil in the sight of the LORD (2 Sam 11:27).

Still David moved further along with his plan. When Bathsheba had finished grieving for her dead husband, David had her brought to his house and she became his wife; then she bore him a son. Although David had completely deceived the nation, he had not covered up his sin in God's eyes.

It always displeases God when we sin. David's sins of adultery, cold- blooded murder, and subsequent cover up were an exceptional evil in God's sight. His sins were considered greater because he was a shepherd over God's people and the one who was responsible to administer justice and righteousness in Israel (2 Sam 5:2; 8:15).

In spite of all these things, it is surprising to see that David never seemed to show any sign of repentance. He tried to maintain integrity in the eyes of the people, and he could now enjoy Bathsheba as his wife . . . but he could not enjoy his fellowship with God.

In 2 Samuel 12, God stirs David's heart toward repentance through the bold confrontation of prophet Nathan.

Wisely, Nathan approaches David indirectly. He cleverly captivated David with a heartrending story:

> "There were two men in one city, the one rich and the other poor. The rich man had a great many flocks and herds. But the poor man had nothing except one little ewe lamb Which he bought and nourished; And it grew up together with him and his children. It would eat of his bread and drink of his cup and lie in his bosom, And was like a daughter to him. Now a traveler came to the rich man, And he was unwilling to take from his own flock or his own herd, To prepare for the wayfarer who had come to him; Rather he took the poor man's ewe lamb and prepared it for the man who had come to him." (2 Sam 12:1–4).

He offered the case to David, the highest judge in Israel. David's reaction was quick and powerful. His anger burned greatly against the man of whom Nathan was speaking about. He told Nathan *"As the LORD lives, surely the man who has done this deserves to die"* (2 Sam 12:5). Nathan tells David that he was the man. The story was not really about a little lamb, but about David's cold-blooded murder of Uriah the Hittite. Nathan told him

> "Thus says the LORD God of Israel, 'It is I who anointed you king over Israel and it is I who delivered you from the hand of Saul. I also gave you your master's house and your master's wives into your care, and I gave you the house of Israel and Judah; and if

that had been too little, I would have added to you many more things like these!" (2 Sam 12:7–8).

He goes on to name David's crimes and their punishment, as told from the mouth of God. Broken over his sin, David confesses it to Nathan. He said, *"I have sinned against the LORD"* (2 Sam 12:13).

Nathan, the prophet of God, represented the convicting power of God's righteous Holy Spirit. In John 16:8, we read, *"And He, when He comes, will convict the world concerning sin, and righteousness, and judgment. . . ."* The convincing or convicting work of the Holy Spirit is seen clearly with Nathan, the prophet, confronting David about his sin with Bathsheba and Uriah. David's secret sin was uncovered and exposed to God's light; there was nowhere to hide. God sees everything.

However, assurance of life was advanced to David. Nathan told David that God has taken away his sin and he would not die. However, God would take the life of his illegitimate son so that the Lord's enemies would have no reason to blaspheme God (2 Sam 12:14). Nathan not only confronted David's sin, he named the painful consequences that the king would endure.

The Consequences of David's Sin
David broke at least four of God's ten commandments in his sin with Bathsheba.

1. He put the god of lust before the God of heaven.
2. He coveted his neighbour's wife.
3. He committed adultery.
4. He indirectly murdered Uriah.

David reaped a bitter harvest as a direct result of the things he did with Bathsheba. Even though he repented and found forgiveness, he still had to face those consequences.

Deep down we think that if we confess our sin fast enough we will be saved from all of the suffering it brings. David reminds us that this is not the case. God is not being unfair when He allows the consequences of our sins to bring our lives to a screeching halt. By doing so the Lord reaffirms His love for us, a love so great that He will do whatever it takes to end our love affair with sin.

David faced the first consequence of his sin soon after it was predicted. The Lord struck the son Bathsheba bore to David with a sickness. On the seventh day of the boy's sickness the child died (2 Sam 12:15–17).

The second consequence David had to face because of his sin is given in 2 Samuel 13. Absalom the son of David had a beautiful sister named Tamar. Amnon the son of David loved Tamar very much but it was a wrong kind of love. It was not an affectionate, brotherly love. It was physical and incestuous love.

Amnon took the counsel of Jonadab, a wicked friend, who asked him to lie on his bed and pretend to be ill. He requested his father (David) to let his sister Tamar to prepare some food for him in his sight and eat from her hand. David sent for Tamar and asked her to do just like Amnon had requested (2 Sam 13:2–7).

Tamar went to Amnon's house and she took dough, kneaded it and made cakes in his sight, and gave it to him. Amnon refused to eat it and he asked everyone to go. Then he asked Tamar to bring the food to his bedroom. When she brought it to him he told her to lie with him. She refused because she said it was a disgraceful thing for such a thing is not done in the whole of Israel. Then he violated her because he was stronger than she was. Then he hated her with a hatred that was greater than his love for her (2 Sam 13:8–15).

When Absalom, Tamar's full brother, found out about the rape, the tension in the family became more volatile. David heard and he was very angry (2 Sam 13:21). But sadly, David's anger went no further. Absalom did not take his revenge immediately on Amnon. Absalom waited two years for David to act. But because of his father's passivity, Absalom's hatred festered into a plot to murder Amnon.

Later, Absalom ordered his servant to strike Amnon and put him to death when he was merry with wine. The servants did as they were told and Amnon died. Thus Absalom took revenge for what Amnon had done to his sister (2 Sam 13:28–29). Then Absalom ran away and stayed in Geshur for three years. David however, brought him back to Jerusalem. Then Absalom led a conspiracy against his own father David. The storm in David's life continued to stir fiercely, as we find Absalom's heart filled with revolt against his father.

In course of time a messenger reported to David of his son's conspiracy:

> "The hearts of the men of Israel are with Absalom." David said to all his servants who were with him in Jerusalem, "Arise and let us flee, for otherwise none of us shall escape from Absalom…" So the king went out and all his household with him. But the king left ten concubines to keep the house (2 Sam 15:13–16).

When David had fled from Jerusalem, Absalom and his men along with Ahithophel entered Jerusalem with him. When Absalom asked Ahithophel what he should do, he advised him,

> "Go in to your father's concubines, whom he has left to keep the house; then all Israel will hear that you have made yourself odious to your father. The hands of all who are with you will also be strengthened." So they pitched a tent for Absalom on the roof, and Absalom went in to his father's concubines in the sight of all Israel (2 Sam 16:20–23).

The place where they pitched a tent for Absalom was on the palace roof—the very place where David had sown the wind of adultery. Thus the words to the Lord spoken through the prophet Nathan when he confronted David of his adultery with Bathsheba came true—

> "Now therefore, the sword shall never depart from your house, because you have despised Me and have taken the wife of Uriah

the Hittite to be your wife . . . 'I will raise up evil against you from your own household; I will even take your wives before your eyes, and give them to your companion, and he will lie with your wives in broad daylight. Indeed you did it secretly, but I will do this thing before all Israel, and under the sun" (2 Sam 12:10–12).

Sin deceives. David gave in to sin, he began to walk down sin's slippery slope of destruction that began with giving in to lust, plots, lies, schemes, intrigue, cover-ups, and finally murder! Although God forgave David and he genuinely repented, his sins cost him very dearly.

David's Honest Confession

David responded to Nathan's confrontation with a wholehearted confession: *"I have sinned against the Lord"* (2 Sam 12:13). David was a great king partly because he did not act with the normal pride of a king. When confronted with the truth, he repented.

David acknowledged his sin. He accepted the truth and the seriousness of what he had done and why it had happened, which is so important for recovery. The memory of it was part of what would protect him from another such failure. He said, *For I know my transgressions, And my sin is ever before me* (Ps 51:3).

He cried out for mercy; he pleaded with God to purify his heart. *Purify me with hyssop, and I shall be clean; Wash me and I shall be whiter than snow* (Ps 51:7). His words show us the true nature of confession when he cried out, *Against You, You only, I have sinned, And done what is evil in Your sight, So that You are justified when You speak And blameless when You judge* (Ps 51:4).

David faced the consequences realistically. He told his officials,

"While the child was still alive, I fasted and wept; for I said, 'Who knows, the LORD may be gracious to me, that the child may live.' But now he has died; why should I fast? Can I bring

him back again? I will go to him, but he will not return to me."
David accepted this painful consequence, refusing to blame
God or becoming bitter (2 Sam 12:22–23).

David's response shows that he believed in the hope of heaven. He
knew his son was gone, but he also knew that one day he would
see him again. Even in the midst of his suffering, David relied on
God's truth. Then David comforted his wife Bathsheba and lay
with her and she gave birth to a son, and he named him Solomon
(2 Sam 12:24).

David felt the pangs of sin deeply and was earnest in his
repentance. Since God looks at the intentions of the heart, David
could be called *a man after his own heart* (1 Sam 13:14). God is
concerned more with who we are, than with what we do.

First and Second Samuel does not paint him as a flawless
character, nor as a perfect model of strength and courage. David had
striking weaknesses. In his love for God, he held nothing back. David
knew that God loved him even though his sin had caused death and
destruction for many.

Psalm 103:12 states, *As far as the east is from the west, so far has
He removed our transgressions from us.* God is bigger than our sins; and
even though there are times when we will have to experience pain and
suffering for our choices in life, we can count on the fact that God
holds nothing against us if we ask for His forgiveness.

Nevertheless, David was Israel's greatest king. Even at his lowest
flagging, his strength of character showed. He was never vengeful with
his enemies. He took full responsibility for his mistakes. Perhaps he
always remembered that he had started out as a mere shepherd. He
held power only by the grace of God and he believed that God had
every right to take the power away.

Chapter 12

ELIJAH
Secret and Strength of Leadership

Elijah was one of the most colourful of all the prophets of Israel. He did more for God's purpose in Israel, than the 7,000 compromising Jews, who merely had a positive testimony that they had not bowed down to Baal (1 Kings 19:18). It is true that they had not bowed down to Baal, but did they take a public stand for God like Elijah? They neither rejected nor projected the living God. However, God used Elijah's stand to challenge and change the lives of many. But others were afraid of displeasing King Ahab, and even Obadiah was one among them (1 Kings 18:3).

The Bible does not give us a detailed description of Elijah as a person. As to his appearance, he is described as a hairy man with a leather girdle bound about his loins (2 Kings 1:8).

We read in James 5:17, *Elijah was a man with a nature like ours and he prayed earnestly that it would not rain, and it did not rain on the earth for three years and six months.* The important thing we note here is, Elijah was an ordinary man with all the passions that any mortal would have, but he was a man of prayer, a prayer warrior. A warrior is a person who not only fights the battle, but also challenges the enemy. His life was an extraordinary one, and he lived in one of the greatest outbreaks of miracles in biblical history. He was a faithful overcomer.

Many years ago, the former Indian President, Dr Radhakrishnan said, 'You Christians claim to have an extraordinary God, but your life is still ordinary'. How true it is! Every one of us should pray, 'Lord, make me an extraordinary person'. What made Elijah an extraordinary person? Let us look into three major secrets of Elijah's strength.

Secrets of Elijah's Strengths

a) Elijah experienced a living God

Elijah knew that his God is a living God. He stood before King Ahab and said, 'As the Lord, my God lives'. By asserting thus he challenged the king. What does the statement 'The Lord, my God lives', mean? It means, experiencing God as a living God. Knowing God is different from experiencing Him as a God who lives in the midst of us. In a situation within the family, you may remember what you spoke to your family members this morning. Because you are living together, you remember what you spoke with each other.

But if you are put forth with a question, 'What did God speak to you this morning?' Can you answer, 'Brother Chandrakumar, I can precisely tell you that this is exactly what God spoke to me?' If you are unable to answer this question, it means you are not experiencing him as a living God.

James says, that even the demons shudder when they hear the name of the Lord. Even the devil knows that Jesus Christ is the living God. Perhaps he knows God, and the Word of God more than you and I do.

If the devil knows the Lord and you also know the Lord, what is the difference between you and the devil? The difference is that, the devil believes that He is the living God, but he doesn't experience Him as the living God. It is just not sufficient to believe in your head that Jesus is the Lord. You have to reach your heart to experience Him as the living God. Today people are expecting something new in their lives. You cannot talk about Jesus to someone unless you experience Him in your life. We need to demonstrate in and through our lives, that we have a God, who lives and who speaks.

In one sensitive place, where preaching is forbidden, people go to concealed houses to hear the Word of God. In one such house, a man came to me for prayer. I told him, 'You need to accept Jesus as your personal saviour if you want me to pray for your sickness.' He said, 'No, no, I am from another religion and I have my ritualistic things on my body and so I cannot accept Jesus.' I said to him, 'Then, you better follow your religion, don't come to me.' I sent him away. Seeing so many people healed in that home, he came back to me again and said, 'Please pray for me'.

I generally do not pray for healing for anyone who refuses to accept Jesus as his or her personal saviour. Hence I asked him, 'Are you ready to accept Jesus?' He said, 'No.' I replied, 'I am sorry I cannot pray for your healing.' The third time he stood in the long queue and came to me and said, 'First you pray for me, then I'll accept Jesus as my Saviour and Lord'. I was moved by his consistency and started praying for him. As I was praying, God revealed the secrets of his life to me. I told him, 'You along with the union members of your company are planning a strike against your authorities.' That shocked the man and he was wondering how I knew all his secrets since he had just entered the house and no one knew him.

I asked him, 'Did you pray to your God this morning?' He said, 'yes.' 'Did your God hear your prayers?' He said, 'I don't know.' Then I asked him another question. 'Did your God speak to you this morning?' He said, 'no.' Then I challenged him by saying to him, 'My friend, I have a God who speaks to me, I have a God who is a living God. This God told me all about your life. You just entered this house and I could tell you all about your life because my God spoke to me'. I asked him, 'Do you want a God who speaks or doesn't speak?' He instantly removed all the ritual things from his body and he said, 'I want this Jesus who is a living God'. It is not a change of name or religion, but a relationship that is required of us when we encounter God.

The secret of Elijah's strength was, he had a personal relationship and a personal experience with the living God. Job said, *"And as for me, I know that my Redeemer lives"* (Job 19:25). Paul said, *"I can do all things through Him who strengthens me"* (Phil 4:13). Isaiah in his vision saw the Lord lifted up with power and authority (Isa 6:1). Jesus said to Mary and Martha, *"I am the resurrection and the life"* (John 11:25).

The first secret of Elijah's life was that he knew God as a living God and the second secret was, that Elijah was a man who stood in th presence of God.

b) Elijah stood in the presence of God

Suddenly, standing before the king, was a unique figure, very much different from the rest of his generation. Quite how Elijah worked his way through the hierarchy to a meeting with the king remains a mystery. It is possible only with God's amazing strength. Jesus told Ananias that Paul was His chosen instrument to carry His name before . . . kings (Acts 9:15). Paul didn't know how this would happen, but it happened. David, an obscure shepherd was brought before King Saul, and Moses confronted the mighty Pharaoh.

God has been raising people out of obscurity and has given them a voice to address the nation's leaders. Doubtless He is able to do it again.

Elijah did not mince words as he encountered the king. He

said, *"As the Lord, the God of Israel lives, before whom I stand . . ."* (1 Kings 17:1). He spoke with all the authority of one who came from the presence of God, so that in meeting Elijah, Ahab was really being confronted by Elijah's God. Pharaoh had a similar experience when he met Moses.

Elijah's tall claim was that he stood before God. The world too often detects our uncertainties. We do not sound like people with confidence, who genuinely know the living God. Our message often lacks credibility because it lacks assurance. We seem to carry our doubts into the battlefield.

Although Elijah stood before God, he was not cut off from his society. He said, 'I stand before God,' but he was also totally involved with what was happening in his nation. Jesus did not hide Himself away from the crowds. He put Himself where it really counted, earning the title 'Friend of sinners' yet remaining both untouched by their sin and unprepared to adjust His message to accommodate them.

The presence of God makes the difference. When we pray, we need to get into the presence of God. The best time for prayer is early in the morning. 'He who seeks me early shall find me.' So, get up early in the morning and pray. What should you do early in the morning? Get up! I know you don't like to get up. Some people just want to lie down and have a horizontal meditation. They pray, 'Lord, thank you for the night's sleep and the rest you gave me,' then they snore back to sleep and then they wake up and pray again. No horizontal meditation will do.

Amos says, *"Woe unto those who are at ease in Zion"* (6:1). There's no real rest for Christians. If you rest, you will rust. Get up from your bed, go to the bathroom, clean yourself up, wash your face, and brush your teeth. Please, don't go to God with a bad breath.

Feel fresh in the sight of God. If the President of your country calls you tonight to dine with him, how would you go? You would have put on your best outfit, a suitable hairstyle, the best perfume possible and you would be fresh and clean. If you can go to a worldly authority so well prepared, how well prepared should you be in the presence of the Lord of lords and the King of kings. We Christians, tend to have no fear of God. We take the love of God for granted. Other people seem to fear their gods more than Christians do. I think Christians don't have the fear of Jesus because Jesus does not hold a spear or a sword in His hand. Go before God with fear and trembling. The presence of God is very important.

Here I want to place before you two important spiritual disciplines: (1) Please do not start praying unless you have felt the presence of God. (2) Whenever you open the Bible never close it without God speaking to you. Because it is God's Word and it will not return back in void. God will definitely speak to you something from the portion that you are reading, but you are not waiting in His presence to listen to Him. Christian life is a life of discipline and the word 'disciple' comes from the word 'discipline'. Discipline pays dividends.

People are in a hurry to quickly pray because they want to get to work or do other things. Some people pray like this: 'God bless me, my wife, my son and my daughter, we four and no more.' Do not be in a hurry when you pray. Do you hurry when you watch cricket? You don't say one, two and I'm going away now. You are sure to relax and watch the complete game, but you don't want to relax and pray. Wait for the presence of God. If you are not able to feel the presence of God, read a few verses of Psalms or Proverbs in the Bible and sing few songs of praise and by then you will be able to feel the presence of God. If you still, do not feel the presence of God, don't start praying.

Make it a discipline in your life that you will not start praying if you are unable to feel the presence of God, but that you would cry to the Lord, saying, 'Lord, what is that which is hindering you from coming to me? What is there between you and me? Why am I not able to feel your presence'. Cry out to Him, God will speak to you perhaps saying, 'Hey, you husband, last night you scolded your wife and turned the other side and slept and she turned the other side and slept, and this morning, do you want me to come to you? No, No! I'm not a cheap God. Go say sorry to your wife, then you come to me'.

Are you a person, who has been watching obscene movies on television or on the internet and has been having all sorts of hallucinations and fantasies and have ended up in a mess? Now do you expect God to come to you as soon as you start praying? Our God is a holy God. Without holiness, no one will see the Lord (Heb 12:14).

Entering into the presence of God involves four aspects: Conviction, Confession, Cleansing and Communion. First, comes conviction. The Holy Spirit of God convicts us of any unconfessed sin in our hearts.

What is confession? Confession is not telling God that you have sinned. He already knows and that is why He has given you that conviction. The word confession means agreeing with God, saying, 'Yes Lord, I have sinned'. Then comes the cleansing through the blood of Jesus and then comes the communion with God. Once these aspects are taken care of, then you feel the presence of God and now whatever you pray, it gets into the computer of God and you can be sure of getting an output. This is exactly what I mean by going into the presence of God.

Elijah was a man who always stood in the presence of the Lord. Before Elijah could stand in the presence of the king, he stood in the presence of the King of kings. That was his strength. If you stand before God in fear and trembling, you can stand before people with power and authority.

That's what Elijah did. Moses requested God, *"If Your presence does not go with us, do not lead us up from here"* (Exod 33:15). As the Israelites walked in the wilderness, the presence of God never left them. The presence of God was in the pillar of cloud in the daytime and pillar of fire in the night. Only when the pillar of cloud and pillar of fire moved, they moved. We need to walk in the presence of God. On the Day of Pentecost, the presence of the Holy Spirit made the difference.

c) Elijah obeyed the Word of God

The third secret of Elijah's strength is found in 1Kings 17:5: *"So he went and did according to the word of the Lord."* It was implicit obedience to God. It was unconditional, unreserved, immediate obedience, without any question and without any wavering.

What is obedience? The Bible says, *"Behold to obey is better than sacrifice . . ."* (1 Sam 15:22). When we look at the spelling of the word O-B-E-D-I-E-N-C-E, the centre word is 'Die'. The centre letter is 'I'. Hence, I must die to myself—that is obedience. Why is it that we do not obey, it is because we are selfish. Selfish ambitions, selfish ego, and self, keeps us away from obeying the Lord. Get out of your selfishness. Be willing to be nothing.

You should be willing to be submissive and servant to others. Only if you humble yourself, can God really help you to be obedient to Him.

God listens to those who listen to Him. When you take seriously what God says to you, you can expect God to give heed to what you say to Him. Jesus said, *"If you abide in Me and My words abide in you, ask whatever you wish, and it shall be done for you"* (John 15:7).

When God spoke, Elijah reciprocated with obedience, and later in the story Elijah spoke and God acted.

Adopt God's Perspective

In the background to this story we see that Elijah had prophesied that, it would not rain for three and a half years. King Ahab was angry and commanded his soldiers to bring Elijah to him. So the soldiers were searching for Elijah. Ahab and Jezebel had no regard for the prophets of God. They had already put most of them to death and would not have hesitated to kill Elijah. Elijah needed a place to hide himself; he was in a crisis at that time when the word of the Lord came to him saying, *"Go away from here and turn eastward, and hide yourself by the brook . . . and I have commanded the ravens to provide for you there"* (1 Kings 17:3).

When God asked Elijah to go to the brook Cherith, God was demanding something strange. Soldiers were searching for Elijah, and God told him to hide himself by the side of a river. It did not seem a wise thing to do.

It is obvious that no one can hide in an open public place like the river. But Elijah never questioned God, because he knew his God would never make a mistake. Sometimes our disobedience is because we do not fully trust God. While I was analysing this passage, I found that it was not raining and there was no water in the river and no one would come to the river to fetch water. If I were in Elijah's place, probably I would have asked, 'Lord, why don't you show me a cave to hide?'

Do you know, why God did not show a cave for Elijah to hide? It is because He knew all the soldiers would be searching for him in the caves. No one would ever think that anyone would go and hide near the river. Though according to human reasoning one would not correlate this with the idea of hiding near the river, God knows what is best in a given situation. It is better not to reason with your intelligence when God tells you to do something, just obey. He's the Lord. Elijah obeyed and went.

Before even Elijah could start wondering how he was going to live in that desolate spot by the brook Cherith, God said, *"It shall be that you will drink of the brook, and I have commanded the ravens to provide for you there"* (1 Kings 17:4). Where God guides, He provides. All of God's promises are certain, sufficient and conditional. God promised food and drink, absolutely sufficient for the sustenance of His servant. It was a conditional promise to the extent and effect: 'If you will, I will.'

Here, I would like to draw your attention to the most important word 'there', in verse 4 as well as in several other incidents in the Bible. What God told Elijah was, that if he wanted the water and food he must go there—into the place of God's choice. Are you 'there', in the place of God's will for you? For *there* is the place of God's provision. When Moses asked God to show His glory, God told him, *"Behold there is a place by me, and you shall stand there by the rock"* (Exod 33:18–21).

Why did God send him to Cherith? The answer was that he should be protected from the soldiers. After a time of ordeal and special service there is always the danger of reaction. Second, to prepare him for further service. Elijah had to still learn greater lessons of dependence upon God and complete trust in Him, of patiently waiting for God's time, and of humility.

God commanded the ravens to feed him. We know that ravens are birds that scavenge on the dead. Any one of us could have said, 'Lord haven't you ever read Leviticus 11:13–15?' It says, 'These, moreover, you shall detest among the birds . . . every raven in its kind.' We could have said, 'Lord, how on earth did you choose such an unclean bird?' Elijah never grumbled, complained or murmured like some of us do. He never questioned God. He simply listened to the voice of the Lord. And he was even willing to take and eat from the ravens.

Although carnivorous birds themselves, ravens lose their ravenous nature when commanded to fulfil the will of their Creator, who is able to make the most unlikely instruments minister to His saints. Our Lord's reference to ravens is instructive: *"Consider the ravens, for they neither sow nor reap . . . and yet God feeds them"* (Luke 12:24). God commanded the ravens to feed Elijah (1 Kings 17:4); all things are possible when God speaks.

God's word to Elijah was unusual. For example, even Jesus gave unusual instruction to His disciples, which He wanted them to obey. He told Peter to go to the sea and throw a hook, and take the first fish that comes up; and to open its mouth to find a shekel (Matt 17:27). On another occasion Jesus said to Peter and John,

> "Go and prepare the Passover for us, so that we may eat it . . . , When you have entered the city, a man will meet you carrying a pitcher of water; follow him into the house that he enters. And you shall say to the owner of the house, 'The Teacher says to you, "Where is the guest room, in which I may eat the Passover with My disciples?"' And he will show you a large furnished, upper room; prepare it there. And they left and found everything just as He had told them; and they prepared the Passover" (Luke 22:8–13).

Jesus said to Peter, *"Cast the net on the right-hand side of the boat and you will find a catch"* (John 21:6).

Why did Jesus instruct His disciples to do such strange things? I think it is because He wanted to develop their obedience. He wanted them to live, not by their own reason and wisdom, but by His Word. The more they acted on Jesus' word, the more they trusted it, and all the more they acted on it. Jesus' mother learnt this lesson too. 'Do whatever he tells you', she told the servants at the wedding in Cana, and their obedience brought about a miracle (John 2:5).

Sometimes God may ask you to do odd things. Like Peter, you

must be willing to say, 'but at Your bidding I will let down the nets' (Luke 5:5). Only when you reach out with Peter's faith and obedience will you enjoy the miraculous shoal of blessing.

The ravens brought him bread and meat in the morning and bread and meat in the evening, and he would drink from the brook (1 Kings 17:6). Elijah did not ask, 'What about my lunch Lord?' Who in the world told you that you need to eat three times a day? I know some people who eat five times a day. My wife and I eat twice a day. When we were ministering in Fiji Islands in 1990, every day we had to pray for the sick and the possessed. So, we decided to fast every day. We continue the fast till today. We have breakfast at 8 o'clock in the morning and we fast the whole day and eat our dinner at about 8 p.m. That's the strength of our ministry.

Perhaps God wanted Elijah to fast one meal everyday to keep the soldiers away from him. God opened the brook just for one man Elijah. In another instance, God heard the cry of Ishmael and opened a brook in the wilderness for him to drink (Gen 21:17).

It happened after a while, that the brook dried up, because there was no rain in the land (1 Kings 17:7). Now Elijah faced a crisis of faith, the brook dried up and he had no water to drink. That's the life of a child of God. Temptations and crises come one after another, but the Lord is with us.

When Elijah found the brook dried, was he depressed? Sometimes we go 'there' in faith, only to find that something 'there' begins to dry up. We say, 'God why did you bring me here, it's too hard for me now. I don't know how much more of this situation I can take in this house, job, home life and, this pressure.' And we make plans to move out. God is watching over you to see if you have faith to stay where He sent you, even when your situation is dry and bleak. Make sure that you are putting your faith on the Word of God and not in the circumstances.

If you obey the Lord, you may go through suffering and pain. You may ask 'Why, why me, O Lord?' Don't ask 'Why me?' but ask 'Why not me?' God may not always answer our 'whys' but surely He tells us whom to trust so that we can endure our trials. Problems are a part of the fabric of life situations. They are real stimulators to success. Every problem is an opportunity to think and act creatively. No problem leaves you where it found you.

The three questions often asked by those in crisis are: Why has this happened to me God? When will my troubles end God? How will I ever come out of this problem? But the most common question is: Why me Lord? Why should it come to me? Why was I ever born?

The prophet Habakkuk appalled by the suffering he saw, cried out, *How long, O LORD, will I call for help, And You will not hear? . . . Why do You make me see iniquity, and cause me to look on wickedness?* (Hab 1:2–4).

Although Habakkuk's 'why' seemed to go unanswered, he eventually came to the place of confidence and hope:

> Though the fig tree should not blossom, and there be no fruit on the vines, Though the yield of the olive should fail And the fields produce no food, Though the flock should be cut off from the fold And there be no cattle in the stalls, Yet I will exult in the LORD, I will rejoice in the God of my salvation (Hab 3:17–18).

In spite of everything falling apart, Habakkuk could rejoice in the Lord.

Come to the Place of Confidence

You too can come to the place of confidence and hope in your time of crisis. As you ask God why, also ask Him to help you come to the place where you can say, 'In spite of . . . I will rejoice . . . .' Our goal is not just to cope with crisis but also to praise God no matter what!

Job said, *"Though He slay me, I will hope in him"* (Job 13:15). David said, *Even though I walk through the valley of the shadow of death, I fear no evil; for You are with me* (Ps 23:4).

For instance, I was a qualified engineer with five university degrees. I left my job, and came out in faith for full-time ministry along with my wife. Our daughter was about a year old at that time. We did not have any bank savings. We used to spend what I had, for the ministry. Still, the Lord wanted us to came out in faith. Our ministry was supported by the offerings that came in and through our ministry. One day there was no money to buy milk for our one-year-old child. Since we were God's ministers, we decided not to borrow money. We felt that the day we borrowed money our God is dead. That is our faith. God had called us, and He is faithful.

My wife is a woman of faith. She poured water into the feeding bottle and added sugar and she prayed, 'Lord, like you changed water into wine at Cana in Galilee make this water into milk'. We gave that sugar water to our daughter and she slept the whole day, without giving any trouble. We believe that the Lord not only changed it into milk but also into solid food and gave it to her.

In another instance, my wife was in hospital after the delivery of our second daughter who is a Downs Syndrome child. It was a Caesarean operation, but in spite of much discount given, the bill came to Rs. 2,176 and I had only Rs. 200 in my pocket.

It was a Saturday morning, I fell on my knees and prayed, 'You know us, Oh Lord, we never borrow money and hence you must provide the money; I am not going to ask anyone'. We did not want to borrow even from our parents and hence did not tell them of this need. I simply told the Lord, 'If you do not provide, my wife may have to remain in the hospital for more days and perhaps she would have good rest'. Monday morning, my wife had to be discharged, I told the Lord, 'If you make the payment now, it is better for you.

If you're going to make it one week later, it is going to be more expensive for you'.

Surprisingly, on Sunday evening a young man with his wife and child walked into the hospital room, and gave me Rs. 2000. I do not usually take any gift or money from anyone unless I know for sure it is from God. Hence I was hesitant to take this money from him. I told him that it was quite a big amount for them to give me. This man never knew about our problem and the amount we needed. He and his wife told me that it was not their money but ours. They further explained that the day they had heard that my wife was pregnant they started saving this money for the last nine months. Can you believe that! Our God is so concerned and mindful of us.

When we put our trust in the Lord, He'll take care of every need. God prepared them in advance to save this money. After paying the hospital bill we were left with Rs. 24, with which we bought coffee and chips for the pastors who came to bless the baby. We may be a zero in the sight of the world, but we are heroes in Christ.

Doubt Sees the Wall, Faith Sees the Way

'Then word of the Lord came to him . . . .' Every time Elijah went through a crisis the word of the Lord came to him. The water dried up. But he never grumbled or complained about his situation. The Lord said, *"Arise, go to Zarephath, which belongs to Sidon, and stay there; behold, I have commanded a widow there to provide for you"* (1 Kings 17:8–9). God first commanded the ravens to feed Elijah, now He commands a widow. In those days, widows were poor and it was not a common practice for any stranger to stay with a widow. Hence it would have been very difficult and a delicate thing for Elijah to do.

Sometimes God puts you in an embarrassing situation. The reason why God put Elijah in a widow's place was because the soldiers will never look for Elijah in a widow's place. God knows the best place. We may have to go through embarrassing situations, but He knows what is best for us at a particular given time and situation. He will never let us down.

God never gave an address or the name of the widow to Elijah. He just said 'go'. Elijah could not go and shout in the street, 'Is there any widow here?' People may throw stones at him.

Your ears will hear a word behind you

Elijah knew his God; he knew God could lead him where He wanted him to go. God guides us wherever we should go. We read in Isaiah 30:21, *"And your ears will hear a word behind you, 'This is the way, walk in it,' whenever you turn to the right or to the left."*

I accepted Jesus as my Saviour and Lord when I was twelve years old, and since then, I have lived a life of faith. During my Engineering studies, I was sent on training to another city. Sunday morning, I was on the street looking for a church. As the Spirit of God guided me I got into a bus, and there I saw a man with a Bible and went close to him. Seeing the Bible in my hand, he asked me, 'Are you going to church?' I asked if I could go along with him, 'Sure,' he replied. I went with him to his church. I received a mighty anointing in that church service and received some spiritual gifts. I was not lazy, giving excuses about not knowing a church. When we ask God for guidance He will surely guide us and take us to a place of blessing. If there is a will there is a way.

Elijah went to Zarephath, behold, the widow was there at the gate gathering sticks. He called to her and said, *"Please get me a little water in a jar, that I may drink"* (1 Kings 17:10). As the drought had not been so keenly felt near the mountain ranges of Lebanon, the widow was ready and able to provide Elijah with water. We know the rest of the story, how the Lord led him where he had to go, whom he had to speak to and what he should do. In every way God guided him.

How did Elijah find out that she was the particular widow whom God had commanded to serve him? Probably she had a different kind of dress. However, there would have been many other widows. I'm sure God spoke to him, and guided him to this particular widow.

After a very fruitful mission in Kuwait, I was getting ready to leave for Dubai in the United Arab Emirates. The receptionist of the Kuwait Continental Hotel where I was staying called me to say that they had received a fax of my entry visa to the UAE. However, when he opened my file, the visa paper was missing. 'Sorry, I can't find it,' he said. He searched for it till the next morning, but in vain.

Anyway, I drove to the airport in faith. But the Kuwait immigration officers wouldn't let me board the plane without a valid visa to the UAE. But I was persistent. I pleaded with a top official at the airport, and persuaded him to let me travel to Dubai, as I was on an urgent mission. 'My God would arrange a visa for me at the Dubai airport,' I told him. He just 'stared' at me, observing me from head to toe, and said: 'Ok, Go,' and signed off the ticket to obtain my boarding pass.

All through the flight, I was in communion with my God. I didn't know what was in store for me in Dubai, but I was confident, my Lord was in control of the situation.

On Thursday, around 5:30 in the evening our Jumbo touched down at the spacious Dubai airport. The sun had just begun sending its twilight rays, declaring the darkness to come. It should have been an 'ordeal' of 23 hours, in the normal sense. But for me it was an exciting experience of a lifetime-ever to keep fresh in the memory.

I rushed to the immigration counter. I revealed my identity to the officer. But it was a blow to me when he said my visa hasn't been filed, and I must leave by the next flight, back to India.

However, I refused to accept defeat. I wrestled with my Master.

For He had said 'The things impossible with men are possible with God'. I clung to the promise. I telephoned my contact in Dubai. But he said that the agent who was supposed to bring my visa to the airport was missing. Further, the next day was Friday when all the offices would be closed and arranging a visa was impossible, he added.

It was a time of real test of my faith. The impeccable Dubai airport is one of the most luxurious shopping centres of the world, but I was not fascinated by it. I decided to spend time in fasting and praying till I got a visa to get out of the airport.

I was to address a meeting on Friday at 6.30 p.m. I tried to contact some top officers at the airport, but no one would permit me, even to go near them. There were already scores of 'stranded' passengers like me at the airport. I had a very profitable time with many of them, sharing my life testimony with them. I commended many in prayer to receive the Lord and all of them got the visa, except me.

I knew, delay was not denial, and endurance has its reward. It was patience on trial. But my faith grew. I knew God wanted me in Dubai. I telephoned a hotel to try an emergency visa for me. They submitted the visa application at the airport at 11.30 p.m. on Thursday. But it was rejected without any reason being assigned. Again they submitted the same at 2.30 a.m and again it was rejected the second time. However, my faith grew further.

I phoned my contact in Dubai again. 'Are you still in the airport?' he asked. 'I cannot understand your faith. Please go back, you don't know Dubai,' he warned me. 'Yes, I don't know the situation here but, I know my Lord, I am confident that I will come out,' I replied. The whole of the next day I was praying and trying to persuade the officers to issue a visa. But no help came from any quarter.

Then, at 2 p.m., I asked the Lord to tell me the next course of action. Soon the answer came. The Lord directed me to talk to a particular lady staff at the airport. I narrated my story to her. What a miracle! She not only spoke my language but she was also a child of God, and she was planning to attend the same meeting I had to address that evening. However, though she was deeply concerned about my plight, she also expressed her inability to help me. Anyway, I insisted that she should play the role of Esther in this situation and plead my case with her officers. At last she took courage and spoke to some senior officers.

To her surprise, she found out that my immigration visa had been refused because the hotel people had wrongly spelt my name. Instead of writing Chandrakumar (a male name) they added an 'I' to the last letter, making me Chandrakumari (a female name). Then I explained the problem to the officers, who were kind enough to allow the hotel people submit the visa application form a third time, correcting the mistake.

Indeed it was a miracle. It was a real expression of faith at work. I was issued an entry visa to the UAE at about 4.30 p.m. on Friday. The meeting was scheduled for 6.30 p.m. I was there at the conference hall sharp on time. When heaven intervenes, you will enjoy the mercy drops. Praise God, His 'wind' moved in mighty force at the meetings, both in Dubai and Abu Dhabi. As we had sown in tears, we were sure to reap in cheers!

Don't accept any defeat in the ministry. Be willing to undergo any suffering. God will bring you out. God showed me the right person at the right time. God showed Elijah the widow.

Those who fear Him lack nothing

> As she was going to get it, he called to her and said, "Please bring me a piece of bread in your hand." But she said, "As the LORD your God lives, I have no bread, only a handful of flour in the bowl and a little oil in the jar; and behold, I am gathering a few

sticks that I may go in and prepare for me and my son, that we may eat it and die" (1 Kings 17:11–12).

From her statement, 'As the Lord God lives . . .' Elijah could easily understand that she was the woman sent by God. She also said that she and her son would eat their last meal and wait for their death. That showed she did not have a husband. This is a further confirmation that she was the widow whom God had prepared for Elijah to stay with. Our God is a God of clarity.

Then Elijah said to her, "Do not fear; go, do as you have said, but make me a little bread cake from it first and bring it out to me, and afterward you may make one for yourself and for your son' (1 Kings 17:13). Elijah asked her to make a cake for him first. Here, Elijah seems to be a selfish evangelist. But probably he was testing her faith. It is easy to give from abundance, but it is difficult to give out of nothing. Give something out of nothing and God will honour that. God sends people on our way to test us. The Bible says: Do not withhold good from those to whom it is due, when it is in your power to do it. *Do not say to your neighbor, "Go, and come back, And tomorrow I will give it,"* when you have it with you (Prov 3:28).

Elijah assured the widow that her meal and oil would never end until the famine ceased. Further Elijah said to her, this is what the Lord of Israel says, *"The bowl of flour shall not be exhausted, nor shall the jar of oil be empty, until the day that the Lord sends rain on the face of the earth"* (1 Kings 17:14). Elijah's faith and prophetic word released faith into her. The widow learnt a lesson that in making God's will her first concern, He made her need His first concern. Though the whole nation suffered due to the famine, Elijah, the widow and her son had enough to eat everyday. This confirms the biblical promise, *Fear the Lord, you his saints, for those who fear him lack nothing. The lions may grow weak and hungry, but those who seek the Lord lack no good thing* (Ps 34:9–10).

"So she went and did according to the word of Elijah, and she and he and her household ate for many days. The bowl of flour was not exhausted nor did the jar of oil become empty, according to the word of the Lord which He spoke through Elijah" (1 Kings 17:15–16). How did Elijah know about it? The word of the Lord came to him. God did not reveal this to Elijah when he was at the side of the brook. God reveals one step at a time. When you obey the first step, He'll reveal the second step.

Let not Dilemma Damage Your Faith

> Now it came about after these things, that the son of the woman, the mistress of the house, became sick; and his sickness was so severe, that there was no breath left in him. So she said to Elijah, "What do I have to do with you, O man of God? You have come to me to bring my iniquity to remembrance, and to put my son to death!" (1 Kings 17:17–18).

Now Elijah had to face another crisis. If only Elijah had a Bible dictionary, he would have looked up 'Zarephath' to find out the Hebrew derivation of the word for its meaning. Incidentally the name of the village Zarephath means 'crucible' or 'place of testing'. Suddenly there was a crisis, the woman's son died. She had already lost her husband and now her son was taken away from her too. In her agony of soul she turned to Elijah and blamed him. Elijah, who had brought faith, blessing and godliness to her home, found himself facing tragedy and hostility.

He said to her, "Give me your son." Then he took him from her bosom and carried him up to the upper room where he was living, and laid him on his own bed (1 Kings 17:19). How did Elijah face the crisis? He did not retaliate. He did not rebuke her for her anger, and neither did he say, 'Well, I am very sorry to hear about your son'. Elijah's response was amazing. He said, 'Give me your son.' In other words, what he was saying to the widow was, 'Give your problem to me. I will not shrug off your problem, I'll identify with it'.

And he called to the Lord and said, "O Lord my God, hast Thou also brought calamity to the widow with whom I am staying, by causing her son to die?" Then he stretched himself upon the child three times, and called to the Lord, and said, *"O LORD my God, I pray You, let this child's life return to him"* (1 Kings 17:21).

Elijah stretched himself upon the child two times and prayed. But the child was not brought to life. Sometimes God doesn't answer us immediately. He expects us to pray again and again.

Elijah took the child, and brought him down from the upper room into the house and gave him to his mother; and Elijah said, "See your son is alive" (1 Kings 17:23). After he prayed the third time, the Lord heard Elijah's prayer and the child came back to life. Elijah was never angry with the widow for accusing him. We learn a great lesson from Elijah not to get angry or to be irritated when we deal with people to whom we minister.

Then the woman said to Elijah, "Now I know that you are a man of God, and that the word of the LORD in your mouth is truth" (1 Kings 17:24). When the flour was increasing in quantity and the oil was not ceasing did she not know that he was a man of God? When we go through personal calamities, that is the time we lose our faith and get dispirited. Do not lose your faith. Encourage yourself and your faith in such situations.

Later on Elijah takes a national problem on his shoulders. He stood on Mount Carmel and said to the Israelites, *"Come here to me"* (1 Kings 18:30). He told his servant seven times to check the sky for rain. Elijah prayed as long as God expected him to pray to fulfil His Word. He just kept on interceding until God answered him. And in secret God fashioned His servant for his future public ministry. Maturity does not come with age, but with the acceptance of responsibility.

We often want to be in the limelight. We want our ministry to be adequately recognized. But what have we proved secretly? What have we done that no one but God and a widow knew about? God wants to hide us away like Elijah and prepare us in humble surroundings, far away from the big platform.

God is looking for people who will reach out where society is hurting, people who will say, 'I'm here to help you in your problems. I'll hold it; I'll give myself to it?'

It's exciting to go forth in faith, trusting God's promises and reaching out into something new. It is harder to sustain that faith when pressures develop. Elijah's response was magnificent. He did not allow his dilemma to damage his faith. How often we give up when we are actually still on course! How often we think, 'Oh God, you told me . . . and it's not working! What's gone wrong?' When God told Moses to get the people out he was met not with enthusiasm, but with opposition.

Do you feel the same way about your situation? Did God tell you that things would happen immediately, or does His plan need more time to unfold? Are you walking by faith or by sight? Have a strong faith and know that God is committed to accomplish what He has promised. Do not back off because of disappointments and delays. There will be no running out of resources. When you come to the end of the rope tie a knot and hold on. That is HOPE (Hold On Patiently Expectantly).

Chapter 13

ELISHA
A Leader with Powerful Faith Encounters

We live in a culture marked by lust, unfaithfulness, rebellion, instant gratification, broken relationships, hopelessness, escapism, depression, disillusionment, discouragement and disappointments.

A study of the life of Elisha helps us to understand some ways in which we can be signals to people who have been in the search for the right direction. It also helps us to deepen our insight and our involvement in the ministry.

Just as God used Elisha's bones to bring a dead man to life long after Elisha's death, the incidents in the life of Elisha still possess the power to awaken the dead churches today. In the following pages I would like to take you through the exciting and thrilling experiences of Elisha's *destiny* to be the next prophet in Israel, his *decision* to accept the call of God, his *discipleship* as a servant and a trainee under Elijah, his *determination* to stay with Elijah till the end, his *desire* to have a *double* portion of Elijah's spirit, and the *demonstration* of miracles as the *daring* new prophet of Israel.

Elisha's Destiny

God commissioned Elijah to anoint Elisha, the son of Shaphat from Abel Meholah to succeed him. So Elijah went from there and found Elisha with twelve yokes of oxen, and he himself was driving the twelfth pair. Elijah went up to him and threw his cloak around him. This he did to show that Elisha would become his successor. And here in this passage, as a transfer of authority Elijah left his cloak for Elisha (2 Kings 2:11–14; Exod 14:21–22; Josh 3:7–13). Elisha took it up, not as a sacred relic to be worshipped, but as a significant garment to be worn.

The cloak was the most important article of clothing, a person could own in those days. It was used as protection against the weather, as bedding, as a mat to sit on and for carrying things. It was even given as pledge for a debt or torn into pieces to show grief.

Elisha didn't volunteer. It was God's idea. But the fact, sovereign and surprising as it is, does not negate the importance of human response. Elijah walked on ahead, giving Elisha time and space to respond. Elisha had been surprised by God's sovereignty; now it was a time for decision. He did not find this easy.

Elisha's Decision

Elisha then left his oxen and ran after Elijah. 'Let me kiss my father and mother good bye,' he said, 'and then I will come with you.' 'Go back,' Elijah replied. 'What have I done to you?' In other words, probably Elijah was saying, 'This is between you and God. He is calling you into His ministry. You will have to make your own decision whether or not you will follow His call'. So Elisha left him and went back.

He then burned the ploughing equipment to cook the meat and gave it to the people, and they ate. There is tremendous festivity and joy in sacrifice. 'Sacrifice is the ecstasy of giving the best we have to the one we love the most.' We don't do God a favour for choosing us for His service.

Then he set out to follow Elijah and became his attendant. (1 Kings 19:15–16, 18–21). Except for God, neither Elijah nor Elisha initiated this. The call was radical and uncompromising. Elisha felt claimed by God and there could be no bargaining or resisting. God is not looking for volunteers. He is looking for conscripts. God handpicks the weak, the ignorant, the helpless, the lost, the least, and the lowest. There are exceptions of course. God does not perceive things as men do, neither does He choose men because they are fit, but fits men because He has chosen them.

When God's call for ministry comes to us, it creates in our minds a clear impression that we have little option. Probably that's how James and John would have felt when they left their father's fishing business to follow Jesus. And even Levi would have felt the same way when he resigned his post as a public tax official in order to align his life with Jesus (Luke 5:9–11, 27–28). To hear God's call is like the touch of God on a man or woman's shoulder. It will shake us and catch us off guard.

Hudson Taylor, the pioneer missionary to China, said, 'God is looking for wicks to burn, the oil and the fire come free.' Will you become one of those wicks? Are you prepared to 'burn on' for God until He decides you have burned long enough and you 'burn out'? The Lord finally burns you out. In the same way God is looking for the knife and the wood, and the sacrifice comes free, as we understand from the story of Abraham and Isaac.

During the days of Elijah, Elisha was not well known as a man of God, though he always wanted to be with Elijah. He was always faithful to Elijah and followed him everywhere. We hear nothing more of Elisha for eight years, until the translation of his master, when he reappears to become the most prominent figure in the history of his country during the rest of his long life.

We all have a calling of some kind awaiting us. You may not have discovered yours yet, but it is there. You cannot be reconciled to God without being recruited into His service, so if you are truly a child of God you also have the privilege of being His servant. You will feel the energy in what you are the one chosen by God. The Holy Spirit's power will be upon you to equip you to perform His task.

Of course Elisha made the right decision. F W Boreham said, *We make our decisions and then our decisions turn round and make us.* Things would never be the same again. In slaughtering his oxen, Elisha gave up his former career, his inheritance and his financial security. In burning the ploughing equipment, Elisha burned his bridges too. There could be no going back. The Lord had let Elijah know that his time was at hand. He therefore went to the different schools of the prophets to give them his last exhortations and blessing (2 Kings 2:1–8).

Elisha's Determination

The chronology of the narrative of the Bible in the two books of Kings suggests that it took around ten years from the incident when Elijah threw his cloak over the surprised shoulders of Elisha, to the next episode of Elisha actually following Elijah, recorded for us in 2 Kings 2:1–18.

For forty years Moses worked in obscurity as a shepherd in the wilderness of the Sinai Peninsula before his call was reiterated at the burning bush (Exod 3:1–2). Saul of Tarsus was called to be an apostle to the Gentiles at his first encounter with the risen Lord on the Damascus road (see Acts 9:1–6; 26:15–18). He began his preaching ministry almost immediately, but most scholars agree that he was to spend the next ten years building a fine work in Antioch, alongside

Barnabas, before he could go for the first time on his apostolic mission. God takes time to prepare us.

While God is in the process of preparing us for his ministry, we must learn to trust God. God is in charge of our promotion. When it comes, it will neither be too late, nor too early. Like the rest of his dealings this would also be on time.

Elijah permitted Elisha to accompany him to Gilgal without saying a word about staying anywhere. But when he arrived at Gilgal, he told Elisha to stay while he would go alone to Bethel. Then later Elijah urged him to stay back at Bethel and again to remain at Jericho while he was leaving for Jordan. But Elisha said, 'As the Lord lives and as you yourself live, I will not leave you.' Elisha was determined to accompany him until he was taken to heaven that day. Elijah neither argued with him nor forced him to remain. Perhaps Elijah was testing Elisha to see how determined he was to have his spirit and power so as to carry on in his place after his departure. So they went together up to Jordan. Your decision always determines your destiny.

The sons of the Prophets at Bethel were probably jealous over Elisha being the personal secretary of Elijah. They already knew that Elijah would be taken away to heaven that day. In a way they would have been happy about it, because after Elijah goes, Elisha would become like any one of them. This kind of jealousy is very much prevalent even today in the ministry.

They asked Elisha, 'Do you know that the Lord will take away your master from over you today?' Elisha of course was aware of it and gave them a cool answer and warned them to be still. Words of discouragement could not be darted into the mind of the determined Elisha. No one could bring an emotional imbalance in his life. Each time they attempted to deter Elisha from following his master, he boldly replied … hold your peace. He was very faithful to his master. God honours faithful servants.

Elisha had only one plan—to follow the master wherever he went.

He did not have any secondary plan nor did he have any means for a livelihood. The journey got tougher and tougher, but Elisha stuck with it. Perhaps he had learnt through his past experience that: Quitters don't win and winners don't quit! You may be going through the trouble, but look for your double!

Thrice Elijah told him to remain behind. Elisha could have very well stayed back and taken rest. But he did not want to leave his master. Elijah did not reveal his final destination as Jordan to Elisha. Anyway he had to go through Bethel and Jericho. But he revealed only the next place of arrival. Likewise God does not give a blue print for our life. God reveals one step at a time to those who seek to follow Him faithfully.

Elisha learnt to walk closely with God and to exercise a faith in order to exercise the power of God. While the company of the prophets 'stood at a distance', just as many of God's people distance themselves from active participation in God's ministry; Elisha sticks close to a man of God who knows how to move in that power. He was not merely a spectator, but an active participant. Some people watch history some people make history. What kind are you?

In order to bring glory and honour to God, Elisha had to take some risks. Anyone who wants to grow in faith has to make some choices, take some chances and encounter some risks. Elisha had to risk some unpleasant consequences.

The first risk was that of being shunned by his fellow prophets. The greatest hindrance or challenge in the life of a child of God who wants to move in the power of God, does not come from being in the company of the skeptics—the atheists, agnostics, and liberals. It comes from our fellow evangelicals, 'the company of the prophets'.

Fifty men of the company of the prophets went and stood at a distance, facing the plane where Elijah and Elisha had stopped at the Jordan. Elijah took his cloak, rolled it up and struck the water with it. The water divided to the right and to the left and both of them crossed over on dry ground (2 Kings 2:7–8).

Elisha's Discipleship

It is more likely that it was a disguised test for Elisha's loyalty and discipleship. For Elisha, leaving was not an option. Two things tied him: his fear of God ('As surely as the Lord lives . . .') and His heart's tie to Elijah ('and as you live, I will not leave you'). Loyalty is a decision of the will. Are you loyal in your friendships, loyal to your marriage, loyal in your place of work, loyal to your nation and loyal to your church and its leaders? God is allowing your loyalty to be tested. Pass the test and God will have many wonderful things in store for you.

During World War II, on 13 May, 1940, Winston Churchill's first statement as Prime Minister to the house of Commons, in America was this: 'I have nothing to offer but blood, tears and sweat.' Those were such harsh times that spawned men and women of character who understood the words Churchill used —constancy, determination, faithfulness, durability . . . no matter the sacrifice or cost.

He said that the words, 'Not in vain', may be the pride of those who survived and the epitaph of those who fell. Churchill's words echo what Apostle Paul wrote: *Therefore, my beloved brethren, be steadfast, immovable, always abounding in the work of the Lord, knowing that your toil is not in vain in the Lord* (1 Cor 15:58).

As believers today, we must renew that same spirit of determination and commitment of faithfulness, to constancy, to endurance—no matter how difficult the path or how much the cost. The great preacher John Henry Jowett said, 'Ministry that costs nothing, accomplishes nothing.'

Elisha's Desire

Elisha had already been anointed to take his place (1 Kings 19:16), but he had not yet received the spirit and power of Elijah. This is what he desired as it is clear from verses 9–11.

When they crossed the River Jordan, Elijah said to Elisha, *"Ask what I shall do for you . . ." And Elisha said, "Please, let a double portion of your spirit be upon me"* (2 Kings 2:9).

Elijah lays down a condition for the granting of Elisha's request; it will be granted if you see me as I am being taken. What Elijah implies is that Elisha's status as successor depends on his commitment to follow his master. If he cannot demonstrate this ability to follow his master then his request will not be granted.

Elisha's Double Portion from Elijah

Carnal ambition would have prompted Elisha to ask for fame, travel and financial security. Elisha asked for none of these. He did not want a 'double portion' of Elijah's air-miles, salary, royalties or bank balance—only a double portion of his spirit.

The 'double portion' is the inheritance of the firstborn son in a Hebrew household when he comes to take on responsibilities as the head of the family upon the death of his father (Deut 21:27). This shows that Elisha wanted to be regarded as Elijah's heir or successor. It also implied that Elisha had weighed the price to be paid if he takes up such a responsibility, which involved a constant confrontation with the king, challenging idolatry and demon worship, putting his life on the line, risking poverty and unpopularity. He was putting first the kingdom of God and His righteousness.

God did not choose you to be a sensation but simply to be a servant. In God's kingdom the way up is down. But this is a generation of Christians who desire for gains without pains. If you want to exercise authority then you must first submit to people who are in authority over you. If you submit, you'll serve. If you serve, then one day you will also rule. In the intervening years of ministry it is good to serve or help a servant of God to fulfil his vision. One day you'll get to fulfil yours. Elisha was evidently good at this. He became known as the one who used to pour water on the hands of Elijah (2 Kings 3:11). That was all he was known for. He wrote no paperbacks and conducted no seminars.

Elisha can be called as the double portion prophet, but he did not receive his double without some trouble. In order to receive this 'double portion', Elisha had to do three things: First, he had to keep walking with Elijah who had it. You need to keep company with men and women of God who have the Spirit of God. Catch their heart, read their biographies and attend their seminars and study the Word of God. Power is imparted in these ways.

Second, he had to keep talking with Elijah. You must be inquisitive to find out some of the secrets of anointed servants of God.

Third, he also had to keep watching. Elijah said, *"If you see me when I am taken from you, it shall be so for you; but if not, it shall not be so"* (2 Kings 2:10). And sure enough, 'Elisha saw this and cried out'. Watch and learn from the lives of men and women of God. See the spectacular intervention of God in their lives and like wise keep yourself transparent to the conviction and correction of the Holy Spirit of God in your life. Develop perception, discernment and sensitivity; your life will never be the same again. Then it came about,

> As they were going along and talking, that behold, there appeared a chariot of fire and horses of fire which separated the two of them. And Elijah went up by a whirlwind to heaven. And Elisha saw it and cried out, "My father, my father, the chariots of Israel and its horsemen!" And he saw Elijah no more. Then he took hold of his own clothes and tore them in two pieces. He also took up the mantle of Elijah that fell from him and returned and stood by the bank of the Jordan (2 Kings 2:11-13).

For a moment Elisha would have felt that he was on the wrong side of the Jordan River with no boats, no bridges and no ferries to help him cross over. Sometimes even when we follow the perfect will of God, we are pushed into such situations where there seems to be no conventional way out. Bernard Edinger rightly said, *Inside the will of God there is no failure. Outside the will of God there is no success.* Those who walk in the will of God will not be disappointed. *The center of God's will is our only safety* —Betsie Ten Boom.

When the conventional way doesn't seem to work out, then we need to look into the supernatural provisions that God has provided us. Since Elisha had asked for a double portion of Elijah's power, this was his first opportunity to test it. In fact, he did the same thing he had seen Elijah do: he slapped the surface of the river with the cloak he'd just picked up. 'Okay,' he said defiantly, 'where is the God of Elijah?' The implication was clear in the question, 'If I'm really Elijah's successor and my time has really come, then what you did for him, do for me!' He didn't want the cloak for show but for action. He didn't want gifts to dangle as ornaments around his neck so he could show off with them. He wanted those gifts as tools to accomplish God's purpose in his life.

> He took the mantle of Elijah that fell from him and struck the waters and said, "Where is the LORD, the God of Elijah?" And when he also had struck the waters, they were divided here and there; and Elisha crossed over. Now when the sons of the prophets who were at Jericho opposite him saw him, they said, "The spirit of Elijah rests on Elisha." And they came to meet him and bowed themselves to the ground before him (2 Kings 2:14–15).

God exalted Elisha in the eyes of the company of prophets by dividing the water at Jordan (2 Kings 2:14–15). Even to Joshua the Lord said, 'Today I will begin to exalt you in the eyes of all Israel, so they may know that I am with you as I was with Moses'

(Josh 1:7). And here, through this miracle the Lord established the fact that He is with Elisha as He was with Elijah.

The concrete evidence that Elisha became the true successor of Elijah is provided when he re-enacts Elijah's miraculous splitting of the waters. The waters of Jordan, of old, yielded to the ark; now, to the prophet's mantle, because of God's presence. When God takes His beloved ones to heaven, death is the Jordan, which they must pass through. The death of Christ has divided those waters that the ransomed of the Lord may pass over. 'O death, where is your sting, thy hurt, thy terror!' (1 Cor 15:55).

Elisha's action brought recognition from the community of prophets at Jericho that the spirit of Elijah rests on Elisha. 'Where is the God of Elijah?' The company of the prophets recognized that Elijah's God was still there even though Elijah was taken away. They said, *"The spirit of Elijah is resting on Elisha"* (verse 15). This provides a fitting conclusion. Do not hinder, but be willing to let God do through you today what He did through others in former days?

Elijah, left Elisha in the most spectacular way, but he did not leave him bereft, impoverished, and powerless. The 'double portion' of his spirit came on Elisha.

Elisha's Daring Faith

The prophets seemed to imply that Elisha's greatness would be shrunk to size when he no longer lived under Elijah's shadow. It was a test of his identity. No longer linked with Elijah, would Elisha simply disappear from the scene, or would he emerge as a significant contributor in his own right?

A great new burden was laid upon his shoulders. People were now looking up to him as they had once looked to Elijah.

The slight variance in the two men's names expresses their difference in style. Elijah, whose name meant 'The Lord is my God', challenged the king and the priests of Baal in dramatic confrontations of power. He lived apart from the people and preached judgement and the need for repentance.

Elisha's name meant, 'God is salvation'. He lived among poor and the outcast. All levels of people had access to Elisha from lowly widows to foreign kings. His extraordinary life included ministry as a prophet, a miracle worker, an adviser to the king, a leader of a school of prophets and an anointed of revolutionaries.

Elijah and Elisha used both words and dramatic events to convey their message. But the prophets, who followed them, relied less on spectacular displays and more on the power of the verbal messages from God.

A position of responsibility is a lonely place. However, if you are truly ordained for your position by God, then you must be prepared to face the loneliness of envious colleagues, patronizing comments and fearful responsibility. Ministry can also be a very lonely calling. We may be shunned or criticized or misunderstood. Seasons of painful isolation can come on account of our faithfulness to God. We must be prepared for this, ready to stand apart and to be misunderstood. If you walk on ahead with a great dream then you have to be prepared to walk alone at times, until others have seen what you see and are prepared to walk where you walk.

Elisha's Demonstration of Miracles

Elisha moved into ministry of the miraculous. God was confirming his calling as a prophet by performing signs and wonders through him.

Elisha had asked for a double portion of Elijah's spirit and incidentally we have a record of about twice as many miracles performed by Elisha. Several of these miracles, especially those in chapter 4, have great similarities to the miracles Jesus performed later.

Elisha became the new leader of the company of prophets (2 Kings 2:15). He went back to Jericho where he miraculously transformed a poison water supply into a clean spring (2 Kings 2:19–22). From Jericho, he travelled to Bethel where he was accosted by a huge gang of youths. Elisha called down a curse on his attackers and two bears from the woods mauled forty-two of them (2 Kings 2:23–25).

Elisha miraculously provided a supply of water when Jehoram's army was suffering from thirst (2 Kings 3:9–20). He performed the miracles of increasing the poor widow's supply of oil (2 Kings 4:1–7) and restoring of life to the son of the woman of Shunem (2 Kings 4:18–37). He miraculously brought about the multiplication of 20 loaves of bread, enough to feed 100 men (2 Kings 4:42–44). Naaman was healed of leprosy (2 Kings 5:1–27). Elisha could make an iron axe head float in the waters of the Jordan (2 Kings 6:1–7).

Elisha's exploits fall roughly into two categories and the Bible seems to group them that way. One set of stories concern people with evident needs and another group of stories were to the nations. He showed a deep sensitivity for the suffering and distressed and sometimes helped them in miraculous ways: healing diseases, raising a young boy from the dead and so on.

Elisha purified poisonous food (2 Kings 4:38–41) and then miraculously fed one hundred men with limited resources (2 Kings 4:42–44). This miracle is similar to Jesus' miracle of multiplying the loaves and the fish. God backed up Elisha's prophetic message with legitimate signs and wonders. Mark 16:20 states that when the disciples preached the gospel, the Lord worked with them and confirmed the Word 'through the accompanying signs'.

Another group of stories were to the nations. Israel was reeling from the corruption brought in during King Ahab's reign. Politically,

Israel was at the mercy of the neighbouring state of Aram (Syria, as known today), which launched periodic raids across the boarder.

Sometimes Elisha helped out Israel's army, using his special insight to detect bands of raiders. Twice, he predicted and allowed Israel's army to break out of an impossible situation and rout the enemy. Yet he refused to become a 'court prophet' serving the king's whims. On at least one occasion, he blatantly insulted a king of Israel (2 Kings 3:13–14). Another time, he anointed a general to overthrow the king in an out right revolution.

The way Elisha treated General Naaman and the king of Israel, contrast sharply with his mild approach to the poor and the oppressed. And Elisha pointedly refused to accept payment from the wealthy general, who was used to paying his way.

Elisha's long career spanned the reigns of six kings and included some dramatic ups and downs with them. When Elisha was suffering from the illness from which he died, at his deathbed, Joash, the reigning king of Israel knelt beside him, weeping and cried, 'My father! My father! The chariots and horsemen of Israel!' (2 Kings 13:14). It means that King Joash recognized Elisha's God as the real defender of Israel (see 2 Kings 2:12); he knew beyond a doubt that with the death of Elisha, Israel's strength and protection would be gone. In any age when there is no prophetic word to God's people spiritual death and apostasy are sure to occur.

Elisha, through whom God had performed many wonderful miracles, eventually succumbed to a fatal illness. Reality dictates that great people of faith die and ironically death sometimes comes through sickness even to those who have themselves had a healing ministry. Among the consequences of the fall of Adam and Eve are sickness and death; no one is exempted from them.

Live like Elisha. He was called to speak and to live prophetically, to move powerfully, to minister to the needs of others effectively, to act fearlessly, to serve outsiders mercifully and then to die gloriously. And that was not the end of his ministry. Even long after his death his bones brought someone to life. Your ministry should not end in your death. It should continue through your disciples, your books and through your multiple contributions to the church and the society.

Chapter 14

NEHEMIAH
A Leader with a Broken Heart, Bent Knees and Wet Eyes

Nehemiah was a man of prayer. In the Hebrew language, his name would be written as *Ne He Mi Ah*. But I would like to call him as knee-miah, since he was on his knees most of his lifetime. He was the prophet of the knee. He did not act without praying, and did not pray without acting. He practised the presence of God. He defeated the plan and the project of the enemy by his vigilance and prudence. He also reformed abuses, redressed grievances, introduced law and order, revived the worship of God (Chapters 7, 8). The name Nehemiah means 'Yahweh has comforted'.

A servant of God is a person who stands with fear and trembling in the presence of God and with power and authority before the people. God and His people are constantly searching for such kind of leaders who are authoritative, spiritual and sacrificial.

In the Scripture, God is frequently represented as searching for a person and not for a group of people or an organization. *"The Lord has sought out for Himself a man after his own heart"* (1 Sam 13:14).

I looked and behold there was no man (Jer 4:25).

"Roam to and fro through the streets of Jerusalem . . . if you can find a man . . . who does justice, who seeks truth . . ." (Jer 5:1).

"I searched for a man . . . who should build up the wall and stand in the gap before Me . . . but I found no one" (Ezek 22:30).

There is a common saying that Satan is sure to find some work for idle hands. God certainly does not. God never goes to the lazy, idle people, when He needs people for His service. He goes to those who are already at work. He has always called busy people to be His servants.

MOSES	-	was busy with his flock at Horeb.
GIDEON	-	was busy threshing wheat by the wine press.
SAUL	-	was busy searching his father's donkeys.
DAVID	-	was busy caring for his father's sheep.
ELISHA	-	was busy ploughing with twelve yokes of oxen.
NEHEMIAH	-	was busy serving the king as the wine cupbearer.
AMOS	-	was busy following the flock.
PETER & ANDREW	-	were busy casting a net into the sea.
JAMES & JOHN	-	were busy mending their nets.
MATTHEW	-	was busy collecting customs.
SAUL	-	was busy persecuting the followers of Jesus.

Martin Luther, John Wesley, Adoniram Judson, William Carey,

Hudson Taylor, Spurgeon, D L Moody, and George Mueller were all busy in their work when the Lord called them for ministry.

Nehemiah As a Spiritual Leader

A person who enquires

As soon as some people arrived from Judah, Nehemiah enquired about the welfare of the Jews and about Jerusalem. This is a typical eastern custom and this touches the hearts of the people. As a result of that, his heart was broken which in turn resulted in days of fasting and prayer.

What do you do with bad news? How do you react when your brother brings you some distressing information about the people you love? Nehemiah's first and immediate response was prayer. He did not turn to prayer as a last resort.

The major part of the ministry of Jesus was one to one ministry with the people. He often interacted with the common people and enquired about their welfare. He enquired with the Samaritan woman about her personal life. He asked the blind man, 'What do you want me to do for you?' So the most important quality of a leader or a servant of God is enquiring the people of their needs.

A person who identifies himself with his people

Nehemiah prays, 'We have sinned against Thee; I and my father's house have sinned . . .' This brought the people closer to him and helped in developing more confidence in him. As a result of that, even the heart of God was shaken.

Ezra too identified himself with the people. Unlike Jesus, he could not take the punishment of the sin of his people, but he took the burden of their sin on himself. He confessed, *"O my God I am ashamed and embarrassed to lift up my face to You, my God, for our iniquities have risen above our heads . . ."* (Ezra 9:6).

Daniel prayed,

> "We have sinned, committed iniquity, acted wickedly, and
> rebelled, even turning aside from Your commandments . . .
> Open shame belongs to us . . . because we have sinned against
> You" (Dan 9:5, 8).

A distinct noticeable person

The king noticed the face of Nehemiah (Neh 2:2). A leader should
be a unique, extraordinary person with an excellent spirit like
Nehemiah. 'Why is your face sad though when you are not sick?'
the king asked him. 'This is nothing but sadness of heart'. Then
said Nehemiah, 'I was very much afraid, but . . .' 'The buts' of the
Bible are often beautiful bridges used to cross from the depths of
despair to the mountains of hope. In this instance, Nehemiah's
'but' was the bridge from the fear of his earthly monarch to faith
in his heavenly king! *And I said to the king, "Let the king live forever.
Why should my face not be sad when the city, the place of my fathers'
tombs, lies desolate and its gates have been consumed by fire?"* (Neh
2:3–4). That in fact could pave the way for Nehemiah to present
his problem to the king.

A person with discernment who knows the plan of God

God will place His plans in the minds of spiritual leaders and reveal
it to them. When the King enquired Nehemiah about his request,
Nehemiah could clearly and boldly talk about God's plan and even
gave a definite time to the King (Neh 2:4–6). He realized during
the time spent on his knees, that God had chosen him to return to
Jerusalem, encourage the remnant that had returned, rebuild the
walls of the city, and thus remove their disgrace.

The king asked Nehemiah, 'What is it you want?' The Bible
tells us that at this point, Nehemiah prayed to the God of heaven.

Aren't we challenged by Nehemiah's daring spirit, regardless of the consequences? If we dare, God will surely bring glory to Himself out of any situation.

Nehemiah was granted his vacation—a free trip home, letters of safe conduct for his journey, timber for the gates of Jerusalem and the house that he would occupy, and even army officers and cavalry to protect him! The powerful, earthly monarch proceeded to inquire humbly of the slave, 'How long will your journey take, and when will you be back?' (Neh 2:6–9). So Nehemiah set a definite time. Since he practised the presence of God, he knew the time and plan of God. He was neither an engineer nor an architect and moreover he had not yet made a survey of the broken walls, and in his human strength and knowledge he could not have set a time. It was God's revelation to him. We must applaud the audacity of his faith. What we know of God's character determines what we expect of Him.

When my wife and I were ministering in certain countries, there were many people who were living together as husbands and wives but not officially married. So when they came for prayer, the Lord gave me the discernment about their lives and when I shared it with them, they confessed and acknowledged the facts. Some of them have been attending the church for two or three years, but the pastors were ignorant of this. The gift of discernment and prophecy play an important role in the life of God's servants.

Here as Nehemiah explains it, 'Because the gracious hand of my God was upon me, the king granted my requests' (Neh 2:8). He believed as the Scripture say, "The king's heart is in the hand of the Lord; He directs it like a watercourse wherever He pleases" (Prov 21:1).

A person who passes his vision on and produces new leaders

Nehemiah was a man of action. He had a great capacity to identify with the troubles of others and the ability to do something about their plight. Nehemiah was unselfish in spirit and tireless in his efforts to improve the people in Jerusalem. His actions demonstrated uncommon courage. He was a master of motivation and organization.

Returning to the people the next day, Nehemiah spoke first to the officials, priests, and nobles, believing that the leadership had to be motivated and they need to be lifted up in their spirit. He knew that if leaders won't lead, the flock wouldn't follow. 'Let us rebuild the wall of Jerusalem', Nehemiah exhorted them as they stood together among the ruins. 'Let us start!' the majority of men responded enthusiastically (Neh 2:16–18).

A person who acquires new abilities, receives new promotions
Nehemiah was appointed as their governor. Nehemiah was a person who owned tremendous leadership skills. He was an organizer and a pragmatic leader.

What had kept the Israelites from doing anything about the broken-down wall for nearly hundred years? Local resistance was one obstacle: powerful politicians were determined to keep the Jews down. Perhaps another reason was the lack of a leader like Nehemiah. In his memoirs, he shows remarkable qualities of leadership: impassioned speech, prayer, organization, resolve, trust in God, quick and determined response to problems, unselfishness. Perhaps his years in the Persian court had been preparing him. He never complained about not having any previous experience of building structures, but adapted himself to new challenges. Organizing a difficult building project and handling fierce opposition seemed to come easily to him.

Nehemiah was more than a good business manager. His prayers punctuate the book. He recognized God's role in all that happened and never would have left his comfortable position in Persia. When Nehemiah received the call from God about repairing the walls of Jerusalem, he didn't run out impulsively and begin doing things in haste. He did his homework first; secretly, at night, he surveyed the damage and gathered information. Also he did not talk with everyone about what God had put in his heart. As a wise leader, Nehemiah kept quiet and didn't discuss his ideas until he had collected all the facts, considered the cost and had prayed about the matter.

We learn a very important lesson from Nehemiah in terms of handling spiritual gifts: when God reveals certain things we need not immediately reveal it to the people or to the concerned person. We need to first of all understand and digest what God has been trying to get through to us, then pray and wait upon the Lord for the right time and for the right situation to bring the matter out. Since some people do not follow this principle, they create confusion among people and mess up the whole situation.

Nehemiah understood that the nobles had a very important role to play in this matter, for if leaders won't lead, the flock won't follow. *"Let us rebuild the wall of Jerusalem,"* Nehemiah exhorted them as they stood together among the ruins (Neh 2:17). *"Let us arise and build,"* the majority of men responded enthusiastically (verse 18). There were, however, some among the nobles who would not support the work (Neh 3:5). We don't know why they were hesitant to help. May be their homes were complete and their families were doing fine. Perhaps they were reluctant to get their hands dirty. If this was indeed the case, they were extremely selfish and shortsighted. To live in a nice house with inadequate defences was an open invitation to the enemy.

We simply cannot afford to sit tight and do nothing because 'our' home is intact. Whether you are a Nehemiah, a noble, or a common man, each and every one must rise up and build, so that you will no longer be in disgrace (Neh 2:17). Believers can accomplish seemingly impossible tasks when they work together in fulfilling God's purpose.

As God's people began rebuilding the wall, the enemies of God became furious and tried to discourage them from doing what God had called them to do (Neh 4:1). Basically, these enemies said that all their work was useless and that even if they succeeded in building the wall, it would fall down. Such an attack can come in the form of peer pressure through insults and cutting remarks. The purpose was, to discourage the children of God from keeping their commitment to accomplish God's will.

Nehemiah used wisdom in patiently dealing with his enemies. When people are moving in God's direction, Satan tries to involve them in all kinds of arguments, strife, and problems as a way to shift their focus from God's purposes. If Satan can divert their attention, then he can keep them from finishing what God had called them to do.

The accomplishment of Nehemiah in leading the people to rebuild the wall around Jerusalem was remarkable. It provides an inspiring case study of the way God works through His people to accomplish seemingly impossible tasks, if they will work together in one spirit. They first need a clear understanding of God's purpose. Then, with effective leaders who can motivate and encourage them, they can become a powerful force.

Nehemiah was a key leader in a critical time in restoring the exiles back to Jerusalem. He was a man of action. He had a great capacity to identify with the troubles of others and the ability to do something about their plight. Nehemiah was unselfish in spirit and tireless in his efforts in uplifting the society. His actions demonstrated uncommon courage. He was a master of motivation and organization.

A person who overcomes the enemies through prayer
The enemies realized that the work would be accomplished with the help of Nehemiah's God (Neh 6:15–16). Sanballat, the governor of Samaria and Tobiah, probably the governor of the Ammonite

lands were persistent in their hatred for the Jewish people and for Nehemiah in particular. First they opposed Nehemiah and his team by mocking at them. Nobody likes to be laughed at. People didn't like it then, and they don't like it today. But Nehemiah's God-given responsibility could not be deterred by the ridicule of the crowd.

Finally Sanballat and his cohorts planned a sneak attack on the labourers as they worked. Nehemiah used several methods to meet the impending attack. First, he asked the people to pray and then set a watch day and night. Second, he positioned the people in places around the wall near their homes and families so that they were prepared to fight for their own wives, children, and homes. He ordered half the labourers to be prepared to fight with their weapons, while the other half built the wall. Eventually even those laying the stones on the wall had a trowel in one hand and a sword in the other. They laboured long, from dawn until the stars came out. They were determined to get the work done, and they did complete it through the power of prayer. That is what Jesus asked the disciples to do. Nehemiah had watchful spies in all places of work round about, who reported atleast ten attacks planned by the enemies. So it was easy to ward them off. They prayed as they worked and watched for the enemy. Let us also watchfully and prayerfully do our ministry, which the Lord has entrusted with us.

A firm, steady, and un-compromising person

Nehemiah said, 'Oh no!' to the Ono valley invitation from Sanballat and Geshem for a compromise (Neh 6:1–3). The enemies tried to dispose off the servant of God through foul play. They asked Nehemiah to leave his work and meet them at a village in the plain of Ono. Their purpose was to kill him. Realizing their malicious intent, Nehemiah told them he was too busy working for the Lord to meet them. In spite of his reply, they tried on four more occasions to trick him into leaving the work, but to no avail. Jesus said, *"We must work*

*the works of Him who sent me as long as it is day, night is coming when
no man can work"* (John 9:4).

If you think it is hard to pray during a crisis, please know that
it is harder still to keep praying when the crisis is over. *But they were
planning to harm me,* says Nehemiah, clearly discerning the intent
of his enemies (Neh 6:2). He also realized that the enemies would
change their strategy but never their motive. Even Satan, who is
behind every destructive attack, will never change his goals; but
he will certainly use new strategies. Watch, therefore, if we do not
know how to keep praying after the trouble is over, we will simply
lurch from crisis to crisis.

Opposition comes through accusation

Sanballat was not the one to give up easily. Chapter 6 relates that he
sent a letter alleging that the frenzied activity of building the wall
was merely a guise for Nehemiah's attempt to set himself up as king
of the Jews. This was an attempt to make Nehemiah respond in fear.
Instead, he quelled the false rumours and asked the Lord to strengthen
his hands so that the task would soon be completed. A servant of
God is not disturbed or discouraged by unjust personal attacks. He
will continue to move toward the completion of the goal.

A person who does not hide or run away from problems

When his life was threatened, Nehemiah said, *"Should a man like
me flee? And could one such as I go into the temple to save his life? I will
not go in"* (Neh 6:11).

Opposition comes through deceit

Shemaiah tried to deceive Nehemiah into locking himself in the
temple for his own protection, but Nehemiah quickly saw through
this deceitful plot. To have followed this suggestion would have

desecrated the temple and brought God's wrath on his servant. Nehemiah knew that God did not send Shemaiah.

Opposition comes from within

Attacks came on a regular basis from the Gentiles around Judah. This was expected. But the unexpected problems from within the camp, must have been discouraging to Nehemiah. First the Jews told him they were tired (Neh 4:10). Next they were plagued by fear. They complained to Nehemiah ten times about their fear.

Chapter 5 describes three more problems Nehemiah confronted. First of all, the builders wanted to leave their work on the walls and go back to farming. They claimed they would soon run out of food, and their families would face starvation. Second, since they could not farm their lands, the builders complained that in order to purchase food they had to mortgage their properties, vineyards, and houses. This, however, was a poor excuse because the entire project was completed in only 52 days (Neh 6:15).

Then, there was the problem of taxes. *"We have borrowed money for the king's tax, on our fields and our vineyards"* (Neh 5:4). They pointed out their children would be taken in servitude and bondage, which they did not want, nor did Nehemiah. This kind of opposition apparently touched Nehemiah's heart, for he became very angry, not at the people in general but at those who were taking advantage of his workers. He quickly responded with a strong rebuke, commanding those who were charging interest to stop the practice immediately (Neh 5: 9). He pointed out to them that they were bringing reproach to the name of God.

A person who prays for himself only at the end

Towards the end of his work Nehemiah prayed, *"Remember me, O my God, for good"* (Neh 13:31). Nehemiah had completed a tremendous job under the direction of God. Now after finishing the job assigned to him, he finally thinks of himself and wants to be remembered by God and blessed by Him. He was so unselfish that he never wanted in the first instance to gather all the blessings for himself. Instead he worked for the benefit of Israel.

Let Us Rise Up and Build

Like the ancient city of Jerusalem, the walls have fallen down around our families and all that remnants of many homes—even those built on Christian foundations are heaps of rubble. It is time for those who care to 'rise up and build'!

One of the most frightening reasons for the disintegration of the family today has been the way God's people have begun to be part of the problem rather than part of the solution.

> Many of us have acclimated too quickly to the chill wind of changing values and have simply buttoned up our topcoats of indifference to prevent the icy blast from touching our hearts, says, Jill Brisco.

Nehemiah knew that the only way the walls could be built was by the mobilization and involvement of every man, woman, and child in the land. There needed to be something for every member of the family to do. He would encourage everyone to build the wall in front of their own house (Neh 3:23). Whatever has happened to us in the past must not be allowed to paralyse our present or hinder our future.

If we will walk around our church or our family as openly as Nehemiah walked around the walls of Jerusalem, surveying the damage, assessing the breaches, and examining the cracks, we can be sure, that our God will put in our hearts some things to do as well (Neh 2:12).

Nehemiah's experience demonstrates how believers can accomplish seemingly impossible tasks if they will work together. They first need a clear understanding of God's plan and purposes. Then with committed leaders who can motivate and encourage them, the people of God can become a powerful, effective force.

As opposition came, Nehemiah faced it squarely. He cried out to the Lord for help and then made sound decisions. He did not allow himself to be intimidated by opposition or the people who caused it. The end result was victory. The people of Jerusalem had their protective walls and the city was safe again.

Chapter 15

ESTHER
A Bold and Beautiful Leader

Some people watch history, while some people make history. A true hero recognizes a crisis and moves to meet it. What makes a hero? Someone would say, 'Be just in the right place at the right time'. People become heroes, because they take quick action at the 'right time', while others stand watching in horror. This kind of courage made Esther a brave heroine in the history of Israel.

Though Queen Esther did not have a specific title of ministry, she was instrumental in saving the entire Jewish nation. She was steadfastly committed to living according to godly principles. This allowed God to use her for His purpose and glory.

Judah was in Babylonian captivity for seventy years. Eventually, Babylon was destroyed by the growing Persian Empire under Cyrus the Great. By his edict, many Jews were allowed to return from Babylon and Persia to Jerusalem in 538 BC under the leadership of Zerubbabel (Ezra 1:1–4; 6:3–5). However, many second and third-generation Babylonian Jews who were settled and prosperous chose to stay back. Many kings succeeded Cyrus, and one was Xerxes I (his Greek name) or Ahasuerus (his Hebrew name).

Esther appears on the scene about sixty years after the decree of Cyrus between the first return of Jewish exiles and the second return led by Ezra in 457 BC. Though Esther is placed after Nehemiah in the Bible, its events actually occurred 30 years before Nehemiah's return to Jerusalem (444 BC) to rebuild the wall. Whereas Ezra and Nehemiah address issues involving the Jewish remnant that returned to Jerusalem, Esther records a development of crucial importance among the Jews who remained in Persia.

A Beauty Contest

In the third year of his reign King Ahasuerus gave a feast, which lasted 180 days. It was attended by thousands of his kingdom officials, coming from all the 127 provinces, stretching from India to Ethiopia (Esth 1:1–4). During the final week of the feasting when the heart of the king was merry with wine along with his friends, he called for his wife, Vashti, to come in and parade her beauty before them. Queen Vasthi refused to come when the king sent for her (Esth 1:12). He became furious and banished his wife forever from his presence, lest the other women of the kingdom get ideas from her insubordination.

Queen Vashti's refusal to parade her beauty before her husband's friends was officially interpreted as nothing less than an act of rebellion against male authority (Esth 1:5–17). As a result, King Ahasuerus fired off a decree intended to reinforce the mastery of every male in the empire over the women in his household.

> So he sent letters to all the king's provinces, to each province according to its script and to every people according to their language, that every man should be the master in his own house and the one who speaks in the language of his own people (Esth 1:22).

It would be perilous to try to judge ancient cultures and customs against modern-day understandings of gender issues. Nevertheless, it seems clear that some of the men of Persia felt threatened by Vashti's self-will. Perhaps they feared the social chaos that might result, if women refused to comply with their husbands' wishes. Many men today display similar fears about assertive, strong willed and independent women. Peter said,

> . . . you wives, be submissive to your own husbands so that even if any of them are disobedient to the word, they may be won without a word by the behavior of their wives, as they observe your chaste and respectful behavior (1 Pet 3:1–2).

One of the most despised and misunderstood words in the English language is the word 'submission'. The Greek word translated as 'submissive' (or 'subjection' in the KJV) is hupotasso. The second part of the word, hupo, means 'under'. The latter part of the word, tasso means, 'to arrange in an orderly manner'. So, probably Peter was trying to say that, wives should arrange themselves in an orderly manner under their husband's covering.

A woman should be a person who is very composed and should have control over herself. She should be a symbol of unfading beauty, of a gentle and quiet spirit. But it is the duty of the husband, to be considerate and treat his wife with respect, as she shares her life with him. Peter wrote, that women should seek "*. . . the imperishable quality of a gentle and quiet spirit, which is precious in the sight of God*" (1 Pet 3:4). The Greek word translated 'quiet' literally means 'immovable' or 'steadfast'.

The Book of Esther shows the value of a woman with strong character. Esther was not only beautiful, but also bold and was determined in her mind, to enter into the presence of the king even at the risk of her life, for the sake of God's chosen race (Esth 4:11; 5:1–3). She was thus able to save her people the Jews from genocide. Esther's life encourages women to speak their minds and assert their will, to combat evil and take a stand for godly principles.

After his anger had cooled, the king regretted his hasty action, but was unable to change the strict Persian law even though he himself had decreed it.

He was counselled to look for a new woman to be his queen (Esth 1:13–22). He allowed an empire-wide beauty search to begin, and the winner of the contest to become his new wife (2:2–4). Among the beauties brought to the palace was a Jewish girl named Hadassah, which means 'myrtle'. She also had a Persian name, 'Esther' meaning, 'star'. She was a beautiful young lady who had been raised by her older cousin, whose name was Mordecai, of the tribe of Benjamin (2:9–11).

The contest lasted some four years but after the King had seen all the available finalists, he chose Esther to become his next queen.

The Queen Risks Her Life

God used this contest to move a woman of His choice, a Jew, into a unique position of power. Then, when all seemed smooth, her crucial moment came. This moment has been echoed many times since. As a successful racial minority in the Persian Empire, Esther's people, the Jews, had not accommodated themselves well into their surroundings. Moreover the Babylonians were jealous of their success and separatism. A vengeful prime minister, Haman, made up his mind to destroy them and so he issued an edict of government-sponsored genocide (3:1–15).

The roots of anti-Semitism, or hatred of the Jewish race, go back many centuries. The forces of darkness influence people to hate God's chosen race, the Jews. As a result, demonic powers have constantly moved throughout history to persecute both Jews and Christians. The Jews have been the subjects of many intense persecutions. History has shown what the Nazi Germany did to the Jews, as well as the widespread persecution of the Jews in Russia.

Haman saw that Mordecai a Jew, who sat at the king's gate along with the king's servants; refused to bow before him, as had been commanded by the king. Mordecai had simply stood for his faith. The Jews were to only bow down in worship to their God. Like once in a foreign land three other Jewish captives—Shadrach, Meshach and Abednego did not bow down to the golden image as the king had commanded (Dan 3:12–18).

Mordecai was a God-pleaser. He was well aware of the fact that refusing to bow to Haman, as ordered by the king, could cause him a lot of problems. But Mordecai was much more concerned with obeying and pleasing God than gaining the favour of a man. He was very careful not to worship anyone but the Lord, showing an understanding that to seek honour or favour from people can be a form of idol worship.

Pursuing holiness and not living like others around us may, incur the hatred and hostility of unbelievers. At the same time, as we look at the final outcome of these two men, we also see the importance of faithfully seeking to please God and not people (Esth 8:8–15). The favour, which we will receive from God, will be greater than the favour of people.

Haman conspired a plot, to have King Ahasuerus exterminate not only Mordecai, but to destroy, kill, and annihilate all of Mordecai's people, the Jews (Esth 3:13). Haman accused them of being a separate people, keeping to themselves, their own laws, and observances no matter what the laws and observances were of all other people in the land.

God had called them to be a separate people, and throughout history they have taken their selection seriously. However, God knew ahead of time of this dark plot against His people and had already put His chosen woman, Queen Esther, in place to do something about it.

Haman asked the king, if it pleases him to issue a decree, to destroy the Jews. He would put ten thousand talents of silver into the royal treasury for the men who carry out this business.

So the king took his signet ring from his finger and gave it to Haman. The king told Haman to do with the people as he pleased. Haman issued a decree in the name of King Xerxes saying to kill, destroy and annihilate all the Jews—young and old, women and little children—on a single day, the thirteenth day of the twelfth month, the month of Adar, and to seize their possessions as plunder.

When Mordecai learnt all that had been done, he tore his clothes, put on sackcloth and ashes, and went out in the midst of the city and wailed loudly and bitterly. In each place and every province where the command and decree of the king came, there was great mourning, fasting, weeping, and wailing among the Jews.

Esther's maidens and her eunuchs came and told her of the state of Mordecai; she immediately sent garments to clothe Mordecai that he might remove his sackcloth, but he did not accept it.

Then Queen Esther summoned Hathach from the king's eunuchs, whom the king had appointed to attend to her, and ordered him to go to Mordecai to find out why he was mourning. Mordecai told Hathach all that had happened, and also gave him a copy of the text of the edict, which had been issued in Susa for the destruction of the Jews. Mordecai told him to give the copy of the edict to Queen Esther and ordered her to go into the king's presence to implore his favour and to plead with him for her people.

Would Queen Esther intervene? Doing so would risk her life. And what difference could she make? She could go to the king's presence only when he called for her, and she had not gone into the presence of the king for thirty days. Yet she alone, of all the Jews, had access to the king. So Queen Esther sent word to Mordecai saying,

> "All the king's servants and the people of the king's provinces know that for any man or woman who comes to the king to the inner court who is not summoned, he has but one law, that he be put to death, unless the king holds out to him the golden scepter so that he may live. And I have not been summoned to come to the king for these thirty days" (Esth 4:11).

Mordecai responded with one of the most beautiful statements on God's sovereignty. 'Do not imagine that you in the king's palace can escape any more than all the Jews. For if you remain silent at this time, relief and deliverance will arise for the Jews from another place and you and your father's house will perish. And who knows whether you have not attained royalty for such a time as this?' Esther responded with action, her courageous words are a classic statement of heroism: *I will go in unto the king, which is not according to the law: and if I perish, I perish* (verses 12–16). She also asked Mordecai to assemble all the Jews who are found in Susa and fast for three days and she and her maidens would do likewise and then she would go into the presence of the king.

That is why it is so vital to surround ourselves with godly friends, who will give us wise counsel and who will fast and pray with us as we face the dangers, decisions, and challenges of life; who would also help us hear the word of the Lord for particular situations.

It is important to listen to wise counsel. But at the same time it is even more important to receive a confirming word from God. We must be careful never to take another person's advice without making sure that it is the word of the Lord to us individually and personally.

Esther was a wise woman. She asked for counsel, but then what did she do? She sought God. Not only did she commit to fast and pray herself, she also called upon all the Jews and her closest companions to do the same. She required her maids and servants to consecrate themselves just as she did.

In the mind of every person there has to be a deep question lurking in his or her heart whatever mission or work they are involved in, 'What am I doing here?' The question has to do with purpose and significance. 'What am I doing in sales, or plumbing, or engineering, or law, or hairdressing, or child care? I want my life to count for God. So what am I doing in this job?' The answer is that God never wastes a life, but has a purpose for His people. God says, *"For I know the plans that I have for you . . . plans for welfare and not for calamity to give you a future and a hope"* (Jer 29:11).

The Power of Fasting and Praying

Esther knew how to receive strength and power from God. In fasting she defied dependency, comfort, and safety; in calling for the support of all of the Susa Jews and her own maidens, she moved from singleness to a community approach.

We receive new strength and courage when we move from our own spiritual resources to the community of believers. We should not hesitate or be afraid to ask others to support us in our times of tough decision-making. Esther's maids were probably not Jews, an indication that valuable friends can be found everywhere.

Esther's choices were limited. She could approach the king and risk being killed for entering his court without permission, or she could do nothing and take a chance on dying with her people. Either way she had everything to lose. It was a difficult decision, and a fearsome one.

Sometimes God has to get us to the place in which we have nothing to fall back on but on faith and trust in Him. Where we cannot trace Him, we have to trust Him. We have to surrender our will to His will, humbling ourselves before Him. Many times, whether we like it or not, we have to take a risk. Risk taking is very frightening. Some people prefer to sit back and let others be the movers and shakers. Once the danger is passed, they step in and help with the project. But God does not always work that way.

On the third day, Esther put on her royal robes and stood in the inner court of the King's palace, in front of the King's rooms. The king was sitting on his royal throne, when the king saw Esther, she obtained favour in his sight; and the king extended to Esther the golden sceptre which was in his hand. Esther came near and touched the top of the sceptre.

At that moment, Esther had the king's full attention and favour. He even went so far as to assure her that anything she asked would be granted, up to half his kingdom. She could easily have asked the king, to revoke his edict regarding the Jews and to deal harshly with Haman who had contrived the plot against the people of his queen. But Esther did not do that. Instead, she was wise enough to wait for a more suitable time and place. She took advantage of the king's good mood and favour to invite him and Haman to a special banquet in their honour.

Esther was wise enough to know when and how to use her tongue, her weapon, to maximum advantage. She understood that the king's public throne room in front of many witnesses including the evil Haman himself was neither the time nor the place to present her case. She waited for the right opportunity and God's perfect timing.

We learn a good lesson from Esther. There is a time to speak, and there is a time to hold our peace. Before we open our mouths we need to pray about the situation and make sure that what we are about to say has been released to us from the Holy Spirit of God. If the Spirit is directing us to speak, He will prepare the way and open the door. He will give us the right opportunity at the right moment.

Queen Esther and God's people had been fasting. God had begun to move in response to their fasting and prayer.

Esther could have ended up imprisoned, killed, divorced, banished, or simply misunderstood. But she was willing to do what had to be done. That is all God expects of us, that we do what He requires of us without fretting and without trying to figure out the end result. He wants us to learn to walk in simple obedience and trust.

All we have to do is please our king and He will take care of the outcome. We are not to worry about God's Word; that's His part. He is an awesome God; He can handle things. He doesn't need our input. All He needs or expects from us is that we do what He has called us to do; and He will do the rest.

That night, God caused King Ahasuerus to be unable to sleep. So he ordered the reading of some of their historical records, and by chance he just happened to begin reading at the place that related how Mordecai had once saved the king's life by exposing an assassination plot.

When the king discovered this truth, he also found out that the act of Mordecai had not been acknowledged (Esth 2:21–23). At that moment Haman had just arrived at the palace, seeking the king's permission to hang Mordecai. The king still thinking how Mordecai should be rewarded asked Haman, 'What is to be done for the man whom the king desires to honour?' The arrogant and self-centred Haman immediately thought Xerxes had him in mind and he lavishly suggested a list of things (6:7–9).

Haman was taken by surprise when the king ordered him to,

> "Take quickly the robes and the horse as you have said, and do so for Mordecai the Jew, who is sitting at the king's gate; do not fall short in anything of all that you have said." So Haman took the robe and the horse, and arrayed Mordecai, and led him on

horseback through the city square, and proclaim before him, 'Thus it shall be done to the man whom the king desires to honor'" (10–11).

In all of this, we see God's divine response to the fasting and prayers of his people.

After this Haman returned home, and narrated the whole incident to his wife and his friends. While they were still talking with him, the king's eunuchs arrived and hastily brought Haman to the banquet, which Esther had prepared.

Accidents or Incidents

The story of Esther runs on a series of extraordinary coincidences. Esther just 'happened' to be chosen as the new queen. The king just 'happened' to be unable to sleep, and when he picked up some readings. He just 'happened' to come across an account of a good deed done by Mordecai, Esther's cousin. The evil Haman just 'happened' to come in at that crucial moment. These coincidences, along with Esther's courageous act changed the events favourable to the Jews.

Hence certain accidents in our lives can be incidents in the will of God. Was God behind these incidents? The Book of Esther doesn't say directly: God is not mentioned even once, and sometimes seems deliberately left out. But believing readers, whether Jews or Christians, can have no doubt. All of life is under God's command, nothing just happens. These incidents were part of God's plan to save the Jews.

God continues to protect the Jews not only because He loves them, but also He had chosen them from the beginning. Mordecai confronted Esther with God's plan for her life. Queen Esther realized that it was God who had made her beautiful and God who had made her queen in order to rescue His people. She responded to God's call on her life, even though it threatened her privileged position and future and perhaps even her life.

Reversing a Bad Situation

When the king and Haman were in the banquet prepared by Esther on the second day; the king asked Esther,

> "What is your petition, Queen Esther? It shall be granted you. And what is your request? Even to half of the kingdom it shall be done." Then Queen Esther replied, " . . . If it pleases the king, let my life be given me as my petition, and my people as my request; for we have been sold, I and my people, to be destroyed, to be killed and annihilated. Now if we had only been sold as slaves, men and women, I would have remained silent, for the trouble would not be commensurate with the annoyance to the king." The king, filled with astonishment and anger, asked: "Who is he, and where is he, who would presume to do thus?" Esther said, "A foe and an enemy, is this wicked Haman!" (Esth 7:2–6).

This shows very clearly that God empowered Esther with the spirit of boldness that she could directly point out the treacherous plans of the Prime Minister in front of him to the king.

Haman had violated that fearful warning of God to Abraham, *"And I will bless those who bless you, And the one who curses you I will curse. And in you all the families of the earth will be blessed"* (Gen 12:3). This violation cost him his life (See Prov 26:27; Gal 6:7–8; Isa 54:17). Pharaoh learnt that the Jews, who were God's chosen race, could not be drowned (Exod 14). Nebuchadnezzar realized that they could not be burned (Dan 3). Darius was shaken by the fact that even the hungry lions did not even come near Daniel, the Jewish Prime Minister (Dan 6). Haman learnt that Mordecai could not be hanged (Esth 7).

Haman was hanged on the same gallows that he had prepared for Mordecai. The plot to kill the Jews began to fall apart:

> On that day King Ahasuerus gave the house of Haman, the enemy of the Jews, to Queen Esther; and Mordecai came before the king, for Esther had disclosed what he was to her. The king took off his signet ring, which he had taken away from Haman, and gave it to Mordecai. And Esther set Mordecai over the house

of Haman. Then Esther spoke again to the king, fell at his feet, wept, and implored him to avert the evil scheme of Haman the Agagite and his plot which he had devised against the Jews (Esth 8:1–3).

She said to the king,

"If it pleases the king and if I have found favor before him . . . let it be written to revoke the letters devised by Haman, . . . which he wrote to destroy the Jews who are in all the king's province" (Esth 8:5).

The king granted the Jews who were in each and every city the right to assemble and to defend their lives, to destroy, to kill, and to annihilate the entire army of any people or province which might attack them, including children and women, and to plunder their spoil (Esth 8:11).

Thus the Jews were given complete protection in the land because of the obedience of Esther and the faithfulness of Mordecai. Like Mordecai and Esther, you may face circumstances about which you have little insight. Who knows what circumstances He might bring you into? But be assured that the same God who worked through Esther is at work in your life today.

I would sincerely exhort women not to give lame excuses like 'Oh not me', 'I can't do', 'I am not talented' or 'I am not eloquent'. This causes a low self esteem or low self-value. You don't have to be eloquent, elegant or talented.

God is looking for availability and not our ability. Women have been active in Jesus' ministry from birth to death and resurrection. Even in the early church, many women were involved in the ministry of Jesus. Mary, Martha and Mary Magdalene were very hospitable to Jesus. Joanna, Susanna and Magdalene even extended their financial support in the travelling ministry of Jesus. Mary not only had the privilege of being the first person to see the resurrected Lord but also received the first apostolic commission to go and declare to the world the message that Jesus is alive. Women even proved faithful at the cross.

God sees in each woman her full potential: the ability to become what He wants her to become with His strength and wisdom, under His lordship. He then calls her and encourages her to reach, *Toward the goal for the prize of the upward call of God in Christ Jesus* (Phil 3:14).

Chapter 16

ISAIAH
A Leader with a Vision
for God's Mission

Do you have a vision from God? When I say vision, I do not mean visualizing a picture or an object of art, but I am referring to a real inward vision. Has God given you a real inward vision? 2 Timothy 1:8–9 says,

> Therefore do not be ashamed of the testimony of our Lord, or of me His prisoner; but join with me in suffering for the gospel according to the power of God, who has saved us, and called us with a holy calling, not according to our works, but according to His own purpose and grace which was granted us in Christ Jesus from all eternity.

I would like to emphasize the phrase, 'He who saved us, called us'. He has saved us not just to say, 'Hallelujah, I am going to heaven'. We are not saved merely to go to heaven but we are also called to serve Him. Therefore, it is not an option, but an obligation, that we all should be His witnesses.

To serve the Lord we need to have a clear vision and guidance from God. 'What does the Lord want me to do?' This should be the first and foremost question we need to ask in order to be an effective and a faithful servant of God because He has called us to do his ministry. Every believer in Christ is a missionary and every non-believer is a mission field. You are called to be a servant of God.

King Darius called Daniel, 'servant of the living God'. King Nebuchadnezzar called Shadrach, Meshac and Abednego the 'servants of the living God'. Daniel was a Prime Minister but he was a servant of the living God. Likewise, we are all servants of God. In one's life there are three callings—

1) A call to live a holy life.
2) A call to be witnesses, servants and ministers.
3) A call to be His full-time ministers.

If you are saved, you are also called to serve Him. Calling comes from the Almighty to a person who is saved and therefore it is like two sides of the same coin. You cannot refuse the call of God once you are saved as the still small voice of God, inspires us to do the will of God.

Have you ever wondered, what is the purpose for which God has called you, out of the millions who do not know the Lord or about the kingdom of God? God has a purpose in every individual's life, and wants that purpose to be fulfilled. The Lord says,

> "You did not choose Me but I chose you and appointed you, that you would go and bear fruit, and that your fruit would remain, so that whatever you ask of the Father in My name, He may give to you" (John 15:16).

Do you not know that you are the temple of the living God, knowing that you were redeemed from the futile ways inherited from your fathers, not with perishable things such as silver or gold, but with the precious blood of Christ, as of a lamb unblemished and spotless, the blood of Christ (1 Pet 1:18–19). So, you are called and you need to have a vision.

The Book of Isaiah in many respects is like a miniature Bible. It has sixty-six chapters; the Bible has sixty-six books. The first thirty-nine chapters correspond to the thirty-nine books of the Old Testament, speaking largely about Israel before the coming of Messiah. The last twenty-seven chapters parallel the New Testament, speaking largely about the Messiah and His messianic kingdom. Most often we find the Book of Isaiah quoted in the New Testament.

Isaiah's Historical Background

Isaiah, whose name means 'The Lord saves', was a prophet to Judah at a crucial point when salvation was most desperately needed. He was born in the middle of 700 BC His father Amos was (according to tradition) the brother of King Amaziah, Uzziah's father. If this tradition is correct, Isaiah was of royal blood and a cousin to King Uzziah.

The Bible says very little about the personal history of the prophet himself; what can be known must be gleaned from his writings and from his historical situation.

The southern kingdom

Ever since the northern kingdom of Israel separated from Judah to the south, the southern kingdom had been on a spiritual roller coaster. Good kings were followed by bad kings; bad kings were followed by mediocre ones. Joash's son Amaziah ascended to the throne in 796 BC and ruled for twenty-nine years. When he was taken as a captive around 790 BC, his sixteen-year-old son Uzziah (who was also called Azariah) ruled for fifty-two years (2 Kings 14:2; 2 Chr 25–26).

Isaiah as a scribe

Judah was at its lowest point. It had been totally defeated during the reign of petty kings, and not until Amaziah his father was released some years later could Uzziah rebuild the nation.

At this juncture, Isaiah was busy in his role as a scribe in the royal court.

As a scribe Isaiah's job was to keep a historical record of the times. This gave him great exposure to the political happenings of the court, and secured for him an excellent education. This explains his extensive vocabulary and command of the language. He had a poetic ability to paint word pictures with beautiful metaphors, showing a real sensitivity to the language.

Isaiah the author

Isaiah the author of this book was highly educated, knowledgeable in international affairs, and on familiar terms with the royal court. As a writing prophet he was excellent both in the extent and comprehensiveness of his message and in his ability to communicate.

The period in which Isaiah ministered extends from around 740 to about 690 BC. During the reigns of Jotham, Ahaz, Hezekiah, and Manasseh, all kings of Judah (2 Kings 15:21). Isaiah's ministry was primarily to the southern kingdom of Judah. Its capital was Jerusalem. His message was generally directed toward Judah's sinful people (Isa 1:4) and particularly to its evil leaders (Isa 1:23). His message to them was twofold: God will bring condemnation on Israel and Judah through the nations, but He will also one day provide salvation through Israel and Judah to the nations.

The Book of Isaiah has been called, 'The gospel according to Isaiah'. It may be divided into three sections: the prophetic (1–35), the historic (36–39) and the messianic (40–66).

The historical purpose of the Book of Isaiah was to warn Judah of the sins that lead to Israel's downfall and to warn of the evil that would lead to their own. The doctrinal purpose is to comprehend all the great truths of the Old Testament regarding salvation from man's sin through Christ's redemptive work as well as the final glorious restoration of this earth.

The Christological purpose of the Book of Isaiah is to bring a complete and comprehensive description of Christ found in the Old Testament. For example, Isaiah refers to Christ as the Lord, the Son of a virgin, the wonderful Counsellor, mighty God, everlasting Father, Prince of Peace (Isa 9:6).

Isaiah's call as a prophet

When Uzziah died, Isaiah was called by God to be a prophet to the southern kingdom. He continued to be a prophet during the reign of Jotham, Ahaz and Hezakiah. His life as a scribe and his descent from royal blood gained him easy access to the court and the priesthood. He had the gift of faith, and never seemed to waver in his commitment.

King Jotham was anti-Assyrian, so the political opposition forced his son Ahaz, who was pro-Assyrian into co-regency. When Jotham died in 732 BC, Ahaz assumed full power.

Isaiah's advice to King Ahaz

Ahaz's sixteen-year rule was a difficult time (2 Kings 16; 2 Chr 28). He had established ties with the Assyrians while Israel and Syria had decided to resist. When Syria attacked Judah, Ahaz did not know what to do but Isaiah advised him that if he would have faith in God, he would have nothing to fear (Isa 7:1–9).

Isaiah told Ahaz to ask for a sign from God, but Ahaz refused as he had already rejected the worship of the true God. He was worshipping regularly at the pagan high places and had even sacrificed his sons to Molech at Ben Hinnom (Ben Hinnom is synonymous with Gehenna, the valley forming the west side of Jerusalem.) Because of Ahaz's sin, the valley ceremonially became unclean and suitable only for dumping trash. The continual fires and stench arising from it formed the perfect basis for Jesus' illustration of hell in His teachings.

Despite Ahaz's unbelief, God gave him a sign. A young maiden would conceive and give birth, but before her child would grow old enough to know right and wrong, Judah would see defeat (Isa 7:10–17). (The Hebrew word for 'young maiden' can also mean 'virgin', and as such became a prophecy for yet another birth, the virgin birth of the Messiah).

Isaiah had opposed Ahaz but was active during Hezekiah's time. We can safely assume that the two did work together, probably quite closely. Surely the success of revival during the reign of Hezekiah must be credited partially to Isaiah's preaching.

After fourteen years of reign in Judah, Hezekiah became very ill. Isaiah told him that he will die, but when Hezekiah prayed, God promised that He would remove the Assyrian threat and add fifteen more years for Hezekiah to live on earth.

The last time we read of Isaiah is when Hezekiah showed envoys from Babylon all of his riches. Isaiah told him that some day all of Hezekiah's wealth and family would be taken captive to Babylon. About a century later, the Babylonians took Judah captive and Isaiah's prophecies were fulfilled.

Isaiah's wife and sons

Isaiah's wife, a prophetess (Isa 8:3), conceived and gave birth to a second child (Maher-Shalal-Hash-Baz) whose name means 'quick to plunder, swift to the spoil'. God told Isaiah that before this child could say, 'My father', Judah would be conquered by Assyria (Isa 8:1–4). The couple's first child was named Shear-Jashub, which means, 'a remnant will return' (Isa 7:3; 10:21).

Isaiah's preaching was visual, emphasizing imminent destruction and eventual salvation. This is why he named his sons 'quick to plunder, swift to the spoil', and 'a remnant will return'. Note also that Isaiah's own name means 'the Lord saves'. His sons were visual reminders to the people that the Babylonians were coming soon, but after a while the Jews would return from exile.

Another reminder was given when God told Isaiah to walk around 'stripped and barefoot' for three years as a visual commentary to the nation that they would soon be marched off into captivity, stripped and barefoot (Isa 20).

Isaiah's prophecy about Christ

We see Christ in this book and hear the prophet crying, 'He is coming' and 'He is coming again'. He is coming as Saviour in humiliation as our sin-bearer, depicted in Isaiah 53. He is coming again in power and great glory, depicted in Isaiah 34.

We see two mountain peaks with a valley between. One is called Calvary; on its hilltop is a cross. But as we look farther we see another peak. It is radiant with the light of a crown. This hill is Olivet. The eyes of Isaiah went farther than the sufferings of Calvary; his eyes caught the kingdom and the glory that should follow.

Yes, Christ, the Messiah is coming and He is coming again. This is a glorious fact, our blessed hope (Isa 60:1; Acts 1:11; John 14:1–3).

Isaiah speaks of Christ's death when he says, though your sins be as scarlet, they shall be as white as snow; though they be red like crimson, they shall be as wool (Isa 1:18). Again, He is despised and rejected by the people (Isa 53:3). This speaks of the first time when He came unto His own, 'And His own received Him not' (John 1:11). But when He comes again we hear, *Arise, shine, for thy light is come, and the glory of the Lord is risen upon thee* (Isa 60:1). Then the Lord shares to us through Isaiah about His coming kingdom. And it shall come to pass in the last days . . . (Isa 2:2–5).

Isaiah 11 and 12, give us a picture of this coming King and His kingdom.

The King Himself (Isa 11:1); His anointing (Isa 11:2); His righteous reign (Isa 11:3–5); His glorious kingdom (Isa 11:6–9); His people gathered (Isa 11:10–16); His kingdom of worship (Isa 12). This is the kingdom that Christ came to this earth to establish, but they would not receive their king (John 1:11;19:15).

We need to hear the prophet say today, *Woe to those who go down to Egypt for help, And rely on horses, And trust in chariots* (Isa 31:1). How great a need there is today for those who will remember the name of the Lord our God, who know the saving strength of His right hand (Ps 20:6).

Isaiah spent his life trying to get Israel to become acquainted with God and His Word. He wanted them to trust wholly in God's guidance. God wants us to recognize Him in national affairs. He calls His people to turn unto Him from whom the children . . . have deeply revolted (Isa 31:6).

Chapters 46–66 of the Book of Isaiah are called the 'Book of Consolation' because Isaiah tells in glowing terms not only of the restoration of Judah but the coming of Jehovah's 'Servant' to be the Messiah King. The restoration is assured for they must return to their own land to prepare the way for the coming Messiah, who is to redeem His people.

Isaiah's Vision for God's Mission

Isaiah teaches us that our God is a holy God. The vision that Isaiah saw is narrated to us in Isaiah chapter 6:1–8:

In the year of King Uzziah's death, I saw the Lord sitting on a throne, lofty and exalted with the train of His robe filling the temple.

Seraphim stood above Him, each having six wings; with two he covered his face, and with two he covered his feet, and with two he flew.

And one called out to another and said, "Holy, Holy, Holy, is the Lord of hosts, The whole earth is full of His glory."

And the foundations of the thresholds trembled at the voice of him who called out, while the temple was filling with smoke.

Then I said, "Woe is me, for I am ruined! Because I am a man of unclean lips, And I live among a people of unclean lips; For my eyes have seen the King, the LORD of hosts."

Then one of the seraphim flew to me with a burning coal in his hand which he had taken from the altar with tongs.

And he touched my mouth with it and said, "Behold, this has touched your lips; and your iniquity is taken away, and your sin is forgiven."

Then I heard the voice of the Lord, saying, "Whom shall I send, and who will go for Us?" Then I said, "Here am I. Send me."

In the above passage we see that when Isaiah was in the presence of God he first had an upward vision, which lead to an inward vision and then to an outward vision. Isaiah's call and commission came to him in the form of a 'vision'. Isaiah was the man of the hour.

In his upward vision, when he saw the awesome holiness of God, he received an inward vision which revealed to him the wretchedness of his life which made him to cry, 'Woe is me for I am ruined, because I am a man of unclean lips . . . .' In response to this confession the Seraphim touched his mouth with a burning coal and brought about the cleansing that he prayed for. After the cleansing, he hears the call of God, 'Whom shall I send, and who will go for us?' It is here; he receives an outward vision for God's mission and responds by saying, 'Here am I send me'.

Upward vision

In the year of King Uzziah's death, I saw the Lord sitting on a throne, lofty and exalted, with the train of His robe filling the temple (Isa 6:1). When the strength within the human being died, he went into the presence of the divine strength. When a king dies it was the responsibility of a prophet to anoint the next king.

When Isaiah was in the presence of God he had an upward vision. In his vision he saw 'the Lord sitting on a throne, lofty and exalted, with the train of His robe filling the temple'. *Seraphim stood above Him, each having six wings; with two he covered his face, with two he covered his feet, and with two he flew* (Isa 6:2).

Seraphim and Cherubim, are the servants of God, they minister to God. Seraphim, plural of seraph is described as a burning, fiery, gliding, angelic being. In the following lines I would like to draw your attention to how the heavenly servants of God served God. It is good to appreciate the service and ministry of our earthly servants of God, but they cannot become our perfect models. The pattern and style of ministry or the experience of any servant of God may not be authoritative, but the Word of God and the ministry of the saints of God in the Bible are authoritative. Isaiah received a vision from the ministry of the seraphim and the Cherubim.

With two wings they covered their faces. This they did as a mark of humility and respect in the presence of God. Probably they considered themselves very insignificant in the presence of such an awesome and holy God. You must prostrate humbly before God and empty yourself of thoughts that make you feel proud or feel that you have obtained something.

God will not fill a half-filled vessel but only an empty vessel. The great evangelist D L Moody bowed down with his head on the floor and said, 'I empty my will before God, it's nothing of my will but it is the will of God'. You must surrender your ambitions into His hands, your will unto His will, your ego, and your whole self unto the Lordship of Jesus Christ.

With two wings they covered their feet. By this act they were conveying a message that though they had the ability to move in all the directions at the same time, they do not depend on their own ability before God. It is not your ability that counts, but it is your availability that matters to God. You may be a weak or unhealthy person. God can still use you in a mighty way, if you are available to Him. Isaiah at the end of the vision (outward vision) said, 'Here am I. Send me'.

With the remaining two wings the seraph flew. That represents serving God. Out of the six wings the seraphs had, they used four wings in terms of their humility and personal holiness, thus giving importance to their personal life. Only with two wings they served God. Today with four wings many are busy serving God and give only two wings for their personal holiness, prayer life and for their family life.

The number one priority in your life should be God. Second priority should be your family and the third priority your ministry. Ministry should never come in the way of your family.

Many pastors and evangelists are always on the move keeping themselves busy all the time. They don't spend enough time praying and reading the Word of God. They tend to have a long lasting relationship and are nice with others, but they don't take care or have a proper relationship with their wife and children. It is not what you do for God that matters, but it is how you are before God that matters. When you go to heaven, God is not going to ask you about the enormity of your ministry or the success of your ministry, or how many souls you won for the kingdom but how you took care of your wife, and your children.

And one called out to another and said, "Holy, Holy, Holy, is the LORD of hosts, The whole earth is full of His glory" (Isa 6:3). This is how the seraphs were ministering to God. Seraphim, all they had to talk about was the wholeness of God. They did not spend their time backbiting or gossiping. How many of us spend time gossiping about others, backbiting and even eves-dropping. Don't waste your time talking about unnecessary things.

The Bible says, 'Every careless word that a person speaks, she/he shall render account for it in the Day of Judgement' (Matt 12:36). Two things cannot come back 'an arrow that is sent and a word which is spoken'. A word once spoken is gone, it is lost. If you have anything to speak, speak about what God did in your life or the holiness of God. That's what the seraphim were doing. They didn't have anything else to talk about except the glory of God.

We must be careful not to talk about a servant of God, if we do, the wrath of God will come upon us. Even though he or she may be making a mistake, it's not your business to talk about servants of God. For them, Jesus Christ is the boss. Jesus will take care of them. If something's wrong in any of the servants of God, go straight to that person and talk to him/her personally and pray with that person. But never talk behind a servant of God.

In Isaiah 6:4, says, *And the foundations of the thresholds trembled at the voice of him who called out, while the temple was filling with smoke.* Here, we see the result of their ministry. At the sound of their voices, the doorposts and thresholds shook and the temple was filled with smoke. We see here that there was a shaking of the place and the smoke came down.

In some churches, they do use incense, why? They believe that the smoke will carry their prayers up. That is why they burn the incense while they pray, but they never realize that the smoke does not go beyond the ceiling, and likewise traditional prayer also does not go beyond the ceiling.

But here, when the servants of God prayed, a reverse thing

happened, the smoke came down from the throne of God. The room was filled with the smoke; the smoke represents the blessing of God. Their ministry was so powerful that the blessing of God came down and filled the place. This is the vision that we should have about God's ministry.

Have you received a vision from God with respect to the purpose for which He has chosen you? Probably you have wasted a major amount of your lifetime. You do not know how long you are going to live in this world. The Bible says, *Therefore brethren, be all the more diligent to make certain about His calling and choosing you; for as long as you practice these things, you will never stumble* (2 Pet 1:10).

Before doing anything for God, we should have an upward vision. First see God in His power and authority. We should see God as omnipotent, omnipresent and as omniscient, the all powerful Almighty God, in power and authority. When we have seen God in His power and authority, then we experience the transfer of His power to us.

Great people of God, in the Bible always had an upward vision before they came into God's ministry. When Ezekiel was alone with God, he had a vision of God. He saw the omnipotence, omnipresence and omniscience of God. *In the thirtieth year, on the fifth day of the fourth month, while I was by the river Chebar among the exiles, the heavens were opened and I saw visions of God* (Ezek 1:1).

Hence the secret of having an upward vision is to be alone with God. Spend time all by yourself in a place where others will not disturb you. It should be just you and the Lord. God can speak to you more clearly when you spend time alone with the Lord rather than in a crowded worship place. So if you have not been with the Lord alone, then now is the time God wants to be with you. So, meet the Lord today and see what the Lord has in store for you.

The omnipotence of God

Ezekiel 1:4–5 says,

> And as I looked, behold, a storm wind was coming from the north, a great cloud with fire flashing forth continually and a bright light around it, and in its midst something like glowing metal in the midst of the fire. And within it there were figures resembling four living beings... .

This particular passage tells about the vision of Ezekiel, that he saw God, as an omnipotent God, the same God who created Adam, who delivered Noah from the flood, the God of Abraham, Isaac and Jacob.

As we read further in verse 13, the appearance of the living creatures was like burning coals of fire or like torches. Fire moved back and forth among the creatures. It was bright and lightning flashed out of it. Fire represents the omnipotence of God. Wherever there was the presence of God, there was fire. When Moses went up on Mount Sinai, he saw a burning bush. The pillar of fire guided the Israelites throughout their journey in the wilderness by night.

The omnipresence of God

In Ezekiel 1:17, Ezekiel was looking at the seraphs and 'Whenever they moved, they moved in any of their four directions, without turning as they moved'. We see the presence of God among the Seraphim and Cherubim. The Seraphim and Cherubim could walk in all the directions at the same time because the omnipresence of God existed with them. Can you drive your car in all four directions at the same time?

God can be present at the same time in every part of the world. Satan cannot be present everywhere at the same time. That's the difference between Satan and God. Satan is mighty, but God is Almighty! Satan does not have a discerning spirit; he cannot discern what you are thinking. Know the character of Satan and whenever you feel that he is trying to devour you, chase him out in the name of Jesus.

You must never give a chance to Satan to come your way. Never give the devil a ride, he will soon take over driving. He can only act on the spot depending on what is happening.

The omniscience of God

Ezekiel 1:18 reads, *As for their rims they were lofty and awesome, and the rims of all four of them were full of eyes around about.* This reveals to us that God at one time can see every single creature in this world, every bird that flies, every fish that swims, and every move of every plant in this world. God sees you and me in every moment of our lives and one day He will hold us accountable for the same.

Inward vision

Isaiah first had an upward vision, which led him to an inward vision. When he was in the awesome presence of God, he saw the greatness and the wholeness of God and became aware of his own unworthiness and realized his sinfulness.

In the presence of God, when Isaiah realized who he was, he wept and said, *"Woe is me, for I am ruined! Because I am a man of unclean lips, And I live among a people of unclean lips; For my eyes have seen the King, the LORD of hosts"* (Isa 6:5). The more you draw close to God, the more you will realize who you really are. The Word of God is like a mirror. The closer we go to the mirror, the better we see ourselves. Likewise, the more you read the Word of God, the more you will know about yourself.

Today, there are very few Isaiahs who introspect deeply and realize that they need to cry 'Woe unto me'. Very often you may see the need for others to change but not yourself. But this one thing you must realize that, unless you change, you cannot bring any change to

society no matter how hard you try. Always be conscious that your
life is a book, a book which people love to read and examine. If you
fail to produce good chapters in your book of life, you cannot be a
blessing to anybody.

Once, after Jesus performed a miracle, Peter realized his Master's
awesome holiness, and fell to his knees saying, 'Depart from me, for I
am a sinful man, O Lord' (Luke 5:8). When Thomas was confronted
with the risen Lord he cried out in all humility and reverence, 'My
Lord and my God' (John 20:28).

Paul said, *For I am the least of the apostles, and not fit to be called
an apostle, because I persecuted the church of God* (1Cor 15:9).

*It is a trustworthy statement, deserving full acceptance, that Christ
Jesus came into the world to save sinners, among whom I am foremost
of all* (1Tim 1:15).

When God asked Solomon what he wanted he fell down on the
ground and said,

> "Now, O LORD my God, You have made Your servant . . . yet
> I am but a little child; I do not know how to go out or come
> in. Your servant is in the midst of Your people which You have
> chosen, a great people who are too many to be numbered or
> counted. So, give Your servant an understanding heart to judge
> Your people to discern between good and evil. For who is able
> to judge this great people of Yours?" (1 Kings 3:7–9).

David said, 'Lord, I am like a weak child. I am like a child, Lord.' The
great men of God humbled themselves and that was the beginning
of their prosperity.

There are three important requisites for a man or a woman of
God: Humility, Honesty and Holiness. You may ask, 'Why holiness
is placed last?' I put it this way to show that without humility and
honesty no one can become holy. Humility and honesty are the
greatest assets to obtain holiness.

Isaiah, who had a supernatural encounter with God, did not feel worthy to be in God's presence. However, God took the initiative and cleansed him. A seraph flew to him with a live coal in his hand and touched his mouth and said, *"Behold, this has touched your lips; and your iniquity is taken away and your sin is forgiven"* (Isa 6:7).

Seeing the awesome presence of God and listening to the worship of the angels, Isaiah realized that he was unclean before God, with no hope of measuring up to God's standard of holiness.

Outward vision

Isaiah then received a divine call from God to go into the ministry as a prophet. *Then I heard the voice of the Lord, saying, "Whom shall I send and who will go for Us?" Then I said, "Here am I. Send me!"* (verse 8). At this time, he gets an outward vision. In response to the cleansing, Isaiah submitted himself entirely to God's service.

The painful cleansing process was necessary before Isaiah could fulfil the task to which God was calling him. Before we accept God's call to speak for Him to those around us, we must be cleansed as Isaiah was, confessing our sins and submitting to God's control. Letting God purify us may be painful, but we must be purified so that we can truly represent God, who is pure and holy. Only after receiving His cleansing was Isaiah commissioned as a prophet.

Today, there are many servants of God who neither have an upward vision nor an inward vision, but they have an outward vision, they want to be sent. That is why they become flat tyres, very soon. They can't stand for long, they just burst out, blow out and burn out. It is necessary to have an upward and inward vision before we can act on our outward vision.

If God has called you for full-time ministry obey the call of God. If the Lord has been calling you, don't be afraid, come out, don't worry about what will happen. Take the first step and say 'Here am I Lord'. After that, He will guide you. This experience of Isaiah should be every disciple's experience. The secret of all of Isaiah's power lay in this vision of the temple.

How I wish that you become pregnant with a vision from God. Have you ever observed a pregnant woman? For twenty-four hours of the day she is concerned with what she has conceived. She cannot do what she likes, she cannot eat what she likes, she cannot say I want to jump, swim and play tennis; because everything that she does concerns the baby. Moreover a pregnant lady is waiting to give birth to something new. She cannot be pregnant long beyond the given time. You should endeavour to give birth to something new in the lifetime that God has given to you.

When Robert F Kennedy the ex-president of America was killed, within two hours the message of his assassination spread to the entire world. But when our Lord Jesus Christ was crucified on the cross, even after 2000 years, the message has not reached the whole world. When Neil Armstrong the first man landed on the moon, the message went across the world; but the message that Elijah went up in the whirlwind has not still reached many parts of the world.

Do you have a target, do you have a vision, do you know what God wants you to do? You should have a specific vision. I understand that Coca Cola company has a vision, and they have a target. Every day 800 million Coca Cola cans or bottles are consumed. They had a target that by the end of the year 2000, every single person in this world should have tasted Coca Cola. We have a better Coco Cola, we have the living water Jesus Christ to quench our thirst eternally. Will you pray and fix up a target that before the end of this year every single person in your country should have heard the gospel, the living water.

If you drink Coca Cola you will thirst again but if you drink the living water, Jesus Christ, you will never thirst again.

There Is Hope

I humbly urge you to be an optimist like Isaiah. While still talking about warnings of imminent destruction in the first half of his book, Isaiah draws our attention to the promises of future salvation.

We are living in such a terrible world where millions of people are going hungry or dying every day. The churches in many areas of the world are so dead that they seem to be of little worth. Believers in many areas of the world are being persecuted and martyred because they worship the Lord. Sin, sickness and destruction are on the increase. Yet, somewhere down the road, stand God and His salvation. As believers in Christ, we know for sure that in the end our Lord will be victorious, and if we remain faithful, we will be victorious with Him. The God who promised restoration to Judah and Israel is the same God we are worshipping today and He will restore our broken world.

It is very important to ask the Lord to help you to conceive your vision. Have a target, have a vision know what God wants you to do today. The world is still waiting to hear the good news.

The times of Isaiah were extremes of religious instability. He addressed his message, prophesying for more than sixty years until, according to tradition, he was martyred during the reign of Manasseh, one of the most wicked kings recorded in the Old Testament. Tradition says the prophet was fleeing from the soldiers of the king and hid in a hollow tree, hoping to escape. But the soldiers, knowing he was in the tree, sawed the tree down and the prophet was sawed in half.

Isaiah trusted in the unbreakable Word of God, rested in the unshakable Power of God, and enjoyed the undeniable Peace of God.

Chapter 17

JEREMIAH
A Faithful and Reliable Leader

God said to Jeremiah, *"Arise and go down to the potter's house, and there I will announce My words to you"* (Jer 18:1). God doesn't always speak to us directly through mere words in the very place we are. Sometimes He speaks to us through certain incidents in certain places. Jeremiah had to go to a potter's house to learn a lesson from the Lord. When he went there, he saw the potter working at the wheel. But the pot he was shaping from the clay was marred in his hands; so the potter formed it into another pot, shaping it as seemed best to him (verses 1–4).

Do You Need a Second Chance?
No matter how marred we become, the Master Potter can salvage us. None of us is beyond the restoring hand of the Lord. God is always willing to take our lives that have become misshapen by sin, abuse, and rebellion and reshape them, making us into new vessels of His choice, shaping as it seems best to Him.

We live in a world filled with men and women who are in need of a second chance. Moses had a second chance and became a leader of an entire nation. Peter denied Jesus, but he returned to the Lord, and the Lord transformed him into a pillar of mighty strength in the church. Saul of Tarsus went about murdering and persecuting the very elect of God, but God Himself called Saul apart and gave him a second chance. When Saul responded to God's call and chose to believe that Jesus was the Christ, the Son of God, his life changed.

The heavenly potter transformed the murderous Saul into another vessel, Apostle Paul, of whom the Lord Jesus said, *"... he is a chosen instrument of mine; to bear My name before the Gentiles and kings and the sons of Israel"* (Acts 9:15). This restored vessel became a mighty Christian leader who wrote much of the New Testament and planted the Christian church as far away as Europe.

God has been giving second chances, to people who are in need of a second chance. The potter can lift up the clay that spiraled or went crooked and redeem it. That is what the Bible and life is all about.

Adam first sinned, but Jesus, the second Adam, went about restoring men and women to that which they were meant to be. He straightened a man's withered hand. He released a man from evil spirits. He raised Lazarus from the dead. When Lazarus came forth, bound hand and foot with grave clothes, Jesus commanded the people standing by, *"Unbind him, and let him go"* (John 11:44).

These words, I think, epitomize the work of Jesus: 'Loose him, and let him go.' He loosed people from their misshapen bondage. He dined with sinners. He said to the prostitute, 'Go and sin no more.' Like the potter, He went about giving a second chance to all who asked. The guilty listened to Jesus and began to see them as worthy vessels.

Who among us would not like to erase some image from our past and start all over? That is the kind of second chance God offers each of us, whoever we are, wherever we have fallen. Great or small, rich or poor, powerful or powerless, we are all fashioned out of clay that can become marred along the way. Being the potter that He is, He can take you in His knowing hands, steady your trembling body, and fashion you again into a new work. Why don't you ask Him to do that for you today?

"*Man looks at the outward appearance, but the* LORD *looks at the heart*" (1 Sam 16:7). The potter's eye sees beyond the shapeless lump of clay to the finished, refined vessel. In this character of the potter we see a picture of the omniscient God. Before we ever came into existence, God saw us and chose us. Ephesians 1:4 tells us that He chose us in Him before the creation of the world, to be holy and blameless in His sight.

The potter in a way is a creator with a vision for the future of the scoop of clay he holds in his hands. Whatever condition the clay is in, the potter will make it better. With the eye of hope he sees within the clay the potential for beauty, for strength, for use. Cheap and formless clay is a simple material. Yet the potter has discovered two great truths about it: first, it improves with age; and second, it responds to blending, shaping, drying, firing, and smoothening.

The Process of Preparation

Like the potter tending his clay, God prepares each of us carefully, for the possibilities are so vast. The potter hopes that from a shapeless lump of clay will emerge a vessel of worth; he is willing to endure the slow, tedious process of preparing the clay. Preparation requires patience by which it gains its unusual strength and resilience.

After the clays are pounded into fine particles, they are spread out in fist-sized piles to dry. Then they are carried to tanks dug deep in the ground where they are mixed with water. Sand sinks to the bottom, the water rises, and impurities are removed as the fine liquid slip is screened very wet between two settling tanks. The potter, his wife, and helpers stir this pure clay mixture with a long wooden oar; they ladle and sieve it back and forth for several days before lading it into shallow settling troughs made of hard clay. The clay cannot be hurried.

After a few days of moisture evaporation, the potter scoops the clay slurry from these troughs into bisque pots for further drying to the plastic, workable state. It is hard work and demanding work. It is tedious and persistent process to bring the clay from its mountainside habitat or rocky field to this smooth and workable state. Though retaining its original chemistry, by this point the clay has given up its own identity.

We, like the clay, should respond to the Master Potter as He patiently prepares us for use. We, too need to give up our own identity, entrusting ourselves fully to the Potter's hand.

Long Periods of Waiting

God's wisdom often includes a slow process of preparation and long periods of waiting. Abraham was seventy-five years old, when God first announced that He would make him the father of nations; childless Abraham was to become the father of innumerable descendants. Yet Abraham and Sarah waited twenty-five years more before they had Isaac, their son of promise.

God's preparation of Apostle Paul also involved a long waiting period. After Paul's dramatic conversion, he was eager to begin preaching the gospel, but God had other plans. He sent Paul into the Arabian Desert, where he spent three years; only after these years of quite instruction was Paul ready to begin his active and sometimes stormy ministry.

We do not always understand God's purposes in our lives. We do not always understand the periods of waiting that He gives to us. But seeing ourselves as clay, we can be confident that our lives are in process and that we are in the hands of a wise and knowing Master Craftsman.

Any stone, no matter how tiny to the touch of the finger, must be removed from the clay before the clay can be worked into a potter's bung, ready for further wedging and forming on the wheel. That minute, but stubborn impediment can wreck the finest of pots, if left until the firing stage. A pretty stone may manage to bury itself under the surface and be covered over by other beautiful traits in the clay vessel—until the final testing. In the firing, the tiniest stone manifests itself. It punches a hole in the pot and rejects the glaze on that spot. If it happens on the lip of a vase, the value of the vase is reduced to almost nothing. If it works through the body of a water pot or a pitcher, it makes the vessel useless, fit only for the discard heap or, at best, a dusty shelf somewhere.

Just as the potter is patient and persistent in making sure that each speck of lime or tiny stone has been removed from the clay, God is patient and persistent in rooting out of our lives, any flaws and sins that would mar us and make us unfit later on.

Times of Refreshment and Rest

Rest for the clay is extremely important. During the rest period, the air escapes from the clay and it forms a more even texture. Rest increases the plasticity of the clay so that it will not crack during the forming of the pot.

No potter neglects the rest period for his clay, for he knows the clay's potential is diminished if it does not rest. No potter hurries his clay through this step, for he knows the clay that is sufficiently rested makes the finest pottery.

For a majority of people, rest is a result of tiredness; it is something that follows exhaustion after the completion of something big. On the contrary, rest is the prerequisite for events to come. It is not the end; it is the beginning. It is not the aftermath; it is the preliminary. It is not a result, but a cause.

It was the sixth day on which Adam and Eve were created, and they were commanded to rest on the next day, the day God rested, the seventh day. Yet Adam and Eve had no part in the great creation. Their rest day was actually their first day.

Just as the potter knows that the texture of the clay will become even only after the clay has rested, God requires the 'evening' effect of rest for our existence and our function.

God knows the importance of rest for His creation. Not only did He give us a model to follow by resting on the seventh day of His creation, but He also set down laws and guidelines in the Old Testament that commanded His people—indeed, all of creation—to rest.

"Six days you are to do your work, but on the seventh day you shall cease from labor so that your ox and your donkey may rest, and the son of your female slave, as well as your stranger, may refresh themselves" (Exod 23:12).

"You shall work six days, but on the seventh day you shall rest; even during plowing time and harvest you shall rest" (Exod 34:21). So strong were the commands, that the penalty for not resting was death. *"For six days work may be done, but on the seventh day you shall have a holy day, a sabbath of complete rest to the LORD whoever does any work on it shall be put to death"* (Exod 35:2).

God knows that our lives need the balance of rest and work, quietness and activity. So He explicitly gave us a time to work and a time to rest. Rest and peace of mind are mandatory for the human body.

Not only does the potter rest the clay to ward off the risk of cracking, but he also rests the clay so that it can be used for a higher purpose. As the clay rests for several days, the water gently permeates the particles of the clay, improving the plasticity of the mass. The potter finds that at the end of the rest, the clay is more pliable and ready to be shaped.

We see ourselves in the metaphor. When we quieten our lives long enough to rest and be still before God, then he is able to shape and direct us. During that time of rest, the great physician is able to work in a way He could not while the person's mind and body were distracted by unrest cares and activities.

Deciding the Vessel

Your eyes have seen my unformed substance; And in Your book were all written. The days that were ordained for me, When as yet there was not one of them" (Ps 139:16). No vase or bowl or cup just happens. All vessels have their genesis in the potter's mind. Each vessel is a response to a clear-cut decision that the potter makes before ever setting the wheel in motion.

I have observed some skilled potters working at the wheel, and not once have I seen a potter change his mind in the middle of forming a vessel (for example, deciding to make a slender pitcher and then turning it into a bowl). Even though the clay may have a natural tendency to spread another way and stubbornly resist being raised, the knowing potter cups his strong hands around the clay and with patience and persistence shapes the clay as his will.

In the beginning the potter conceives a clear image in his mind of the shape, the purpose, and the name of the vessel he has chosen to form at that moment on the wheel. Just as the potter decides to make a vase or a cup or a plate from the lump of clay on the wheel, so God decides for what purpose He will make each of His vessels. Our God is not a capricious artist, randomly shaping His pots. Our God is a potter who shapes us with great care and thought. Our God is a potter who knows beauty and harmony, order and symmetry. Our God is a potter who finishes a vessel and asserts, 'This is my vessel; it is very good'.

Forming the Vessel

I will give thanks to You, for I am fearfully and wonderfully made (Ps 139:14). Gradualness is the heart of the transformation process and the key to the human process. The goal of the potter is to bring the completely finished vessel off the wheel in the desired shape, with the proper toughness—a useful vessel, identifiably the work of the master potter but serving those who may not have ever met the potter.

The process of becoming more than we were yesterday, that is, entering the will of God may be as gradual as the generating of the clay form. Hence the pot that is half-formed and gradually moving into its final dimensions is no less in the will of God than the beautiful teapot that has been serving for years.

The potter does not push and pull us aimlessly. Like a mother urging her moist, newborn infant from the womb, the potter uses every rhythm and every muscle, pushing, urging, stretching, exerting much labour to bring each of his vessels into the world individually. The Potter has chosen us as His clay and purified us; He has conditioned us. He has patiently left us to rest undisturbed for a number of days, and just before He positions us on the wheel to centre us, He takes us from our rest and exercise us one more time. He keeps kneading us till we are ready for further progress.

Insufficient kneading will cause the clay to fail at the wheel, and too much kneading is not only a waste of time, but may be damaging as well. Only the experienced potter knows when his clay has had enough, for he knows what he is trying to accomplish by the kneading process.

The clay is kneaded primarily for three reasons: air pockets and bubbles in the clay have to be driven out; if the clay has hardened at all during the resting period, it is necessary to add water and knead the clay until it is the proper consistency for final working; and kneading equalizes the moisture content throughout the clay.

Our Response That Counts

We, like the clay, should respond to the Master Potter as He patiently prepares us for use. We, too need to give up our own identity, entrusting ourselves fully to the Potter's hand. Sometimes we resist this preparation, wanting to avoid the pain that we fear the process may inflict on us. Or we become impatient with the time the Potter takes to prepare us.

In life as well, the quiet ability to follow, to co-operate, may be the inherent key to success. Our response is what counts—our response to the Word of God and our response to what we have been given.

It is our glorious duty then, to accept the cup that we have been given and to use it for all it is worth. Formed by the Master Potter, we need not complain if we have been given a mole or a freckle or a nose unlike our neighbour's. Our complaining about the way the potter has made us is a serious affront.

> Who are you, O man, who answers back to God? The thing molded will not say to the molder, "Why did you make me like this," will it? Or does not the potter have a right over the clay, to make from the same lump one vessel for honorable use and another for common use? (Rom 9:20–21).

The role of the clay is to accept the decision of the potter and to receive his transforming design.

How often we human beings, unlike the silent clay, complain of our limitations and over look the finer qualities we have been given. Have you ever envied someone for being more handsome than you? Have you ever tried to do something because deep inside, you wanted to be like someone else who could do that thing well? Stop looking at others and be yourself. Whatever you are on the road of life, you are in the process of becoming the unique person God wants you to be. All of us are on the way to becoming more unique, and none of us have arrived yet.

If we want to know and do God's will, we must first accept

ourselves and then be receptive to change.   From then on He will continually and gradually change us. His will is revealed in stages, as demonstrated by the generating of the clay pot. Seldom does anyone see all of God's will at once. We see only so far, and we know only so much.

Chapter 18

EZEKIEL
A Leader with Dramatic Vision Encounters

In Ezekiel 37:1–14, we read about an exciting vision of the 'Valley of Dry Bones', was given to Ezekiel to reassure the exiles of Israel; with regard to the restoration of their land and thus to extol the great name of the Lord Almighty among them.

Pivotal, Potential and Prophetic Message from a Graveyard

God teaches valuable lessons from a graveyard too. The epitaphs and art tend to reflect what was going on in society at large and how people responded at the time of death. For almost six centuries before the birth of Christ, God took His prophet Ezekiel to a graveyard in order to teach a very important spiritual lesson. In fact, this lesson was so pivotal that it had the potential to change the outlook of not only the prophet of God, but also of the people of God.

Ezekiel was the son of a priest and a member of Jerusalem's

aristocracy. When he was just 25 years old, the Babylonians besieged Jerusalem and took many of the Jewish people into exile. Ezekiel was one among them. When he arrived in that foreign land, he was moved by the pathetic physical, emotional, and spiritual condition of his fellow Jews. Overwhelmed by what he saw he merely sat still for seven days (Ezek 3:15). It was there that he received his call to be a prophet in Babylon.

Ezekiel's call as a prophet began with a dramatic encounter with the Lord that left him astounded and speechless (Ezek 1:26–28). Many a time, God calls people for special tasks through such encounters. Even Daniel received his gift of prophecy while he was a slave in Babylon.

Nine years after Ezekiel's exile he received the word that his wife had passed away in Jerusalem. The following year, the exiles were given the news that Jerusalem itself had been completely destroyed by the Babylonians. Naturally, dejection, discouragement, helplessness and hopelessness was the wide spread mood among the exiles at that time.

During that time of exile, the word of the Lord came to Ezekiel and he began to prophesy. His message from the Lord influenced the people to interpret their sufferings as the judgement from God; but it was a message of hope and future restoration after judgement.

However, Ezekiel was given no assurance that his words would make any difference to his listeners. The Lord told him forthrightly that they were a hard–hearted group of people who would not listen to him because they were unwilling even to listen to the Lord (Ezek 3:7). For the most part, they were 'impudent and stubborn children' (Ezek 2:3–4). But the Lord's purpose was no longer to rescue His people from judgement. Instead He only wanted to make sure that events were interpreted from His perspective now that judgement was under way. God told him,

"Son of man, I am sending you to the sons of Israel, to a rebellious people . . . who are stubborn and obstinate . . . ; neither fear them nor fear their words; though thistles and thorns are with you and you sit on scorpions, neither fear their words nor be dismayed at their presence for they are a rebellious house. But you shall speak My words to them whether they listen or not . . ." (Ezek 2:3–7).

Ezekiel responded faithfully to the Lord even amidst such a difficult, discouraging and depressing situation.

God is in search of people who are wholly committed to Him, faithful, living in victory over conscious sin, determined to carry the cross each day, dying to self in each situation, whose tongues are under the control of the Holy Spirit, who do not seek the honour of any human being, who hate materialism, who have dedicated themselves for the cause of Christ, with a love and passion for perishing souls, who have no complaints whatsoever against anyone, giving thanks in all circumstances and who live in unity with each other and thus represent Christ in an unbelieving world.

After being away from their homeland, the Israelites felt like dry bones and seemed to have lost all their hopes of returning. But God affirmed through Ezekiel that He would bring them back to Jerusalem (Ezek 37:11–12). Ezekiel's ministry was twofold, to remind the exiles of their sins and to encourage them concerning God's future blessings. Ezekiel says, *The hand of the LORD was upon me, and He brought me out by the Spirit of the LORD and set me down in the middle of the valley; and it was full of bones* (verse 1).

There is so much we can learn from this verse and from the way the Lord dealt with Ezekiel. We need to consider every word of the Bible in its context and understand the original meaning. Even every punctuation mark counts and with the help of the Holy Spirit of God, we need to analyse the hidden meaning behind every word and every sentence of the inspired Word of God.

Ezekiel responded faithfully to the call of God. He did not seek, as many of us today do, a five–star ministry accompanied by pomp and popularity for comfort, money and security. Such a great man of God like Ezekiel was willing to even go to a graveyard and preach the Word.

Ezekiel's Unconditional Obedience to the Call of God

Let us analyse how it was possible for Ezekiel to be obedient to the call of God even to go down to the valley and preach to the dry bones: The very first word that I want to consider in the above verse Ezekiel 37:1, is the word 'out'.

Very often when God wants to speak to us something specifically or teach us a lesson, He takes us out of our dwelling places, or takes us into new life situations. God took Jeremiah *out* of his house to an ordinary, illiterate potter's house in a village to teach him a lesson that there is a second chance. There is definitely a way out of the difficult situation that you are in right now. No matter how marred your life has become, the master potter can salvage your life situation. You are not beyond the restoring hand of the Lord. God is always willing to take control of your life that has become misshapen by sin, abuse, and rebellion and reshape it, making you to be a new vessel of His choosing, shaping as it seems best to Him.

We live in a world filled with men and women who are in need of a second chance. Moses had a second chance and became a leader of an entire nation. Peter denied Jesus, but he returned to the Lord, and the Lord transformed him into a pillar of mighty strength in the church. Saul of Tarsus went about murdering and persecuting the very elect of God, but God Himself called Saul apart and gave him a second chance. When Saul responded to God's call and chose to believe that Jesus was the Christ, the Son of God, his life changed.

The heavenly potter transformed the murderous Saul into

another vessel, Apostle Paul, of whom the Lord Jesus said, *". . . he is a chosen instrument of Mine; to bear My name before the Gentiles and kings and the sons of Israel"* (Acts 9:15). This restored vessel became a mighty Christian leader who wrote much of the New Testament and planted the Christian church as far away as Europe.

God has been giving second chances, to people who are in need of that. The potter can lift up the clay that spiraled or went crooked and redeem it. That is what the Bible and life is all about.

God brought David *out* of the cattle field to the battlefield. David was willing for this move in his life. David's father Jesse gave him a very simple ordinary job of carrying some foodstuff to his brothers in the battlefield. David never knew what was on the other side and that he was going to win the greatest battle ever in the history of Israel by killing Goliath. David had a constant communion with his heavenly father in the cattle field but he was also obedient to his earthly father. Young people should take note that obedience to your parents can bring you great blessings.

As we are learning about the word 'out', we also learn that behind every physical move there is a spiritual reason in the life of every believer in Christ. The Lord will not let anything happen in your life without any purpose. Hence, you should never resist any move that you come across in your life even though it may look very insignificant or may not be convenient or conducive for you at that particular point of time. Always keep yourself open to any change or move in your life trusting that the Lord will not allow anything wrong to happen in your life. Pray that the Lord should help you get *out* of your rigidity and stubbornness and a bureaucratic attitude.

God brought Joseph *out* of his house. He too was obedient to his father in the task given to him to meet his brothers. God lifted up Joseph from the pit and elevated him from the prison to the palace as the Prime Minister of Egypt—a position he later used to save his family from famine and to keep the dream of God's people alive. If this ordinary shepherd boy had not obeyed the call to move *out*, he would not have become the Prime Minister of a great nation like Egypt, which was even a foreign land to him.

God called Elijah *out* to go to the riverside to hide himself. In the background to this story we see that Elijah had prophesied that, it would not rain for three and a half years. King Ahab was angry and commanded his soldiers to bring Elijah to him. So the soldiers were searching for Elijah. Ahab and Jezebel had no regard for the prophets of God. They had already put most of them to death and would not have hesitated to kill Elijah. Elijah needed a place to hide himself; he was in a crisis at that time when the word of the Lord came to him, *"Go away from here and turn eastward, and hide yourself by the brook . . . and I have commanded the ravens to provide for you there"* (1 Kings 17:3).

When God asked Elijah to go to the brook Cherith, God was demanding something strange. Soldiers were searching for Elijah, and God told him to hide himself by the side of a river. It did not seem a wise thing to do.

It is obvious that no one can hide in a public place like the river. But Elijah never questioned God, because he knew his God would never make a mistake. Sometimes our disobedience is because we do not fully trust God. While I was analysing this passage, I found that it was not raining and there was no water in the river and no one would come to the river to fetch water. If I were in Elijah's place, probably I would have asked, 'Lord, why don't you show me a cave to hide?'

Do you know, why God did not show a cave for Elijah to hide? It is because He knew all the soldiers would be searching for him in the caves. No one would ever think that anyone would go and hide near the river. Though according to human reasoning one would not correlate this with the idea of hiding near the river, God knows what is best in a given situation.

It is better not to reason with your intelligence when God tells you to move *out*, just obey. He is an omniscient God. Elijah obeyed and went. Before even Elijah could start wondering how he was going to live in that desolate spot by the brook Cherith, God said, *"It shall be that you shall drink of the brook, and I have commanded the ravens to provide for you there"* (1 Kings 17:4). Where God guides, He provides.

All of God's promises are certain, sufficient and conditional. God promised food and drink, absolutely sufficient for the sustenance of His servant. It was a conditional promise to the extent and effect, 'If you will, I will'.

The second word that I want to consider in the chosen passage in Ezekiel 37:1–14, is the word 'there'. Ezekiel said,

> The hand of the LORD was on me *there*, and He said to me, "Get up, go *out* to the plain, and I will speak to you. So I got up and went *out* to the plain; and behold, the glory of the LORD was standing *there*, like the glory which I saw by the river Chebar, and I fell on my face (Ezek 3:22–23).

Even in the Lord's dealing with Elijah, I would like to draw your attention to the most important word 'there', in 1 Kings 17:4. What God told Elijah was, that if he wanted the water and food he must go there—into the place of God's choice. Are you 'there', in the place of God's will for you? For 'there' is the place of God's provision. When Moses asked God to show His glory, God told him, *"Behold there is a place by Me, and you shall stand there on the rock"* (Exod 33:18–21).

It is not what you have, but *where you are* that matters to God. You may have a great potential and may do great exploits for God, but if you are not *there* where God wants you to be, God will not accept you or approve your ministry.

So far we have been analysing how it was possible for Ezekiel to be obedient to the call of God going down to the valley and preaching to the dry bones. We have seen in detail two important words (out and there) that influenced him in obeying the call of God in his life.

The third word that I want to consider in the chosen passage is the word 'hand' *The hand of the LORD was upon me . . .* (Ezek 37:1). The word used for 'hand' in Hebrew language is *yad* (yawd), which indicates 'power', 'means' or direction. This means that the power of God was upon Ezekiel and God directed him in all his ways.

As I travel around the world, I see one common thing among the believers and that is, they are seeking for power and anointing from God. Indeed, it is very essential for you to have the anointing, but along with that you also need the direction from God through the Word of God. The most essential need is to live a holy life. Mere anointing cannot substitute for personal holiness. Without holiness no one will see the Lord . . . . What good will it be for a man if he gains the whole world, yet forfeits his soul? Or what can a man give in exchange for his soul? (Heb 12:14b; Matt 16:26). Holiness means being separated from sin and fully dedicated to God.

It is good to thirst after the Holy Spirit's anointing and His spiritual gifts, but don't stop there. You need to thirst after righteousness and pursue holiness. Holiness is always given. It is given by grace and received through faith. But it is given only if the person is in proximity to the Holy God.

Holiness means clean and blameless walking with the feet; clean and blameless talking with the tongue; and clean and blameless thinking with the mind, every minute detail of life under the scrutiny of the Holy Spirit of God. When you live a holy life, people can see the divine presence of God in you.

Holy Desires, Clean Passions, Pure Thoughts

Paul writes, 'I pray God your whole spirit and soul and body be preserved blameless unto the coming of our Lord Jesus Christ' (1 Thess 5:23). Sanctification is the work of God through the Holy Spirit that affects the entire nature of man. The body has its own appetites and cravings, which are capable of being perverted through indulgence. When your spirit is brought into a right relationship with God it becomes the controlling force in your life. As you allow the Spirit of God to work in you, you will find that your desires become holy, your passions clean, your thoughts pure, and that your delight will be in fulfilling the will of the Lord. You need to stop focusing on the wrong desires of your heart and the improper appetites of your body and maintain contact with God on a day-to-day regular basis.

In the Book of Ezekiel 11:1–23, God revealed to Ezekiel that when His temple becomes filled with corruption and idolatry His glory must go because God is holy and pure. He cannot co-exist with evil in the inner sanctuary, whether that sanctuary is in a physical temple as in Ezekiel's time or the church today.

If you are a believer in Christ, and if you deliberately yield or open your heart to spiritual darkness, then, although you may have the anointing, you have allowed entry points for bondage or control in your life. These things will cause God's glory to depart from you.

When your mind is filled with the all-pervasive presence of God, it will not only be cleansed from defilement but it will begin to reflect the mind of God. You will find yourself not only meditating on God but also thinking His thoughts and filled with His wisdom and knowledge.

Holiness may not be popular, but it is powerful. Without it you shall see neither God nor a revelation of His glory. You claim to be headed toward a holy heaven to spend eternity in the presence of a holy God. Do you realize that 'Our God is a consuming fire?' (Isa 33:14).

You need to become aware that holiness is not an attitude of God; it is an attribute of God, an energy so forceful that He cannot help repulsing anything that is inconsistent with the divine nature. To live a holy life should not only be the deep desire of your heart but a pleasing attribute of your life.

We have clearly seen above that simple anointing is not enough but you need to live a holy life and receive direction from God and God's Word. There were great men of God who had the *anointing* but lost the sense of *direction* and thus became failures.

For example, Saul was a prophet and he was an *anointed* man of God, but did not receive *direction* from God or rather disobeyed the direction that was given to him by God. God took away His loving kindness from Saul (1 Chr 17:13).

Saul said to Samuel, 'God has departed from me and answers me no more.' *Now the Spirit of the LORD departed from Saul* (1 Sam 16:14). The prophet Samuel said to Saul, "*As you did not obey the LORD and did not execute His fierce wrath on Amalek, so the LORD has done this thing to you this day*" (1 Sam 28:18).

Saul himself confesses his sin by saying, "*I have sinned . . . because I feared the people and listened to their voice*" (1 Sam 15:24). Saul died for his trespasses (1 Chr 10:13–14). In fact he committed suicide. Is it possible for an anointed man of God like Saul to commit suicide? Yes it is possible when there is no *direction* from God.

The Bible says, "*Now then let the fear of the LORD be upon you; be very careful what you do, for the LORD our God will have no part in unrighteousness, or partiality, or the taking of a bribe*" (2 Chr 19:7).

Is it possible for a spirit-filled man like David to become an adulterer and a murderer? Yes it is possible when there is no *direction* from God.

The fourth word that I want to consider in the chosen passage in Ezekiel 37:1, is the word 'He'. The word 'He' brings glory and honour to God. Great servants of God in the Bible used the word 'He' instead of the word 'I' which only gives an impression of self-elevation. I believe that there is no word called 'I' in the dictionary of a believer in Christ.

Ezekiel said, *He brought me out . . . . He caused me to pass* (Ezek 37:1–2).

The Psalmist says, *He makes me lie down in green pastures; He leads me beside quiet waters* (Ps 23:2).

The fifth word that I want to consider in the chosen passage in Ezekiel 37:1, is the word 'Spirit'. The word 'Spirit' in Hebrew is *Ruwach* (rooakh) which primarily means 'to blow' or 'to breathe'. When the wind blows, you cannot see it but can feel it; likewise, though you cannot see the Holy Spirit of God, you can definitely feel the moving of His Spirit in your life. The word 'Ruwach', also has an implied meaning and that is 'to smell' or 'to perceive' or 'to receive a quick understanding or a sensible exaltation'.

Before it rains, we can predict that there would be rain right from the very smell of the wind. In the same way, we can perceive the Holy Spirit of God and He will give us wisdom and direction. The power of God, the direction from God and the understanding of the Holy Spirit of God helped Ezekiel to be obedient to the call of God. I would humbly urge my readers to seek for these three spiritual strengths that Ezekiel had.

We very clearly see in Ezekiel 37:1, that the triune God was involved in the call that Ezekiel received. The hand of the Lord (Son of God) was upon him, He (Father) brought him out by the Spirit(Holy Spirit). It is amazing to realize the fact that Father,

Son, and the Holy Spirit are collectively involved in our day-to-day life.

In the very first chapter of Ezekiel God revealed Himself in all His three potentialities. Ezekiel was then among the captives who had been carried way with Jeconiah, and had his dwelling near the river Chebar, Chaborus, or Aboras, a river of Mesopotamia, which falls into the Euphrates a little above Thapsacus, after having run through Mesopotamia from east to west.

In verse 4 of chapter 1 of the Book of Ezekiel, you see that there is a fire as well, a light that is brighter than the sun. This fire represents the omnipotence of God. There, in the midst of that whirlwind, there is great fire—why? Because our God is a consuming fire, our God is light!

In verse 17, the wheels that can move in all the four directions describe the omnipresence of God in apocalyptic terms.

Verse 18 tells us that those wheels were full of eyes. This speaks to us of God's omniscience, the all-seeing nature of God. Even though the children of Israel were in Babylonia, a faraway country, God could still see what they were doing. His eyes are in every place, beholding the evil and good. He is a powerful and a glorious God, constantly moving and working in His world.

Under the power of God Ezekiel was directed through the Spirit of God, in order to understand the then situation of the people of Israel. Despite the fact that the Babylonians had invaded Judah twice, fulfilling the warnings of the prophet Jeremiah, the exiles still didn't understand either why God had allowed these events to happen or why they had been deported to Babylon. They failed to grasp the fact that their nation's troubles were the result of their idolatry and other sins against the Lord.

In many ways, Ezekiel was used by God to make this truth clear to the people over a period of at least 20 years. But the people remained willfully blind to their condition. Their hardness of heart is the core to explain why the phrase, 'You (or they) shall know that I am the Lord', is repeated more than sixty times in the Book of Ezekiel.

The impending judgement foreseen in Ezekiel's vision has a message for us today. It demonstrates that God shows mercy, but at the same time He looks for repentance. Those who resist Him and remain committed to sin will encounter His wrath, but those who feel sorry and repent over their own sins and the sins of their own people will know His comfort and forgiveness (compare James 4:8–10).

It is easier just to 'go along and get along', especially when it seems as if everyone else is in agreement. It can be terribly hard to stand against the crowd. Yet Scripture shows that it is better when God's people honour His truth rather than the shifting winds of public opinion.

Ezekiel was a desperate man among desperate people. He longed for people to see what God had planned for them, and he was willing to do whatever God told him to do in order to see it. Some Christians are actually afraid of what God may do if they give Him control. They fear the changes He may bring about.

Can These Bones Live?

And set me down in the middle of the valley; and it was full of bones (Ezek 37:1). God put him in the middle of dead people who were reduced to mere bones. Ezekiel did not resist the move. Without being choosy he was readily available to go anywhere God wanted him to go. He says, 'I saw a great many bones on the floor of the valley, bones that were very dry' (verse2).

The dry bones are a picture of the Jews in captivity scattered and dead spiritually. The Lord asked him, 'Son of man, can these bones live?' Ezekiel replied, 'O sovereign Lord, you alone know.' Peter said,

'Lord you know all things . . .' (John 21:17). The disciples said to Jesus, 'Now we can see that you know all things . . .' (John 16:30).

What was God really saying to Ezekiel in that valley of dry, sun bleached bones? It was to ascertain that God is always in control—even of dry bones. There is nothing useless for God. Don't ever think that 'it is finished' and the story is over. God can create a new story out of your old story and that can become your history.

Do you want to know about these dry bones? Evidently there had been a battle fought in this valley many years before, and many people were killed. Their bones lay scattered about in the sand, bleached white, so dry and parched that even a dog would not pick one up. All the moisture and marrow had gone out of them over the years and become very dry.

Like these dry bones, do you find yourself helpless, hopeless and without Christ in this world? (Eph 2:12). God is at hand to help you. When God asked whether these bones could live, probably he meant whether men with blood, breath and bodies could stand where these bones lay in the dust?

This is the whole issue of Scripture: 'Can the Ethiopian change his skin or the leopard his spots? Can we do good that are accustomed to do evil?' (Jer 13:23). Can the fragrance of the rose issue forth from the sepulchre? Can the cursing tongue praise the Lord? Can hate be turned to love and pride and arrogance to humility.

Ezekiel gave only one answer, 'O Lord God, Thou knowest'. The preacher certainly has no power to accomplish such a miracle. The bones themselves have no power to raise themselves. In the same manner, a dead sinner has no more power to give himself spiritual life than a dead body can raise itself. Jesus said, *No man can come to me except the Father which hath sent me draw him* (John 6:44). No man will move toward God until God moves him. *Thy people shall be willing in the day of thy power* . . . (Ps 110:3). He can transform your discouragement into hope, depression into joy, and spiritual compromise into renewed commitment to him. These dry bones can live!

I want to share a wonderful miracle that took place in one of my ministerial trips to one of the sensitive nations. I was taken to the intense care unit ward of a hospital to pray for a man who was in coma for several days surviving only by a life support system. The doctors attending to him had given up all hope and had even prepared a place in the mortuary. Since the doctor had planned to take him off the life support system that afternoon around 2 p.m., the relatives were summoned to see the man before that. It was 12:30 that afternoon when I arrived in the hospital. I saw the man's wife bitterly and helplessly crying for she knew in a couple of hours when he would be removed from the life support system he would be a dead man.

I started comforting the woman by saying that there was only one way to get life back to her husband and that is by putting her trust in the Lord Jesus. She was immediately willing to do so and prayed the sinner's prayer and accepted Jesus in her heart as her Saviour and Lord. Then I told her, 'Madam, now that you are a child of God, you are going to pray for your husband, I am going to help you to do that'. I clearly reiterated to her that in the name of Jesus, there is a possibility that God could bring him back to life. Then we went near the man's bed and I put her hand on his body and put my hand over her hand and I told her to join with me and we said together, 'In the name of Jesus!' That is all. The man started to breathe and his body moved up and down violently. Suddenly life came into him. Jesus turned the hopeless situation into one of hope and joy.

In one hour's time they shifted him to the ordinary ward from the Intensive Care Unit. The situation turned humorous when the nurses attending on him in the afternoon shift could not find his body in the mortuary, as they knew very well about this man's predicament. Instead, they found him very well seated in bed in the ordinary ward and supposed that it was his ghost.

I was preaching in the same place that evening. After I preached, I gave an altar call for people to come for prayer and there was a man standing in the corner with a child in his hands. I asked this man, 'Sir, what can I do for you?' He said, 'Sir, I am the doctor who was taking care of that patient in the hospital for whom you came and prayed. As a doctor I knew for sure that there was no life left in him. Medically and clinically there was absolutely no possibility that he could ever come back to life. But, now I know that it is because of the living God, Jesus that he came back to life.' Then I asked him, 'Doctor I am happy to hear that, now tell me what it is that you want me to pray for?' He was carrying a child in his hand and he said, 'Sir, my child has a chronic disease. If your Jesus could heal and bring back to life that man who was dead, then I believe Jesus can heal my child too'. I admired his great faith and I prayed for his sick child.

If you too would put your trust in Jesus and receive Him as your Saviour and Lord, He will do miracles in your life. If you believe in the recreating power of God, He can recreate that which needs to be recreated in your life.

Ezekiel preached to the dry bones with faith that if God wanted them to come to life then they would definitely come to life. Without such obedient faith Moses never would have gone back to Egypt, Abraham never would have ascended to Moriah, the priests carrying the ark never would have stepped into the Jordan River expecting it to part, and without it you will never experience what God can do in you and with you.

Turn Loose or Relinquish Your Past

Life comes from God, not from the past or from favourable circumstances. Have the battles of your past turned your life into a valley of dry bones? Here is the good news: God through Jesus Christ can bring you back to life. Will you let him do that?

We should not become captives of the past. Destroy the chains of failure that bury you to the past. The real challenge to a life of faith is relinquishing the past. Giving in to the past enslaves one to the past that does not allow living in the present because the past controls one's mind, emotions and understanding. It is true that the past has produced some negative consequences, but with the help of the Lord, we must be able to deal positively with what had happened and now become overcomers.

Completely disillusioned, the Jews expressed their feelings that there is nothing God can do to help them. They felt that they would never recover. Perhaps they thought if God couldn't help them when Jerusalem fell and the temple was destroyed, and the last king of Israel imprisoned, in what way was He going to help them in this situation? From their human perspective, it was an impossible situation.

The Lord said to him, *"Son of man, these bones are the whole house of Israel; behold, they say, 'Our bones are dried up, and our hope has perished. We are completely cut off"* (Ezek 37:11). God does not want His people, not one of them to be like a lost dry bone. He wants us to have life. Jesus says, 'I have come that you may have life and have it abundantly.' As he promised the people of Israel, he would look for the sheep to bring back to His fold to life. We need to hear the Word of God and have life breathed back into our souls (Ezek 34:11–12).

You see, it wasn't Ezekiel that raised those dry bones to life; it was the power of God, which comes from the speaking and hearing of His Word. It wasn't the preacher that I listened to that brought life into my heart, but it was the power of God. As Paul wrote to the Romans, consequently, faith comes from hearing the message, and the message is heard through the word of Christ (Rom 10:17).

Despair into Hope, Death into Life

God fulfils His promise to the prophet that He will look for His lost people and restore them to a right relationship with Him. It is a promise we can take hold of in our day-to-day situations.

What God did in the cemetery that day, was strong proof that God can turn carnality into spirituality, despair into hope and death into life. But only He can do it. In Ezekiel 37 God does it all. He sent Ezekiel, and gave him the words to speak and caused the bones to live.

The quickening work of the Holy Spirit is the only one, which brings dead sinners to Christ. He must first regenerate the dead heart. In so doing, the sinner will then 'hear', 'see' and 'receive', Christ in truth. Ezekiel says, 'So I prophesied as He commanded me, and the breath came into them, and they lived, and stood upon their feet, an exceeding army' (Ezek 37:10). Such a work of the Spirit in the heart is essential to any saving work of God in the sinner. Otherwise, our ministry will be nothing more than the shaking and rattling of dead bones, covered with lifeless flesh. This is the greatest and the most remarkable of all changes that a man can undergo—to be brought out of the grave of spiritual death and made to rejoice in the light and liberty of spiritual life.

Ezekiel was now surrounded, not by bones but by human corpses. The next step was that God told Ezekiel to prophesy to the breath, or wind, or spirit (same word in Hebrew) to come into the dead. And just as God breathed the breath of life into the first human, He caused these to come to life by His breath. It was a beautiful and compelling display of the fact that spiritual life, and physical life, comes from God. He is the giver of life.

Revival Breaks

The first thing that happened was a sound of rattling and clicking like the tide going out over a million pebbles as the bones started snapping back together again. The next thing that happened was thousands of re-assembled skeletons putting on bodies. And then the colour came back to cheeks, and the spark to the eyes and the breath of life to the lungs (Ezek 37:7) This is beyond curiosity or entertainment. And just so the meaning is not lost, the vision is interpreted.

The bones are the nation, the dream, and the idea of Israel, God's chosen people and even though they appear to be dry, dusty and dead, God can breathe life into them and they be restored to life. There is a cause to hope, when hope seems hopeless. The dream will not die. And as long as there is hope, there is life.

There was a noise

The noise or the sound of rattling represents restoration and renewal. The people were in a state of spiritual stagnation. They felt spiritually and emotionally dry, and they doubted that anything would or could be done about it. It was as if they were dead to any new hope or spiritual vitality. But they did recognize their spiritual condition and the need for renewal.

Obviously, one does not attempt to repair something if it is not believed to be broken. You cannot be ready for a new work of God in your life, until you are willing to acknowledge the fact that you have a name, that you are alive, but you are dead (Rev 3:1). When do we stand in the need of prayer for a spiritual renewal? It is when we have something against our brother or sister and have not gone to them to make it right. We cannot be right with God and wrong with our fellow beings at the same time. God teaches about the possibility of spiritual renewal among God's people even when circumstances seem least promising.

There was a shaking

First comes the renewal (noise), after renewal comes the shaking and after shaking comes the revival. . . . *The bones came together, bone to its bone* (Ezek 37:7). This cannot happen without a shaking. When there is a shaking, there is oneness and unity. Even on the Day of Pentecost all the people were together when there was a noise and a shaking of the place (Acts 2:1). Paul exhorts us, not to be conformed to this world, but to be transformed by the renewing of our mind, that we may prove what the will of God is, that which is good and acceptable and perfect (Rom 12:2).

After shaking comes the revival. The word 'revival' comes from the word 'revive' meaning to regenerate or re-strengthen. God explains His concept of revival in the Book of Ezekiel. It involves: Separation from the world; Cleansing from filthiness and idols; A new heart and spirit; An outpouring of the Holy Spirit leading people to listen and obey the Lord; A personal relationship with God; And a blessed fulfilment of God's Word and His purpose in our lives (Ezek 36:24–29).

John, the Baptist paid a price for the revival at that time. He, from childhood was separated and was prepared. He even died for it, and his whole life was a sacrifice. We are called to be similarly devoted to the Lord and to His purpose in our lives.

We need revival, not revivals. When Christians have a spirit of prayer, we should expect revival. When pastors make it their goal, we should expect revival. When Christians are willing to sacrifice, then we should expect revival. If we don't experience revival, it's because we haven't asked for it. Revival always come as a result of devoted prayer.

The Lord commanded Ezekiel to preach upon those bones and say to them, *"O dry bones hear the word of the LORD"* (Ezek 37:4).

I suppose if one wanted dry, dead bones to live, the very last thing one would do is to preach to them. But this is God's way and God's command, 'Preach the word of the Lord to them' (1 Cor 1:21; Rom 1:16, 10:13–17; James 1:18). This is because the Word of God is the Word of life. Christ is the Word of God and one cannot separate the Word incarnate from the Word written and spoken.

'So I preached as I was commanded.' Wouldn't there be a great revival if all preachers would forget the programmes, the entertainments, the methods and the eloquence and preach the Word of God as they are commanded!

'There was a noise' or a rattling! If the true Word of God is preached in the power of God's Spirit, there will be a stir of interest, of life, of joy, of faith. But there will also be the stir of opposition, persecution, and trouble.

O breath, and breathe upon these slain that they may live (Ezek 37:9). Ezekiel did more than just preach; he prayed to the Spirit of the Lord to give life (John 3:5–8). Doctrines and facts (as true as they are) do not save nor give life. Jesus said, *I am the resurrection and the life; he that believeth in me, though he were dead, yet shall he live* (John 11:25). So it is Jesus who gives us eternal life.

There was no life

Even though they were shaking, they were lifeless. The Lord said, 'Call breath to fill the dry bones' (Ezek 37:8–9). Some people have just received a shaking, but are not in the fullness of the Holy Spirit of God. If you are not filled with Holy Spirit, then you are dry.

When the bones came together they were stiff, dead and flat and they could not move. But when the spirit came they stood up. Soldiers were ready for the fight! They were no more dry but alive (Ezek 37:10). Such experiences of dry bones coming to life, are not just sparks in the night, soon extinguished; but they are signs of the dawn which is coming and will finally banish the darkness forever. The dynamic vision of Ezekiel can be yours too! Claim it now!

Chapter 19

DANIEL
An Uncompromising Leader with an Excellent Spirit

God raised up a young man named Daniel. He was about seventeen years old when he had been captured and taken to a foreign land to serve a worldly king. God's movement most often begins with young people. On the Day of Pentecost, the disciples who experienced the anointing of the Holy Spirit were around thirty-three years. Joseph was 30 when he came to power; Daniel was 30 when he became the Prime Minister of Babylon. Ezekiel was 30 when he began to prophesy. Jesus was 30 when He entered into the public ministry. I was 27 when I started off with full-time ministry. God calls many people while they are young to be involved in a powerful ministry.

Daniel exhibited a remarkable servant spirit and an amazing endurance to unfair treatment, giving us a living example of how to respond when one suffers wrong for doing right. James Russell Lowell said, *Truth forever on the scaffold, wrong forever on the throne.* It is important to remember that showing patience while suffering for Christ finds favour with the Lord. Many of us might have faced various situations of suffering for doing right. We need to wait patiently to see the hand of the Lord working miracles for us. If we are not 'patient', we will turn out to be 'patients'.

King Nebuchadnezzar wanted to select some young people to serve in his palace (Dan 1:3–7). So he ordered Ashpenaz, the chief of his officials to bring in some of the sons of Israel, including some of the royal family and of the nobles, youths in whom was no defect, who were good looking, showing intelligence in every branch of wisdom, endowed with understanding, and discerning knowledge, and who had ability for serving in the king's court; and he instructed him to teach them the literature and language of the Chaldeans. If they needed people who are without blemish and good looking, gifted in all wisdom, possessing knowledge and sound understanding, how much more would be expected of those who are needed for God's kingdom.

We need to be well equipped for the furtherance of God's kingdom. Today the media has been captured by the devil. The Christians are still lagging behind in adapting the latest media technologies and the needed infra structure including the Internet in the spread of the gospel.

An Uncompromising Attitude

The commander of the officials assigned different names to Daniel and his friends. Names were extremely important in biblical times, for they conveyed something of a person's identity. Thus God sometimes gave a person a new name to indicate a changed life. However, the names the commander of the officials assigned to Daniel and his friends were the names of Babylonian gods. The name Belteshazzar given to Daniel has been taken from 'Bel', a title for the Babylonian god Marduk (verse 7).

He could only change their names, but not their faith:

> But Daniel made up his mind that he would not defile himself
> with the king's choice food or with the wine which he drank; so
> he sought permission from the commander of the officials that
> he might not defile himself (verse 8).

Daniel did not want to take the delicacies or wine from the table of the king for he knew that partaking in them could defile his body, the temple of God. As much as we take care of our spirits, we need to take care of our bodies too. Daniel was not a compromiser, but an overcomer.

We understand that even Paul was determined not to be a compromiser from his statement, we live, we move and we exist in Christ (Acts 17:28). When we are born again, the risen Lord Jesus becomes the source of our Christian life; in Him we are positioned and in Whom we live, move and exist. Paul further goes on to say that if any man is in Christ, he is a new creature; the old things have passed away; behold all things have become new (2 Cor 5:17).

When Daniel was brought to Babylon, he was just about sixteen or seventeen years old and at that tender age, he decided to take a firm stand for the Lord in a foreign land.

Throughout the history of the church, God has raised up individuals at different times through which great movements have begun. God can always do tremendous things through just one person, who has decided not to be a compromiser, but to be an overcomer whole-heartedly. The area of Daniel's test was related to food and drinks, but he took note of God's commandment regarding the same. From the beginning, Daniel's integrity was his strength. He had such an explicit blameless character that his enemies had to create a new law against praying to God in order to find fault to accuse him.

Daniel was strongly determined that he will not defile himself with the things of this world. Our decision determines our destiny.

We need to make decisions every day not to allow our minds to be corrupted or our bodies to be defiled. We need to develop a strong determination to live a holy life. What is meant by determination? It is de-termination of what we have been doing. If we have been living an unclean life, then we must de-terminate from it towards living a·clean life.

As you read this book, may I urge you to make a strong decision not to corrupt your body or mind; not to look at the things which corrupt; not to read the filthy writings and not to watch the sensual, corrupt programmes in the television that do not edify our intellect or our spirit.

Temptation is all around us. Our consumer-oriented society advocates greed and pride. The cinema posters and advertisements glorify rebellion, drug abuse and illegitimate sex. In Daniel's life we see that he made a determined choice. He requested the head of the eunuchs to provide only the vegetables and water and nothing else from the table of the king. But the commander was afraid that the king would be angry with him. Daniel didn't give up. He asked the commander to watch over him and his friends and he was sure that they would not differ in their appearances from others even if they feed only on the vegetables. In Daniel 1:9, we read that God had brought Daniel into favour and good will of the chief. It is unmistakably true that when we glorify Him through a holy life, He will definitely put us in favour with the authorities. Holiness can lift us to the heights. God will prosper us if we live a holy life.

Daniel was the chief among the three top commissioners of the kingdom. Perhaps, Daniel's pure and noble life of dedication and integrity brought him to this position, where he continued to distinguish himself among the commissioners and satraps because he possessed an extraordinary spirit (Dan 6:3). In the days gone by, King Darius was aware of the gracious and noble statesman—like qualities of Daniel.

Every detail in the life of Daniel confirmed him as a faithful servant and a true friend. More than all these qualities, the king saw in him 'an excellent spirit'. Three times in the Book of Daniel, God calls him 'The Beloved'. In the Book of Ezekiel, the Lord names three great men and Daniel is one among them (Noah and Job follow). So we see here God Himself is testifying about Daniel.

The Danger That Threatened Daniel

The king was looking for a faithful man to be his Prime Minister and he was so impressed with Daniel that he decided to appoint him over the entire kingdom, second to none except the king (Dan 6:13). This promotion brought real trouble to Daniel, because the other commissioners and officers were filled with jealousy, envy and fear.

It is the Lord who gives prosperity and promotions to those who are faithful to Him. But people are definitely going to be jealous about it. How are we fighting it out in our secular lives? When we live a humble, honest and holy life, enemies are sure to crop up against us. People will definitely throw stones at the tree that bears fruit. God has chosen and appointed us to bear fruit (John 15:16).

We shall never become victims of their jealousy, but victors if we remain faithful to the Lord. The Holy Spirit will take control of us. Daniel was a Spirit-filled man. Not only were they jealous, but they were also gripped with the fear that Daniel would not tolerate any corruption or indiscipline, in administering the affairs of the empire. They found themselves in a dangerous position. So, they wanted somehow to get rid of Daniel. Sometimes this may happen to you in your school, college, or in your work place. This often takes place in the official hierarchy where you are expected to compromise with them or to get out of their sight. Sometimes they may even give false reports against you to get rid of you. How do you react in such situations? I know that this is one of the biggest problems we are facing in this sin-sick, corrupt, adulterated, wicked world. But in all these situations, are we faithful to our Master? Are we able to be overcomers or do we become compromisers?

Do we seek to please people or God? Paul, while exhorting the Corinthians, clearly states that his ambition and that of his followers, was to be pleasing to the Lord (2 Cor 5:10). He exhorts the Colossians to walk in a manner worthy of the Lord, to please the Lord, in all respects bearing fruit in every good work (Col 1:10). Jesus Himself said in John 8:29, *"I always do the things that are pleasing to Him."* If so, how much more do we need to seek to please God?

We read in Daniel 6:4, that the commissioners and other officers tried to find a ground of accusation against Daniel in regard to the government affairs; but they failed as they could find no evidence of corruption. He was found faithful and no negligence of duty was found in him. Daniel knew all about this. Yet, as we read in verse 10 he continued praying on his knees three times a day, praying and giving thanks before his God.

Daniel had lost much of his Jewish heritage. Certainly he could not worship God in the way God's law commanded, through sacrifices at the temple in Jerusalem. He did, however, point himself toward the Promised Land three times a day in prayer. Not even the threat of death could make him vary this practice. This made the accusers' job easier. They complained to the king, *"Daniel, who is one of the exiles from Judah, pays no attention to you, O king, or to the injunction which you signed, but keeps making his petition three times a day"* (Dan 6:13).

It is quite interesting to note what they state: 'One of the exiles from Judah.' That means, there were other Jews also in that kingdom who had all compromised with the rest of the world in not praying to God. Daniel alone took a stand for the living God. He was the only overcomer among the other Jews or in today's terms, the so-called 'Christian'.

Even if you are the only person to take a stand in your office, do it boldly. God is looking for an individual to stand in the gap. A sincere, faithful and uncompromising person is of more value to God than a million compromising Christians or Christian believers. God honoured Daniel's consistency and patient endurance.

It is very surprising to note their prejudice against Daniel (Dan 6:13). Rather than call him by his title of commissioner, they describe him as 'One of the exiles from Judah'. Also, notice how they exaggerated the truth, saying 'Daniel . . . pays no attention to you, O king'. They knew the close friendship between King Darius and Daniel and so they tried to strain that relationship in their accusations.

As soon as the king heard this statement, he was deeply distressed and set his mind on delivering Daniel. Till sunset he kept exerting himself to rescue Daniel (Dan 6:14). What motivated the king to agonize over this case? Apparently, King Darius though not a believer, was an honest man who wanted to do the right thing and was also a friend of Daniel. In spite of their different religious beliefs, the two men found an uncommon closeness and loyalty to one another. He wanted to save Daniel, so he paces, about thinks and wrestles in his mind for hours. He was looking for a loophole in the law. At the end of the day, Darius' searching yields nothing; and the accusers say impatiently, *"Recognize, O king, that it is a law of the Medes and Persians that no injunction or statute which the king establishes may be changed"* (verse 15).

Then the king, with his head lowered slowly pronounces the orders: 'Throw him to the lions.' But before leaving he speaks to Daniel and says, *"Your God whom you constantly serve will deliver you"* (verse 16b). The King knew the prayer life of his Prime Minister. Does your boss or your teacher know that you are a man or a woman of prayer?

The Power That Delivered Daniel

Darius had remarkable faith in Daniel's God. Daniel's obedience to God cost him something. He had to be thrown into the lion's den. Yet, Daniel exhibited iron trust in God, without panicking, he quietly allows the guards to toss him into the pit. And they closed the opening of the den with a stone that is sealed by the king and his nobles (verse 17). Now all they can do is to wait. The Pharisees also tried to secure the stone at the mouth of Jesus' tomb in the same way (Matt 27:62–66). Both these incidents show us that they control the situation. God allowed them to do what they wanted, but He showed in both cases that in the end, things are under His control only.

Then the king went off to his palace and spent the night fasting and no entertainment was brought before him; and his sleep fled from him (Dan 6:18). He would have debated inwardly all night. Reason would have said that, Daniel was a dead man. Perhaps the king hoped that Daniel's God could have saved him. And his anxious heart longed to know what was happening in the den.

Being unjustly accused and unfairly punished is a painful experience. But when you confront those hungry lions and hear the back door shut behind you remember that you are not alone. When Daniel was put in the lions' den, two faces watched among the shadows. One was the face of God who had the power to close the lions' mouths; the other was the face of an earthly being, who desperately wanted to know if his beliefs are true. Together they make two good reasons to endure his suffering with courageous faith.

> Then the king arose with the dawn, at the break of day, and went in haste to the lions' den. And when he had come near the den to Daniel, he cried out with a troubled voice, " . . . Daniel, servant

of the living God, has your God whom you constantly serve,
been able to deliver you from the lions?" (verses 19–20).

The king addressed Daniel as the 'servant of the Lord'. Many of us
are interested in big titles, but they cannot help us. It is our holiness
and commitment to the Lord that matters. The king knew Daniel
as a servant of the Lord.

> Then Daniel spoke to the king, "O king, live forever! My God
> sent His angel and shut the lions' mouths, and they have not
> harmed me, inasmuch as I was found innocent before Him;
> and also toward you, O king, I have committed no crime"
> (verses 21–22).

It is interesting to note here that Daniel did not curse the king
instead he blessed him, for he had already forgiven the king. Daniel
was sure that he did not commit any crime. At the age of sixteen or
seventeen, Daniel had decided not to defile himself. He was almost
ninety years now and even in this old age and all through these years
he did not defile himself.

While Darius tossed and turned in bed, Daniel had slept
peacefully with the lions. This is what faith in the living God does.
It gives peace and poise in the midst of terrifying situations. Daniel
was more at rest in the prison with the lions than King Darius was in
his palace with all his comforts and luxuries (Dan 6:18–20). Are you
in some den of lions? Do you believe that the lions cannot harm
you unless God tells them to, and if He tells them to do so, it will
only be for your best, as Romans 8:28 assures us.

When the king came to the den he cried out with a lamenting
voice to Daniel, *"Daniel servant of the living God, has your God, whom
you constantly serve, been able to deliver you from the lions?"* (Dan 6:20).
Is God able? Of course, He is. Amazing! For one night, God had
removed the killer instinct of the lions and the next morning Daniel
stands next to the disarmed beasts, chatting with the King. Unharmed,
Daniel is finally lifted from the den (verse 23). We note here that

God sent His angels to shut the lions' mouths. When we compare Psalm 91:11–13 with Hebrews 1:14, we see that ministering angels are always guarding, protecting and watching over God's children.

Now King Darius sharply reacted to Daniel's accusers by ordering them and their wives, and children to be tossed into the lions' den. However the lions did not ignore them like they did with Daniel. Before they even reached the bottom of the den, the lions overpowered them and crushed all their bones (Dan 6:24). Vengeance is not ours, but God's. Thus was Daniel doubly vindicated, and the words of Solomon were strikingly fulfilled: *"The righteous is delivered from trouble, But the wicked takes his place"* (Prov 11:8).

Finally, Darius responds to Daniel's God. Possibly through this miraculous episode he might have become a believer, for he issues a decree to the empire that reflects an unreserved faith in the living God.

> "I make a decree that in all the dominion of my kingdom men are to fear and tremble before the God of Daniel; For He is the living God and enduring forever, And His kingdom is one which will not be destroyed, And His dominion will be forever. He delivers and rescues and performs signs and wonders In heaven and on earth, Who has also delivered Daniel from the power of the lions" (verses 26–27).

Darius' edict is a tribute to Daniel's influential, godly character. Through this man of faith, God's name is proclaimed all over the world (Heb 11:32–34). And it all began with Daniel's quiet prayers in his bedroom. The decree of the King sets forth the character of the true God: He is the Creator; all others are without life in themselves. He has a kingdom, for He is the Creator who governs all. His kingdom shall not be destroyed; all others come to an end. His dominion is without end; no human power can prevail against it. He delivers those who are in bondage. He rescues His servants from their enemies when they call upon Him for help. He works wonders in the heavens and miraculous signs upon the earth. And to complete all, He has delivered Daniel, giving before our eyes the fullest proof of His power and goodness in rescuing His servant from the power of the lions.

Faith That Sustained Daniel

We learn valuable lessons from here for the times when we accuse others of wrongdoing. First, take care that you aren't guided by your prejudices. Prejudice has no place in confrontation. And second, stay with the facts. Don't exaggerate and paint a bleaker picture than what's really there. If you'll take to heart this negative example of the satraps and commissioners, you will learn to value fairness and practise it.

God does watch His own. Daniel stood firm in his faith even as he faced terrible times of temptations in that foreign land and that indeed pleased God. Daniel's faith was consistent with His godly reputation. Through his consistent walk with God and faithful endurance of injustice, he impressed not only the king but also the entire kingdom. If we are to have that kind of influence, we need to remember two principles from Daniel's story.

First: When God proves our faith, He often puts us in difficult places from which we cannot escape. Like Moses facing the Red Sea with Pharaoh at his back, Daniel faced some deadly lions with no defence and no escape. It's in those types of situations that we must trust God totally. And it's in those situations that God works most spectacularly.

Second: When God touches those without faith, He often uses our faithful reaction that others cannot ignore. Were it not for Daniel's faithful trust in God during his predicament, Darius would never have believed. Likewise, our faith while we suffer unjustly often makes an indelible mark on unbelievers who want to know if our God is real. These two lessons can be summed up in one statement: The inescapable platform of pain provides the undeniable proof of faith.

Daniel was younger to Ezekiel. Ezekiel 14:4 speaks about Noah, Daniel and Job. Ezekiel wrote this about thirteen years after the incident happened in Daniel chapter 1, may be when Daniel was about thirty years old. Notice the impact that Daniel had made! God speaks about three men in the history and one of them was a living man—Daniel.

God picked up Job, then Noah and then we might expect God to pick up perhaps Moses—but He picked up a man who was living at that time. Think of that! Suppose God in His testimony talks about a couple of OT saints and then points to your name, how would it be! God picked up Daniel and put him in the category of Noah and Job. Here is Daniel who was righteous in the sight of God. God could write it down and speak through Ezekiel and God knew that it would not go to Daniel's head—he would not get puffed up and loose his testimony. That teaches about Daniel's tremendous humility. God had such confidence in the humility of Daniel that He could speak about him while he was still alive.

This present study places a challenging and searching illustration of the value and power of private prayer. Daniel 6:10 should be read in conjunction with Matthew 6:6. It is private prayer that is emphasized. The importance of making and maintaining a regular day-to-day communion with God is highlighted here. Our public ministry will only be effective and vital, as we know what it is to pray in private. The value of our service before people is determined by the measure of our fellowship and communion with God in the secret place of prayer.

Daniel's Strong Faith in Hard Times

Daniel knew what it was like to stand fast in his faith, even when circumstances made it difficult. As a young Hebrew, he had been instructed in God's Word and ways, learning to exercise his faith during a time when things were much easier. But when the time came for his faith to be tested, Daniel stood strong, believing God to see him through, no matter what the situations were (Dan 1:8–16).

Daniel's life is an example for all of us. In studying the Book of Daniel, we see that living as God wants us to live means that we will have to live out our faith during times of adversity and want, as well as during times of prosperity and peace. With Daniel as an example, we see that it is indeed possible to stand strong for righteous standards, despite pressure to sin. God will give us a means of escape, without us having to compromise our faith. We must believe, as Daniel did, that God will show us favour and gives us wisdom through 'creative alternatives' in such times of pressure.

We are living in the days of terrible moral compromise. We must refuse to go along with the crowd to do evil and to worship the false gods of this world (Dan 3:12). Instead, live in such a way that no charge (except your commitment to your faith) can be found against you (Dan 6:4–9). Continue to practise your convictions (Dan 6:10–16), maintaining a clear conscience by living a blameless life (Dan 6:21–22).

Chapter 20

JONAH
A Leader Who Lost the Sense of Direction

The ship was readily available; he had the right amount of money and bought a ticket at short notice without any advance reservation, but to the wrong place. This was the experience of Jonah.

We do not know much about the actual personalities of most of the Old Testament prophets. We usually see much emphasis on the prophet's message with a few occasional glimpses of the person behind it. Jonah's prophecy consists of only eight words *". . . yet forty days and Nineveh will be overthrown"* (Jonah 3:4). The rest of the passages in those four chapters unveil God's work in Jonah's life. Action and attitudes play the major role in this exciting drama. It is the only complete missionary book in the Old Testament.

Jonah was the son of Amittai. His birthplace was Gath-hepher, a town of Galilee near to Nazareth. The significant thing for us to notice is that our Lord Jesus Christ set His seal upon the story of Jonah and used Jonah's experience in connection with the fish as a type of His own resurrection (Matt 12:39–41). It is a very solemn story; it contains much encouragement for every servant of the Lord.

Disobedience to the Call of God

God shared His anguish about Nineveh with Jonah. *"Arise, go to Nineveh the great city, and cry against it, for their wickedness has come up before Me"* (Jonah 1:2) This was the heart-cry of God. But probably in Jonah's judgement Nineveh deserved to be destroyed. Nineveh was a large, important city in Assyria, situated on the River Tigris. It posed a grave military threat to tiny Israel. The Book of Nahum gives a clue about the people of Nineveh. It describes them as a ruthless, bloodthirsty people. The Assyrians themselves left monuments of their cruelty with long, boastful inscriptions describing their torture and slaughter of people who opposed them. God sent Jonah there, but obviously, he did not want to warn Nineveh's citizens as they were about to be destroyed. He suspected they would repent and God would forgive them.

Israelites had reasons to hate and fear Nineveh. But God loved Nineveh. He wanted to save the city, not destroy it. He knew Nineveh was ripe for change. So, as a matter of fact, God's instruction to Jonah contained the expectation that he should love his enemies in Nineveh. But he refused to go to the people he hated. Instead, he tried to run away from the Lord.

Jesus told His followers, *"Love your enemies and pray for those who persecute you"* (Matt 5:44). While everyone talks good about that command, loving your enemies is not an easy thing. Some people doubt whether it is even right.

Jonah needed to develop an attitude like God's toward his enemies. Insistently, God led Jonah to this understanding of His own mind and heart. The Book of Jonah is a story of a miraculous change in Nineveh, but even more a story of miraculous change in Jonah.

We read in the 3rd verse of the first chapter, he rose from the very presence of God and even as the Lord was speaking to him he ran away to Joppa to take a ship to Tarshish. This shows that however

close you may be to God, even spending much time in the presence
of God, it is possible to disobey or do things contrary to the will of
God. It was Jonah's deliberate, defiant disobedience.

Jonah lived at the time of King Jeroboam II (2 Kings 14:25)
when Israel was strong and prosperous. So Jonah must have lived
a comfortable, undisturbed life. In such a complacent atmosphere
the Word of God suddenly came to him (Jonah 1:2). While all the
other OT prophets were called to prophesy to the people of Israel,
Jonah received an alarming call to leave his sheltered and comfortable
lifestyle, cross the borders and preach God's judgement to a heathen
people living in wickedness.

It is not enough if you give yourself only to the restoration of
your church or your city. God is calling you to be a light to the
nations, *"For so the Lord has commanded us, 'I have placed You as a
light for the Gentiles, that you may bring salvation to the end of the
earth' "* (Acts 13:47). God had plans for Jonah, but he ran. God has
a plan for your life. He says, *'For I know the plans that I have for you
. . . plans for welfare and not for calamity to give you a future and a
hope'* (Jer 29:11). Are you running away from God's plan for your
life? If Jonah had been listening to his conscience and to the Spirit of
God, he would have obeyed God. But instead he chose to take note
of circumstances. The availability of a ready escape route can be an
attractive option when God asks us to do something, which we do
not like. Jonah failed to realize that the devil could have supplied a
whole fleet of ships headed for Tarshish. When God says 'go', we
must never say 'no'.

Unlike Jonah, Paul was determined to do the will of God and
therefore experienced God's guidance in every step he took. On
one occasion he wanted to preach in Asia, but the Holy Spirit
stopped him.

Consequences of Disobedience

God does not usually intervene to halt our self-motivated actions, but the account of Jonah is a warning that He can do so. The first action to affect the situation was to send a storm. God's anger was made known. Jonah was going to find that, disobedience has consequences. There are times when God causes the wind to blow in our direction. To our surprise, we find that God is at work in the strangest places. We have to acknowledge that God is sovereign and works where He chooses.

Jonah's disobedience not only affected him, but also the people in the ship. It brought about tears, fear, and anxiety in the fellow travellers and a heavy loss of cargo. This is what happens, when we disobey the Lord in our day-to-day life. The whole family suffers due to the disobedience of one member. Jonah's disobedience also caused a delay in proclaiming God's message to the needy people of Nineveh, who were on the verge of destruction.

Jonah lost the sense of direction. Not knowing who had the answer, they all started calling on their gods. But the man, whose God had the answer was fast asleep, not bothered about the problem. Today the world is being confronted by many terrible storms— morally, economically, and ecologically. The enormities of unsolved problems toss people into paralysing fears. Where are we and what are we doing? Are we too complacent in our comfort zones? The prophet Amos warned: *"Woe to those who are at ease in Zion . . ."* (Amos 6:1). There could be no resting for Jonah while a message from God had to be conveyed to Nineveh. His refusal was putting other lives in jeopardy.

Many of our churches, have become like holiday camps where we enjoy ourselves. The people around us are plagued with problems, incapacitated with fear of the unknown and worried about the uncertainties of their future. We must proclaim to the people of this world that Jesus is the answer for their future and all their fears; there is no other way, but Jesus is the only way.

With whom did Jonah have fellowship when the fellows in the ship were undergoing this turmoil? He had gone below the deck and was sound asleep. Sometimes people who make a lot of mischief appear calm as though they have done nothing. This is true of God's children too. Have we been asleep in the back of the boat for fear that we might be identified? A man, who did not believe in or know of the true God, exhorted Jonah!

God over-ruled the casting of the lot and Jonah was revealed as the source of the problem. He was then subjected to a fierce interrogation: *"On whose account has this calamity struck us? What is your occupation? And where do you come from? What is your country?"* (Jonah 1:8).

When he boarded the ship, Jonah thought he was escaping trouble, but now the consequences of his disobedience were coming to light. It is not good attempting to conceal our true identity. The truth will eventually come out. Soon the sailors made the connection between Jonah's disobedience to God and their own predicament. Jonah's sin was disclosed. Sin frequently tries to deceive with secrecy. *". . . be sure your sin will find you out"* (Num 32:23).

He who conceals his transgressions will not prosper, But he who confesses and forsakes them will find compassion (Prov 28:13).

Jonah recognized and acknowledged that it was his disobedience that caused this problem. We must recognize our sin. He did not defend himself or give any excuse. He said, *"Pick me up and throw me into the sea, then the sea will become calm for you, for I know that on account of me this great storm has come upon you"* (Jonah 1:12). Perhaps, Jonah knew that the time God had given him to repent was over. No more forgiveness was available and punishment was inevitable, *A man who hardens his neck after much reproof Will suddenly be broken beyond remedy* (Prov 29:1).

But the men in the ship probably were sympathetic, perhaps forgave him and did not want to throw him into the sea. So they rowed hard to reach the shore. But the sea was becoming even stormier against them (Jonah 1:13). People cannot approve an act, which is disapproved by God.

There is a song that says, 'With Christ in the vessel we can smile at the storm . . . .' But they could not smile at the storm because Christ was not there, only sinful Jonah was. Today some Jonahs are there in the church causing confusion, chaos and corruption and so the church is not able to sail smoothly towards God's destination.

If you recognize that you are a Jonah in your church or in a similar situation, then get out of that situation or take your hands off, so that your church or your family would be able to accomplish peacefully God's plan in their lives.

When they threw Jonah into the sea, the storm and the raging of the sea stopped. This proved to the heathen people, that, Jonah's God was the true living God. Therefore they offered a sacrifice to the Lord and made vows. When anyone has an encounter with the living God, he or she cannot be the same again.

God makes best use of our disobedience to teach everyone of us, some deep divine realities. God can use both an obedient and disobedient believer to accomplish His purposes.

The sailors justified their act of throwing Jonah to death as a sacrifice that would effect the calming down of the troubled seas. But God in His providence had other plans. First He commanded a storm. Now He commands a fish of suitable size to house Jonah for three days and three nights. Yes, God can command anything for your sake. He commanded Aaron's staff to become a snake, grains of sand to turn into gnats, locusts to populate Egypt, the Red Sea to open up, the walls of Jericho to fall, lions to shut their mouths, the fire not to touch His three men, the fire to come down from heaven, the rain to stop for three years, and the ravens to feed Elijah. Is there anything He cannot command?

Through his experience, Jonah discovered that, it was difficult to get away from a God-given mission. We can get out of touch with the Lord, but we cannot get out of His presence. Disobeying the Lord was a costly thing for Jonah and when a servant of God resigns, the Lord waits and invites them to re-sign. So please do not resign but re-sign.

God Is not Quick to Give Up

When Jonah disobeyed the call and command of God, and started moving away from God's will in his life, God did not desert him or give him up. There were other obedient prophets available for His service at that time. God would have been justified in saying, 'I cannot trust Jonah anymore, Amos is much more reliable, let me send him to Nineveh'.

Of all the available prophets, God had chosen Jonah. Having started in him this great task, He was determined to complete it. He loved Jonah and stood by him as He stood by Abraham, Moses, David, Elijah, Peter and others when they acted contrary to the plan and purpose of God. God has an amazing faithfulness towards backsliders. So please do not look down upon or keep away from a backslider.

Both the salvation of his soul, and the physical salvation required that he be removed from the fish. Jonah's salvation was complete when the fish decided that three days of discomfort in its digestive system was sufficient and when it deposited Jonah on dry land. Of course! The Lord commanded it to do so. He was not left with a long swim—the rescue was complete.

God caused Jonah to stay inside the fish for three days and three nights; that was the length of time the ancients thought it took to come back from Sheol (the place of the dead). Jonah said, *"I cried for help from the depth of Sheol"* (Jonah 2:2). The significant thing for us to note here is that our Lord Jesus Christ set His seal upon the story of Jonah, and used Jonah's experience in the belly of the fish to describe the time He would be *"in the heart of the earth,"* preceding His resurrection (Matt 12:39–41).

We have no liberty today to reinterpret God's message so that people may find it more palatable. The message of human sin and disobedience will always be unpopular and cause people to be offended. Those who fail to proclaim the truth, as found in Scripture, are warned that the preaching of another gospel will lead to eternal condemnation (Gal 1:8).

Commissioned and Conquered by God

In the first chapter, we see that Jonah was captured, cornered and convicted by God and people. In the second chapter, we see him being conquered by God. Now, he receives his second commissioning from God. On hearing the call for the second time, he promptly obeyed. He was responsive now whereas he had been reluctant before.

Though Jonah's message contained no hope of mercy, yet there was a tremendous response. The reality of their repentance was not just in word, it was followed by clear evidence that they were really sorry for their sins.

In one day Jonah brought a city of a million people to its knees in repentance before God. His story has few, if any, parallels in history. No study of revival can possibly be complete which overlooks Jonah. The revival that broke out in Nineveh set forward God's foretold judgement on that city for some two hundred years. Yet, all the way through the Book of Jonah we are exposed to the stark reality that God is doing His perfect work with a very imperfect instrument.

The people of Nineveh illustrate perfectly that no matter how far a person or people may seem to be gone, they still may repent. Jonah delivered God's message to the people of Nineveh, and they actually repented of their evil ways (Jonah 3:3–10). In fact, the king of Nineveh and his nobles issued a decree, commanding the people and beast to observe an absolute fast and to put on the garments of repentance and mourning.

God saw that the people of Nineveh were serious about turning away from their evil practices, and He promised that He would not send judgement upon them (verse 3:10). This teaches us a lesson that we should not give up on a person or people just because they are sinful. Nineveh was very sinful; but she came to her senses, and God spared her. Our God is a merciful Judge!

Thus, God responds in compassion to a genuine change of heart taking place from the king down to the man on the street. There is no destruction from heaven, but there is great displeasure on earth! From Jonah's view point the Lord had apparently 'changed back' by not bringing upon the Ninevites the destruction He had threatened (Jonah 3:10). This was all right for God, and fine for the city, but not so good for Jonah! The idea of God 'relenting' (Jonah 3:9; 4:2) turns our attention to Balaam's words in Numbers 23:19, *"God is not a man, that He should lie, Nor a son of man, that He should repent."*

In fact, the word 'relent' in the Hebrew has none of the pejorative sense that a change of mind has in our language. Also in Scripture, God's pronouncements of judgement are often conditional: for example, Jeremiah was warned of the possibility of destruction coming upon a Godless nation (Jer 18:7–8).

Looking back at the text again, it is clear that Jonah's problem arose precisely because God is consistent with His revealed character.

He says, *"I knew that You are a gracious and compassionate God, slow to anger and abundant in lovingkindness, and one who relents concerning calamity"* (Jonah 4:2). Despite God's affirmation the prophet still struggled to come to terms with the multifaceted nature of God's character, especially with His freedom to do what He wants, when He wants. Our long-held beliefs sometimes take years to impact us personally. As for Jonah he was indignant with God who insisted on being Himself!

Jonah responds to God's compassion by bursting a boiler in anger; resigning not only from his job, but also from life itself! The entire book ends with a powerful question: *"And should I not have compassion on Nineveh the great city"* (Jonah 4:11). Did Jonah eventually come through to share more of God's compassionate heart? It seems the question is left hanging in mid-air for us to answer in our day. The prophet Jonah was much like the NT Pharisees and some religious people of our day. Probably Jonah had a 'holier than thou' attitude. Even though Nineveh had repented, Jonah was angry because God did not destroy the city.

God used a plant to teach Jonah about mercy, compassion, and forgiveness. Jonah was more concerned about the plant God had created than about the people of Nineveh. God revealed to Jonah, how small his own heart was and how large the heart of God is which cares for other people and reaches out in healing and restoration. Our response should never be like Jonah's, but like Christ's.

Are you running away from God? God supernaturally blocked Jonah's way so that Jonah would repent and obey God's call. God may not cause you to be swallowed by a great fish if you run from His call, but you may find yourself in a series of adverse circumstances that have been designed by God to get you back on the right path. Doors may be shut, jobs may end, finances may dry up, and relationships may become bitter as part of God's way to lead you back to His purposes for your life.

Perhaps you are living a closed life, trying to play a part that does not belong to you. There is a voice in you that says, 'You're through, finished, burned out, no more chances'. Perhaps you can identify rather easily with prophet Jonah who tried to run away from God's destination for him. *Just as there are few atheists in fox holes, so there are few rebels in fish stomachs,* says Charles R Swindoll.

There is good news for you! A better way to spend the rest of your life. God says, *"I will make up to you for the years That the swarming locust has eaten"* (Joel 2:25). If God can take a disobedient prophet, turn him around and set him on fire spiritually, He can do the same with you. Openly and freely declare your needs to Jesus who cares so deeply for you. If you are ready to run toward that Nineveh called tomorrow, Jesus is ready with His salvation, already accomplished on the cross.

Chapter 21

Charisma Without Character
Is Catastrophe

A scorpion, being a poor swimmer, asked a turtle to carry him on his back across a river. 'Are you mad?' exclaimed the turtle. 'You will sting me while I'm swimming and I'll drown.'

'My dear turtle,' laughed the scorpion. 'If I were to sting you, you would drown and I would go down with you. Now, where is the logic in that?'

'You're right,' said the turtle. 'Hop on!'

The scorpion climbed aboard and halfway across the river, it gave the turtle a mighty sting. As they both sank to the bottom, the turtle said, 'Do you mind if I ask you something? You said there'd be no logic in you stinging me. Why then did you do it?'

'It has nothing to do with logic', the drowning scorpion sadly replied. 'It's just my character.'

Character is that part of a person that makes him or her different from others. Character being the crown and glory of life, lies in the will of a person. It is simply a habit long continued, a noble possession of man. *A man of character will make himself worthy of any position he is given* —Mahatma Gandhi.

It is not what we do for God that counts, but what we are before Him that matters. What we are determines the value of what we say and do. As the saying goes, *'Unless there is within us that which is above, we shall soon yield to that which is around us.'*

Charismatic leaders have attractive personalities. Charisma is not necessarily flamboyance, loudness, or dynamism. It may be a meek and quiet spirit in the midst of a sea of boastful commercialism and slick advertising. A pocket watch and a public clock both serve the same purpose, to tell the time. If a watch goes out of order, only the owner is affected; but if a public clock goes wrong hundreds of people are misled. So, as responsible citizens of this country, let us be examples and let not our lives be a stumbling block to others.

Peter Kusmic said, *Charisma without character is catastrophe.* The circumstances amid which we live determine our reputation; the truth we believe determines our character.

Reputation versus Character

Reputation is what we are supposed to be. Character is what we are. Reputation is the photograph; character is the face. Reputation is earned in a moment; character is built through a lifetime. Reputation is what men tell over our tombstone; character is what angels say about us before the throne of God. A man's reputation is before men but character is what we would do as if no one would ever know.

Character and Integrity

Integrity is what we gain by walking in God's light. *It is far more worth than precious gold to do what's true and right* —Dennis J D. Integrity is a state or quality of being complete. It is integration of a personality. In spite of severe persecution and discouragement Job held onto his integrity.

A good test of a person's character is his behaviour when he makes mistakes. No one goes crooked as long as he stays on the straight and narrow path. Our character is shaped by what our minds take in; we should not be like a waste paper basket. Men are more than what happens to them. Character evolves through man's beliefs, attitudes, intentions or motives and actions by which a man acquires more from history. Our reasons do not count as the real 'explanation' of our behaviour. You can easily judge the character of a man by how he treats those who can do nothing for him or to him.

Choices and Character

Choice is the starting point of action; it is source of motion but not the end for the sake of which we act. Little choices determine habit. Habits carve and mould character.

Why do even men of great reputation fall?

Anyone can fall if his intention is to act contrary to his basic convictions or moral principles of God, and if his judgement has been clouded by 'desire' or overwhelmed by 'passion'. Man develops character though his concrete decisions. Our decision determines our destiny. Circumstances do not make a man; they reveal what he is made of.

Theodore H Epp said, *Lust is the bud, sin is the blossom, and death is the fruit.* That is why it is important to nip temptation in the bud before it can blossom into sin and death. David was a great man but sin defeated him. The Bible says, wherefore let him that thinketh he standeth take heed lest he fall.

You may ask, 'Can a thing like this happen to me?' Yes it can. In some unguarded moment, Satan can slip up on your weak side and set before you a temptation so alluring, that by your own strength you'll not be able to overcome it. Our trouble is not that we are tempted, but that we don't turn to God for deliverance and turn to someone for counselling when the temptation is before us.

Courage Sustains Character

Courage has to be sustained by the encouragement of others. Courage is the keystone in the sustenance of our character. We should have the boldness to stand for what is right, be honest and just. In times of crisis we need the attitude of fortitude to keep us from being overcome when things run over us.

In the Bible, we find evidence of God using trials to refine Paul's character. Paul even learnt to rejoice in his sufferings because he found that suffering produces endurance, and endurance produces character, and character produces hope.

Character is what we are in the dark. The hardest trial of our character is whether we can bear a rival's failure without triumph. A man shows his character by what makes him laugh. In the destiny of every moral being, there is an object considered more worthy by God than anything else; that is character. It exercises a greater power than wealth, and secures all honour without pining for fame. It carries with it an influence and commands the general confidence and respect of mankind.

Keeping character is easier than recovering. Character is made by many acts; but a single one can lose it. The toughest thing in life is to remove the stains from a man's character. *Character is like a tree and reputation is like its shadow. The shadow is what we think of it; the tree is the real thing* —Abraham Lincoln.

The fragrance of our rich and delightful character will continue to linger about the place where we lived. Purity in your heart produces power in your life. Righteousness produces beauty in your character. Do what you can, where you are, with what you have.

Chapter 22

Attitudes That Influence Leadership

An attitude is an emotional and motivational force towards a psychological object. Sometimes we try to picture attitude as 'value', 'belief' or 'opinion'. Attitude is different from them. Belief is its cognitive base and action its cognitive side. In fact attitude is part of the broad value system. We value something depending on our beliefs and attitudes.

Belief is a thought process, which includes a clear perception of value. We form an opinion based on our beliefs and attitudes. But attitudes keep changing with the onset of new environmental influences.

The Nature and Choice of Attitude

Nicolo Pagnini a very famous, gifted violinist was playing a difficult piece of music to a packed audience. A full orchestra surrounded him with magnificent support. Suddenly one string of his violin snapped and hung down from his violin. Though he was shocked and was perspiring, he continued to play the music beautifully. To the conductor's surprise, a second string broke and in a short time a third one broke; now there were three limping strings dangling from Nicolo's violin, but still, the expert performer completed the difficult composition on the one remaining string.

The audience jumped to its feet and shouted 'Bravo! Bravo!' As the applause was over, the violinist asked the people to sit back down. He held the violin high for everyone to see and signalled at the conductor to begin the orchestra and he placed the violin beneath his chin and played the final piece on one string as the audience and the conductor shook their heads in silent amazement. This can be called as an attitude of fortitude—Pagnini and one string! We must have this kind of perseverance. What is perseverance? It means first to take hold; second to hold on and last to never let go.

The longer we live, the more we become convinced that life is 10 per cent what happens to us and 90 per cent how we respond to it. We are more than what happens to us. We should never forget the fact that people are constantly watching us. They are watching our reactions more than our actions. A man or a woman of God should not react, but respond lovingly. How do we respond to our life situations? We respond as we interpret the meaning of actions upon us.

Dr Victor Frankel, the bold, courageous Jew who as a prisoner endured years of indignity and humiliation by the Nazis. In the beginning of trial, he was brought into the courtroom. His captors had taken away his home and family, his cherished freedom, his possessions, even his watch and wedding ring. They had shaved his head and stripped his clothing off his body. He was interrogated and falsely accused. He was destitute, a helpless pawn in the hands of brutal, prejudiced, sadistic men. For all practical purposes there was nothing that he could do. But suddenly, Dr Frankel realized that, he still had the power to choose his own attitude. No matter what anyone would ever do to him, regardless of what the future held for him, the attitude of choice was his to make. He could either hold on to his bitter feelings or change to forgiveness, to give up or to continue, hatred or hope, determination to endure or the paralysis of self-pity. It boiled down to Frankel and one string!

In reality we must admit that we spend more of our time concentrating and fretting over the strings that snap, dangle and pop—the things that cannot be changed—than we do giving attention to the one that remains our choice of attitude. An attitude can be defined as an organization of interrelated beliefs around a common object or a situation with certain aspects being at the focus of attention for some people and the other aspects for others. Belief is its cognitive base and action its cognitive side. All beliefs are predisposition to action. Each belief within the organization of attitude, is conceived to have three components such as cognitive, affective and behavioural.

A cognitive component represents a person's knowledge about what is good or bad, true or false, desirable or undesirable. An affective component takes a positive or a negative position with respect to the object of belief when its validity is seriously questioned, as in an argument. The kind of action a behavioural component leads to is dictated strictly by the content of the belief. Jastrow has pointed out that the human mind is a belief-seeking rather than a fact-seeking apparatus.

Virtually all theories agree that an attitude is not a basic irreducible element within the personality, but represents a cluster or syndrome of two or more interrelated elements. Someone said, 'A person's social behaviour is mediated by at least two types of attitudes—one activated by the object and the other by the situation.' A person's opinion is a verbal expression of his belief, attitude or value. The concept of sentiment is more or less synonymous with attitude.

Certain environmental influences produce certain attitudes and hence these may not remain steady, but change with the development of new environment influences. The change may take place consciously or unconsciously. It is imperative that we consider the impact of our attitudes towards the complexities of our life situations in the following chapters.

Attitude towards Irritation

We need to consider the reality of our reactions to irritations. Some of our common irritants are: traffic jams, long queues, crying babies, misplaced keys, nosy and noisy neighbours, peeling onions, flat tyres, all the in-laws and outlaws including the mothers-in-law and the daughters-in-law.

The secret of overcoming irritation lies in adjusting. There is a three fold truth in adjusting: (i) I can change no other person by direct action; (ii) I can change only myself; (iii) When I change, others tend to change in response to that. In this regard we can learn a great lesson from the Oyster and its pearl. Pearls are the product of pain. It is the symbol of stress—a healedwound—a precious tiny jewel conceived through irritation, born of adversity, nursed by adjustments. Had there been no wounding, no irritating interruption, there could have been no pearl.

The Bible says, 'When all kinds of trials crowd into your lives, my brothers don't resent them as intruders, but welcome them as friends. Realize that they have come to test your endurance. But let the progress go on until the endurance is fully developed and you will find you have become men and women of mature character.'

You must learn to be patient in stressful situations; otherwise you would become a patient. In order to keep mole hills of tensions from becoming mountains of stress you can develop certain precautionary measures such as (i) allow for a margin of error, (ii) put things in perspective, (iii) plan for delays, (iv) think ahead, (v) be prepared even for the worst and (vi) live for the moment.

Attitude of Blaming Others

This is an aggressive attitude that reacts to circumstances with blame. Most of the time, we blame others for our failures and the blunders we have committed. Sometimes we even tend to blame God. Blaming is a system of avoiding responsibility. We have an impulse to blame because it promises an escape. Spiritual growth and maturity comes to a Christian only by owning responsibility and working at resolving it.

We should have no excuses for our failures and no escapes for our mistakes. This is precisely the way to minimize our failures and cut down our mistakes. Even if someone else is at fault, the responsibility of a Christian is to kindly and lovingly exhort that person, with showing much concern for that person for his background and life situation. The most powerful rebuke is not a loud, negative blast, but a quiet, positive model.

Charles R Swindoll says,

> Blame never affirms, it assaults. Blame never restores, it wounds. Blame never solves, it complicates. Blame never unites, it separates. Blame never smiles, it frowns. Blame never forgives, it rejects. Blame never forgets, it remembers. Blame never builds, it destroys. Let us admit it—Not until we stop blaming others will we start enjoying health and happiness again. Rather, if we own the mess we are in, there is hope for us and we will receive help.

Attitude of Rationalization

Rationalization is a dangerous attitude which has been corrupting the lives of many common people as well as leaders. The dictionary defines rationalizing as, 'Providing plausible but untrue reasons for conduct'. In other words, it is what we do when we substitute untrue explanations for true reasons. One sin rationalized becomes two.

Sometimes we cloud our actual motives with a smoke screen of excuses that sound very nice. There is much difference between good sound reasons and reasons that sound good. Often we do this to justify ourselves in the eyes of others. Rationalization is a mental technique, which allows you to be unfair to others without feeling guilty. Sometimes rationalization causes people to gloss over open and obvious sin.

So the principle is, if you're wrong in what you are doing, humbly accept it and stop doing it. No amount of rationalization will make it right or convince anyone. If you are sure what you are doing is right and not in any way a contradiction with the Word of God and if your conscience is clear then relax and be bold to express yourself with confidence. The main thing is that you please the Lord with a clear conscience.

Attitude of Self-Pity

'Self-Pity is when you begin to feel that no man's land is your island,' said Dana Robins. Self-Pity makes you to be absorbed in yourself and you are fascinated by your own egos. You need to understand that the world was not created for you personally, and that it is your pride and self-centredness that lies at the root of your problems. *Self-pity is a prison without walls—a sign pointing to nowhere*—Anon.

Take your eyes off yourself. When 'I' is put to death, the Spirit of Christ can control your life and make it beautiful. It is as addictive as alcohol—and just as deadly.

Despair and Discouragement

Self-pity is always counter productive. It is destructive. If continued it will lead to discouragement, which in turn is often the most direct route to despair and the ultimate self-destruction—suicide.

We should not become prisoners of ourselves. When doors are slammed against us, we are prone to draw into ourselves. Distrust begets distrust. Perhaps some people have lost faith in themselves because they feel God is far away from them. We must trust God where we cannot trace him.

Deliverance from Depression

The body and the will have their part to play in mastering mental depression. Hence the first step is to get out of the depressed situation. Some effort from those depressed is called for. The old maxim, 'You never know what you can do till you try', holds well. The ability and the will to try are made largely out of past efforts that have brought good results. Surprisingly, time and again we have completed tasks, which we first thought were beyond our capability.

The second step is to look up. We need to look beyond what we can accomplish in our own strength with a positive attitude.

Counter Crisis with Courage

Courage has to be sustained by the encouragement of others. Courage is the keystone in the sustenance of our character. We should have the boldness to stand for the right, honesty and justice. In times of crisis we need the attitude of fortitude to keep us from being overcome when things run over us.

God Is Never Out of Duty

Hence, the best thing would be to rest in peace, re-evaluate your life and spend your time in prayer and meditation upon the Word of God. Never allow self-pity to over take you. In essence, self-pity is a bitter resentment of one's condition and an attempt to get back on others or to manipulate others into giving (showing) sympathy.

If you are a person entangled in self-pity, and would like to come out of it, try to do the following: Think about the positive and negative things in your life. Can anything good come out of my illness or problems? Can I get a much broader and realistic view of the present situation? How can I make the best use of this situation?

There are many such attitudes we should take care of. In which areas do we face our greatest struggles? For example are we more often negative than positive? Or are we stubborn and closed rather than open and willing to hear? Is our attitude toward people very different from us? Are we proud and prejudiced? I would like to exhort us through the words of Paul who said, 'Have this attitude in you, which was also in Christ Jesus . . . who emptied Himself taking the form of a bond-servant . . . .' May the Lord help us to exercise the attitude of servanthood like Jesus.

Therefore, the single most significant decision you can make on a day-to-day basis is your choice of attitude. It is the 'single string' that keeps you going or cripples your progress. *It alone fuels your desires or assaults your hope,* says Charles Swindoll. When your attitudes are right, there is no barrier too high, no valley too deep, no dream too extreme and no challenge too great for you.

Chapter 23

Amazing Unity in the Devil's Camp Challenges Christian Leadership

Today we largely encounter instant coffee, fast food, and a quick fix Christianity. People want to do everything with the agility of the lizard not waiting upon the Lord. Reality is the difference between what we wish and what exists. Today's Christian seems to be long on looks but short on substance. The focus has been shifted from loving the Master to love that is on the Master's table.

We must shift our focus from perceiving God as a means to an end to recognizing that He is the end.

Our focus should move from

Success to Significance
Fancy to Faithfulness
Believing to Following
Silence to Speech
Weeping to Singing
Ignorance to Discovery
Guilt to Responsibility
Despair to Hope

Individualism to Partnership
Conformity to Courage
Dominion to Servanthood
Peace keeper to Peace maker
Good Friday to Easter.

The present crisis in Christianity can be eliminated only when we replace it with a Christianity centred in Christ. Today so much effort is put into chasing away the evil and cursing the darkness. But more than that we need to build a lighthouse in the midst of the gathering storm.

Disunity in the Body of Christ

The greatest problem that we face in the Body of Christ today is disunity. The Corinthian Church was a problematic church. In no other Epistle did the apostle deal with so many problems. Of those problems the first one he addressed was disunity (1 Cor 1:10, 11; 13:11). If this problem of disunity can be dealt with I believe all the other differences can be easily ironed out.

Opposition comes from within

Even while Nehemiah was engaged in building the walls of Jerusalem, opposition came from within. Attacks came on a regular basis from the Gentiles around Judah. This was expected. But the unexpected problems from within the camp, must have been discouraging to Nehemiah. First the Jews told him they were tired (Neh 4:10). Next they were plagued by fear. They complained to Nehemiah ten times about their fear.

Chapter 5 describes three more problems Nehemiah confronted. First of all, the builders wanted to leave the building work on the walls and go back to farming. They claimed they would soon run out of food, and their families would face starvation.

Second, since they could not farm their lands, the builders

complained that in order to purchase food they had to mortgage their properties, vineyards, and houses. This, however, was a poor excuse because the entire project was completed in only 52 days (Neh 6:15).

Then, there was the problem of taxes. *"We have borrowed money for the king's tax, on our fields and our vineyards"* (Neh 5:4). They pointed out their children would be taken in servitude and bondage, which they did not want, nor did Nehemiah.

Three bottles on the way to heaven

A story is told of three huge bottles placed on the way to heaven. An angel was taking a saint of God across these bottles and the saint observed that one bottle containing one religious group was tightly closed and another bottle containing another religious group was also tightly closed, but the bottle containing Christians had no lid and it was wide open. The saint exclaimed to the angel that it was not fair to keep only the Christian bottle open, paving the way for them to go to heaven anytime. The angel replied saying, as such there is no problem in that because if one Christian tries to climb up to heaven the other will pull him down and that is why they did not bother to close the bottle. How true it is in Christendom today!

The enemies within us weaken us more than the enemies outside. Jesus said that a kingdom or city or house that is divided against itself would not stand (Matt 12:25). Will then a church that's divided against itself stand?

Unity begins from the top, with the leaders

Psalm 133 begins with an exclamation: *"Behold, how good and how pleasant it is for brothers to dwell together in unity!"* 'Brother', here can be understood to mean the children or the people of God. The theme of brotherhood emerges early in Scripture; and from the very beginning it is clear that God places a high priority on how brothers treat each other (Gen 4:9). In this passage the question of responsibility for one another first emerges.

The Psalmist brings before us two pictures: Oil that 'runs down' and dew that 'descends'. The flow of oil starts with the 'head' of Aaron, the high Priest. The dew starts descending from Mount Hermon. Of all the mountains that existed in Palestine, Mount Hermon is mentioned here because it is the highest of all of them (9100 ft).

The garments of Aaron and the mountains of Zion refer to the assembly of God's people. Aaron and Hermon speak of leadership. Unless unity starts from the top with leaders, it won't be lasting.

Recognize the one and the only enemy

Satan is a common enemy for all of us. We need to unite at least to fight this 'one and the only enemy'.

Jesus wanted His disciples to recognize this common enemy. Once John came to Jesus reporting, 'Master, we saw someone casting out demons in Your name; and we forbade him because he does not follow with us'. Jesus replied, 'Do not forbid him; for he who is not against us is for us' (Luke 9:49–50).

Christians in other camps, though they may not follow Christ exactly like us, are not our enemies. Probably they have not received the grace and the light that we have received. Perhaps we need to teach them the faith and the fullness that we have received over the many years of our ministry involvement. I am not saying that we should compromise with every one, but accommodate those who have a desire to serve the Lord and help them to do it in accordance with the Word of God. We all belong to the same Father and serve the same Lord. The one and only enemy is the Satan.

The Bible describes the Christian unity through seven-oneness factors: *"One body . . . one Spirit . . . one Lord . . . one faith . . . one baptism . . . one God and one Father"* (Eph 4:4–6). But because of the lack of understanding of these uniting factors, the church has been more divided than united. Probably if one more factor is considered then there is a possibility of unity. It is recognizing the factor 'one enemy'!

Jesus is commending Satan for his unity. He asked, *"If Satan casts out Satan, he is divided against himself; how then will his kingdom stand?"* (Matt 12:26). When the expelled evil spirit found that the house he had once occupied was vacant and well furnished, he did not selfishly say, 'Let me tell no one about it. I will enjoy this facility as the sole occupant'. Rather he went out to quickly mobilize seven other spirits and made a triumphant re-entry (Matt 12:43–45).

He was even willing to take with him worse spirits than him to dwell in unity with them. What selfless co-operation among demonic spirits! If any one of us had been given an opportunity to discover such a house clean and swept and freely available for occupation, a vast majority of us could have told our wives to keep it a secret and would have quietly occupied the house just for ourselves. Unfortunately we have become such selfish Christians. That is why the gospel is yet to reach the whole world.

One more important graceful attitude that we discover in the devil mentioned here, is that he was willing to take seven spirits worse than him to adjust and dwell in unity with them. When some pastors want to chose their committee members, they try to choose people who are very close to them and those who are very supportive to them and if possible they will choose their very close relatives including their family members. Which pastor is willing to choose someone whom they think is not good?

In the several years of my counselling ministry to the pastors, I have always advised the pastors not to send away anyone who is a troublemaker out of their church. It is better to patiently adjust and help that person to overcome his weakness like Barnabas who took

Mark and nurtured him for two years. Later Mark was able to once again minister along with Paul. Some people when they are sent out of the church, may give more trouble than when they were inside.

There would have been at least 2,000 evil spirits inside that man who was dwelling in the mountains and tombs of Gadarenes. We discover an amazing unity among these evil spirits. They were so united in their prayer to Jesus! There was one mind, one spirit, one target, one goal and one purpose. There was no dispute among them whether to be sent into swine or donkeys or goats! (Mark 5:9–13).

Just imagine if all the 2,000 spirits wanted to go in different directions into different creatures, it would have been a herculean task for Jesus. They made the task easy for Jesus. But many Christian leaders are not able to unite even for prayer, what a shame! If Jesus were here today, He might be forced to think that it was easy to manage the evil spirits than to manage some pastors and leaders today because of the disunity.

The greater the challenge the deeper the commitment

There are three groups of people: Those who make things happen; those who watch things happen; and those who know not what is happening and what they are supposed to do.

Without information there is no transformation. People are not inspired enough because they are not informed enough, what they hear from pulpits does not convey anything clear to them. As they listen to so many preachers day and night and do not study the Word themselves, there is more confusion than transfusion. *"If the trumpet give an uncertain sound, who shall prepare himself to the battle?"* (1 Cor 14:8)

Under the leadership of Nehemiah we find that 'all the people gather togethered as one man' (Neh 8:1). How did it happen? Nehemiah explained to the leaders and the people the gravity of the situation and challenged them about the need of the hour. The people caught the spirit of the leader and responded positively and overwhelmingly. It is said that the people had a mind to work (Neh 2:17–18; 4:6). The greater the challenge the deeper the commitment!

Leaders of God's people must have one hand on the Bible and the other on the newspapers. Only when they interpret the message of the Bible against the background of the news of the world, they will be relevant on the pulpit. This will give prophetic edge to their sermons.

Work Towards the Common Purpose

In order to achieve unity, first of all we need to recognize our common enemy and then work towards the common purpose and that is to save the perishing souls. Once, some women were fighting tooth and nail among each other aboard a ship. Such a fight overwhelmed a passenger who was sitting at the edge and he slipped and fell into the sea. The moment the women saw that, they forgot their fight and got united in their efforts to rescue the man.

If our fighting leaders come to a realization that, day and night so many are perishing and entering into a Christless eternity, then they will unite together with one common purpose. You need not feel insecure and threatened that you may loose your church. Anyway it is not your church. Jesus said, 'I shall build My Church.' He did not say that you shall build His Church or rather He shall build your church. The Church is His business because it is His Body. Even if you and I are not there He will anyway build His Church.

Hence let us come to a realization of the supremacy and the urgency of the task and the commission that we have received, keep aside our petty differences and put our heads and shoulders together to finish the work. When Fanny Crossby was asked which she considered the top most of her 8000 or more hymns, she instantly replied,

> Rescue the perishing;
> Care for the dying;
> Snatch them in pity
> From sin and the grave!

Today there are so many unions without unity and so many committees without commitment. The Lord Jesus stated it so vividly in His high priestly prayer:

> "I do not ask on behalf of these alone, but for those also who believe in Me through their word; that they may all be one, even as You, Father, are in Me, and I in You; that they also may be in us, so that the world may believe that You sent Me" (John 17:20–21).

So let us recognize our common enemy and work towards the common purpose of bringing people to Christ. Amen.